The World's Landscapes
edited by J. M. Houston

1 China

£1.25 net   25/– net

The World's Landscapes
edited by J. M. Houston

1 **China** Yi-Fu Tuan
2 **Wales** F. V. Emery
3 **The Soviet Union** W. H. Parker
4 **Ireland** A. R. Orme
5 **New Zealand** K. B. Cumberland and J. S. Whitelaw
Other titles in preparation

The World's Landscapes

1 China

Yi-Fu Tuan
Professor of Geography, University of Minnesota

Longman

GEOGRAPHY

LONGMAN GROUP LTD
London

*Associated companies, branches and representatives
throughout the world*

© Longman Group Ltd 1970

First published 1970

SBN 582 31153 5

Printed by offset in Great Britain
by William Clowes and Sons, Limited, London and Beccles

Editor's Preface

Despite the multitude of geographical books that deal with differing areas of the world, no series has before attempted to explain man's role in moulding and changing its diverse landscapes. At the most there are books that study individual areas in detail, but usually in language too technical for the general reader. It is the purpose of this series to take regional geographical studies to the frontiers of contemporary research on the making of the World's landscapes. This is being done by specialists, each in his own area, yet in non-technical language that should appeal to both the general reader and to the discerning student.

We are leaving behind us an age that has viewed Nature as an objective reality. Today, we are living in a more pragmatic, less idealistic age. The nouns of previous thought forms are the verbs of a new outlook. Pure thought is being replaced by the use of knowledge for a technological society, busily engaged in changing the face of the earth. It is an age of operational thinking. The very functions of nature are being threatened by scientific take-overs, and it is not too fanciful to predict that the daily weather, the biological cycles of life processes, as well as the energy of the atom will become harnessed to human corporations. Thus it becomes imperative that all thoughtful citizens of our world today should know something of the changes man has already wrought in his physical habitat, and which he is now modifying with accelerating power.

Studies of man's impact on the landscapes of the earth are expanding rapidly. They involve diverse disciplines such as Quaternary sciences, archaeology, history and anthropology, with subjects that range from pollen analysis to plant domestication, field systems, settlement patterns and industrial land use. But with his sense of place, and his sympathy for synthesis, the geographer is well placed to handle this diversity of data in a meaningful manner. The appraisal of landscape changes, how and when man has altered and re-moulded the surface of the earth, is both pragmatic and interesting to a wide range of readers.

The concept of 'landscape' is of course both concrete and elusive. In its Anglo-Saxon origin, *landscipe* referred to some unit of area that was a natural entity, such as the lands of a tribe or of a feudal lord. It was only at the end of the sixteenth century that, through the influence of Dutch landscape painters, the word also acquired the idea of a unit of visual perceptions, of a view. In the

German *landschaft*, both definitions have been maintained, a source of confusion and uncertainty in the use of the term. However, despite scholarly analysis of its ambiguity, the concept of landscape has increasing currency precisely because of its ambiguity. It refers to the total man–land complex in place and time, suggesting spatial interactions, and indicative of visual features that we can select, such as field and settlement patterns, set in the mosaics of relief, soils and vegetation. Thus the 'landscape' is the point of reference in the selection of widely ranging data. It is the tangible context of man's association with the earth. It is the documentary evidence of the power of human perception to mould the resources of nature into human usage, a perception as varied as his cultures. Today, the ideological attitudes of man are being more dramatically imprinted on the earth than ever before, owing to technological capabilities.

In a book of this modest length, yet covering such extensive and intricate data, much could have been said that has necessarily been omitted. And as it is a pioneer work, the author has only touched in some fields that still await more research. Enough has been said in this work, however, to indicate that the Chinese landscapes are peculiarly the creation of the Chinese culture, indigenous and ancient. Yet, today, Communist China is a notable illustration of how the espousal of new social values can quickly alter the face of a whole nation. The countryside is being altered as dramatically as the cities, making the Chinese case of unique interest in its speed and scale of operation.

J. M. Houston

Contents

Editor's Preface   V

List of Illustrations   X

Introduction   I

Part One THE ROLE OF NATURE AND OF MAN

Chapter 1 **Nature: landforms, climate, vegetation**   9
The chequerboard pattern: tectonics and landforms   9
The unstable earth   13
  Tectonic and hydrologic changes in western China   13
  Loess in the middle Huang Ho basin   14
  Deposition and subsidence in eastern China   17
Changes in the course of the Huang Ho   18
Climate of western and northwestern China   19
Climate of humid and subhumid China   21
Climatic fluctuations   23
Natural vegetation   24

Chapter 2 **Man's role in nature**   29
Soil processes: natural and man-induced   29
Effect on vegetation cover   31
Causes of deforestation   37

Part Two
LANDSCAPE AND LIFE IN CHINESE ANTIQUITY

Chapter 3 **Prehistoric scenes**   45
The well-watered landscape of the prehistoric north   46
The appearance of agriculture   47
Late Neolithic landscapes   48
  Yang-shao   48
  Lung-shan   51

Chapter 4	**Early regional development**	53
	The wet environment of the North China plain	53
	Shang culture	55
	The cities	55
	The countryside	57
	Western Chou: landscape and life	59
	Eastern Chou	62
	Irrigation works and agricultural techniques	62
	Commerce and transportation	64
	The development of cities	65
	Nomads and landscape desiccation in the North	69
	Cultures of Central and South China	69

Part Three   LANDSCAPE AND LIFE IN IMPERIAL CHINA

Chapter 5	**From the Ch'in to the T'ang dynasty**	75
	The Ch'in empire and landscape	75
	The Former Han empire: population and land use	79
	Agricultural techniques and landscapes	81
	Territorial expansion: new products and scenes	84
	The Later Han empire: population changes and migrations	85
	Land use on the great estates	86
	The Period of Disunion	88
	Buddhist contributions to the landscape	91
	Sui dynasty: population change and engineered landscapes	94
	T'ang dynasty: changing frontier scenes	95
	The economy and landscape of prosperity	98
	Sensitivity to nature and conservation	100
	Forested landscapes of T'ang China	101
	The development of cities	102
Chapter 6	**Architecture and landscape**	109
	The 'ahistorical' landscape	109
	The bridge	109
	The house	113
	The courtyard	115
	Nature preserves, parks and gardens	121
Chapter 7	**From the Sung to the Ch'ing dynasty**	126
	The Sung period: agricultural economy and landscape	127
	Effect of the Northern Sung industrial revolution	130
	Commerce and the shaping of the Sung cities	132
	The northern antithesis: Cambaluc or Ta-tu	135

Ming and Ch'ing urbanization 135
Changes in rate of population growth 137
North China under the Mongols 137
Population growth and agricultural expansion: Ming and
    Ch'ing dynasties 138
Landscape changes in three areas 140
    North China 140
    Ssu-ch'uan basin 142
    Southern (Yangtze) highlands 143

Part Four TRADITION AND CHANGE IN MODERN CHINA

Chapter 8 **Stability and innovation: 1850–1950** 147
Types of landscape: c. 1930 148
    Loessic uplands 150
    North China plain 151
    Ssu-ch'uan basin 154
    Yangtze plains 155
    Southwest China: Yun-nan 159
    South China 160
Types of population and landscape change 162
    Natural population increase and landscape change 163
    Natural and manmade disasters 164
    Expansion and adaptation at the frontiers: Tibet,
        Mongolia, Manchuria 168
Impact of the West 177
    Early industrialization 177
    South Manchuria's 'industrial landscape' 178
    Urban manufacturing 179
    Treaty ports 179
    Impact of modernized cities on countryside 182

Chapter 9 **Communist ideology and landscape** 186
Stages in agrarian reform 186
Two villages in transition 192
Afforestation, erosion control, and water conservancy 195
The development and relocation of industries 198
The growth of cities 201

References 205

Index 221

List of illustrations

1   China: places mentioned in the text   2–3
2   Limestone spires and flooded rice-fields near Kuei-lin in Kuei-chou
    province   4
3   Huang Shan after rain, southern An-hui province   5
4   Chequerboard pattern and structural axes of China   11
5   Loess topography   15
6   The Hsi Ling gorge of the Yangtze   18
7   Natural vegetation of China   25
8   Pijun Temple in the Western Mountains of Peking (Peiping)   35
9   Expansion of areas with walled cities, from Western Chou to Ch'in
    dynasty   66
10 Late Chou and Ch'in major constructions   76
11 Mountains on the west side of the Nan K'ou Pass, with part of the
    Great Wall   78
12 Tea caravan on the Djesi La Pass near Tachienlu   90
13 Pagoda in An-hui province   93
14 Ch'ang-an under T'ang dynasty   107
15 Two bridges: suspension bridge across the Mekong River and a
    'moon' bridge in the Summer Palace, Peking   111
16 Pottery model of five-storey house with courtyard (Han dynasty)   118
17 Street and entrance courtyard to a town house   120
18 Hang-chou (Quinsai) in the thirteenth century   134
19 Terraces and stepped pyramids in northern Shen-hsi   149
20 Loess country, near Cheng-hsien, Ho-nan Province   150
21 Settlement pattern on the North China plain   152
22 Terraced rice-fields in the Ssu-ch'uan basin   154
23 Watery landscape of streams, canals, and ponds in the middle
    Yangtze plains   156
24 Settlements, canals, and linear ponds in the Fenghsien district of
    the Yangtze delta.   158
25 Topography, land use and settlements in the New Territories,
    Hong Kong   161
26 Terraced fields built with collective efforts, Kuang-hsi   162
27 Prayer flags at the summit of the Jetrun La Pass on the caravan
    route from Ch'eng-tu to Lhasa   169

28 Shanghai in 1936   181
29 New housing project in Shanghai in the post-1949 era   183
30 Farms and fragmented farmsteads in South China before consolidation into larger units   188
31 Ploughed field east of Chi-nan in Shan-tung province   190
32 Consolidated rice-fields in Hu-pei province, central Yangtze valley   191
33 Iron and steel works in Ch'ung-ching, Ssu-ch'uan province   203

Acknowledgements

We are grateful to the following for permission to reproduce photographs:

Barnaby's Picture Library: Fig. 8; Museum of Fine Arts, Boston, Mass.:
Fig. 17; J. Allan Cash: Figs. 5, 11, 20, 27; Camera Press: Figs. 6, 26; Marc
Riboud-Magnum: Figs. 2 and 30; Paul Popper Ltd.: Figs. 12, 13 and 15;
Fig. 17 is in the Museum of Fine Arts, Boston, and Fig. 16 is in the Collection
of William Rockhill Nelson Gallery of Art, Kansas City; Figs. 3, 19, 22, 23,
29, 31, 32 and 33 are from photographs by the author.

The cover photograph is by kind permission of Marc Riboud.

Introduction

The Chinese earth is pervasively humanized through long occupation. Signs of man's presence vary from the obvious to the extremely subtle. The major changes that have been imposed on the country in the last two decades are obvious. The building of roads, bridges, dams, and factories, and the consolidation of farm holdings are altering the Chinese landscape before our eyes, and these alterations seem all the more conspicuous because they introduce features that are not distinctively Chinese. In contrast, traditional forms and architectural relics escape our attention because they are so identified with the Chinese scene that they appear to be almost outgrowths of nature. If this may be said of earth-coloured city walls, old pagodas and temples, it is even more true of rice fields and villages in the rural landscape. In viewing the densely packed areas such as the Canton delta, the Ssu-ch'uan basin, Chiang-su province, and parts of the North China plain, we need to make an effort of the imagination to see them as forests or marshes that have been slowly transformed through the centuries to the quintessential patterns of the traditional Chinese tapestry.

Even in the rugged parts of China, in areas which look like untouched wildernesses, subtle evidences of the human presence occur. Consider, for example, the landscapes depicted by Chinese artists. To the inexperienced eye they appear either unreal, the pictorial symbol of Taoist nature mysticism, or, if real, then the depiction of a remote nature that is devoid of artifice except for the retired scholar's hut. Yet to those who have seen more of China than her cities the paintings are no mere works of fantasy; they owe their expressive grammar at least in part to the special character of the Chinese environment. The physical setting of the Chinese differs from that of West Europeans and North Americans. Such topographic types as scarplands and vales, rounded hills and lowlands, and broad undulating plains are lacking in China. Most Chinese spend their lives on flat alluvial plains of varying size. On such young deposits even the hills, their lower flanks covered by rising alluvium, look like steepsided mountains. The tense contrast of the vertical and the horizontal, without the transitional zone of soft relief that characterizes the foothills, is a common trait of Chinese topography. In Kuei-chou province of southwestern China limestone spires stand vertically above small, flat plains. Nature here more than matches the seeming extravagance of art. In North China too, lime-

1. China: places mentioned in the text

stone and metamorphic rocks, such as those in the Ch'in-ling Mountains, provide sharp, dramatic relief. In South China, volcanic rocks weather into steepflanked mountains, their structural and topographic alignments camouflaged by intense stream erosion. As to the famous scenic areas, photographs of Hua Shan in southeastern Shen-hsi or Huang Shan in southern An-hui simulate classical paintings of the T'ang and Sung dynasties (Fig. 3).

When a Chinese artist stresses the need for careful observation of nature, he may sound surprisingly like a professional geographer analyzing a landscape. Kuo Hsi, a much acclaimed painter of the eleventh century, illustrates in his work and writing this recognition of the need to attend to the facts of nature. In the following passages, he first notes that mountains differ in their soil and vegetation cover, and then proceeds to describe the location of settlements in relation to natural features.

Some mountains are covered with earth, while others are covered with stones. If the earthy mountain has stones on top, then trees and forests will be scarce and lean, but if the stony mountain has earth on top, the vegetation will flourish. On a mountain where the soil is rich, there may grow a pine a thousand feet high. Beside water where the soil is lean, there may grow a shrub only a few feet high.

An inn and hut stand by a ravine and not by a delta. They are in the ravine to be near the water; they are not by the delta because of the danger

2. *Limestone spires recalling Chinese landscape painting and flat, flooded rice-fields near Kuei-lin in Kuei-chou province*

3. Huang Shan after rain, southern An-hui province

of flood. Even if some do stand by the delta, they are always in a place where there is no danger of flood. Villages are situated on the plain and not on the mountain, because the plain offers land for cultivation. Though some villages are built among the mountains, these are near to arable land among the hills.[1]

Mountains, according to Kuo Hsi, may or may not have a soil cover and their vegetation will differ depending on the nature of the surface. Thickly forested mountain scenes are rare in Chinese landscape painting in comparison with the portrayal of bare slopes that support a few hardy conifers. Kuo Hsi does not blame man for the removal of trees, nor for its almost inevitable consequence, soil erosion, which will change the mountain slopes from 'earth' to 'stone'. On the other hand, the evils of excessive tree-cutting were recognized at the time; and we now see that the eleventh century was one of the more notable periods in the history of deforestation in China. It is not too fanciful to think that the rugged and wild landscapes, admired by artists for their pristine beauty, owe their distinctive mien at least in part to human destructive-

2

ness. Again, the entrenchment of alluvium appears not infrequently on Chinese paintings. As with bare mountains, the sunken stream beds may have natural causes. On the other hand the floods that cut into the alluvial plains may owe their destructive power to rapid run-off over the deforested catchment basins.

The meaning that landscape has for us varies also with our degree of involvement with nature. The explorer seeks out the intransigent wildernesses with which China is so richly encumbered. His experience of the world is vast in space and constricted in time. The peasant's world, on the other hand, is spatially limited, being circumscribed largely by the scattered fields that are within walking distance of his village. In a lifetime the land known to him personally may be no larger than 20 square miles. But in this unit of the earth his involvement is total. To him it is not a view, certainly not an aesthetic or physical thrill; it is a resource, but less a resource than a nurturing personality whose seasonal moods order his pattern of life. The landscape of the gentry is that of the landscape artist and gardener. Of Taoist and Buddhist inspiration, it is less a view than an enveloping atmosphere to which the scholar-official can escape for short periods of time. Its aesthetic character denies the social and biological facets of man's being. The landscape of the artificer is his own handiwork; nature he perceives largely as opportunity. His landscape consists in monuments to the human will and power: the Grand Canal, the geometric cities; and in modern times, iron and steel works, dams and reservoirs, and shelter belts that challenge the desert. But the meaning of landscape is far richer than these few perspectives suggest. For the natural environment itself changes through time – slowly as the result of natural processes, rapidly as the result of human action – so that people do not encounter the same objective reality from one period to the next. And of course attitudes themselves alter so that the same facts, at other times, are perceived differently and call for new responses.

In this book my chief task is to describe some of the major changes in the Chinese landscape; but from time to time I find it helpful to draw attention to those forces in nature and in history that have induced the Chinese to shift their foci of interest in the world around them.

Part One
The Role of Nature and of Man

Chapter 1
Nature: landforms, climate, vegetation

Since our main concern is to trace some of the changes over the face of the Chinese earth wrought through human agency, it is usual to start with a section on the natural setting. The state of nature before the arrival of man is often conceived to be – at least implicitly – in a condition of quasi-equilibrium. Man appears, and through his power for action, upsets the quasi-equilibrium and progressively transforms the primordial state so that eventually, in places, an entirely artificial world is superimposed upon it. A slightly different way of characterizing this view is to describe nature as the 'stage' or the 'setting', and man as the 'actor'. Nature is assumed to be stable and given a passive role. Man is the free and active agent. As a position that one may provisionally accept in order to follow a special line of inquiry it has great value: however, for China the acceptance of a too rigid dichotomy runs the risk of unnecessarily warping reality. Nature in China has not been notably stable. It cannot be viewed simply as the passive, immobile stage. This is evidently true if we take a broad time span so as to include human prehistory, and it remains a relevant fact even if we restrict ourselves to the recorded period.

The chequerboard pattern: tectonics and landforms

China's physique has been described as resembling a chequerboard. Even a brief study of a good relief map supports this characterization. In western China we can easily discern the juxtaposed units of plateaux and basins separated by narrow, sharply demarcated mountain chains. In eastern China the units of the chequerboard are perhaps less clear but several are outstanding, as, for example, the well-defined central Manchurian plain, the North China plain, the lake basins of the central Yangtze Valley, and the Ssu-ch'uan basin; even the great northern loop of the Huang Ho is suggestive of a chequerboard unit. This basic physiographic characteristic of the Chinese land mass appears to be the result of the intersection of two major sets of structural lines: one set extends from northeast to southwest, the other – less well defined topographically – displays an east to west trend. The structure of China, viewed as the complex interplay of several distinctive tectonic areas, was clarified by the generalizations of J. S. Lee (S. K. Li).[1] In what follows we shall describe present landforms in the framework of the major structural trends, for this procedure will allow us to proceed towards an understanding of the landforms as something other than a catalogue of set pieces in the earth's crust.

Consider first the northeast to southwest trends. They may be seen as a succession of upfolds (geanticlines) and downfolds or geosynclines in the earth's mantle. The upfolds produce mountain chains and islands, the downfolds the seas, the plains and basins. These together form concentric arcs on the eastern border of the Asian continent. Beginning from the east, the first of such trend lines is a geanticline which finds topographic expression in the islands of Japan, the Ryukyu islands and Taiwan. Westward is a depressed segment of the earth's crust, covered in varying depth by water: the Sea of Japan, the East China Sea and Taiwan Strait are the main units. On the edge of the Asian mainland we encounter another complex upfold which begins with the mountain ranges of Sikhote Alin in the Soviet Union and continues south westward into the Liao-tung and Shan-tung peninsulas. A branch, or perhaps a separate unit, of the geanticline appears at the south end of the Korean peninsula and reappears, across the sea gap, in southeast China. The alignment of the main mountain ranges in these upfolded zones reflects the general structural trend except where the trend is interrupted by major cross-faulting as in Shan-tung peninsula, and, of course, where it appears to be completely broken and dips under the sea. In detail, the landforms of the geanticlines show great diversity, since they depend not only on structure but also on the rock material, and on the intensity of weathering and erosion. Thus the Liao-tung peninsula and the east Manchurian highland lie mostly under 3,000 feet, are hilly rather than mountainous, and have a local relief of only a few hundred feet. In contrast the mountains of southeastern China, though not much higher, are much more rugged. The granite and volcanic rocks have, under tropical climate, yielded steep, dramatic forms; these, when wrapped in mist and appropriately crowned by Buddhist monasteries of the Ch'an sect, evoke the full flavour of Chinese landscape painting.

The chief lowland of China corresponds to a downwarped strip of the earth's crust (Fig. 4). It extends from northeast to southwest, and is rimmed by high lands except for two breaks in the geanticline on the eastern side: one is the narrow neck of water, dotted with islands, that separates the Liao-tung peninsula from the Shan-tung peninsula. Another is the low coast between Shan-tung and the northeastern terminus of mountains in southeast China. The lowland is made up of three units, set apart from each other by mountain barriers, the Jehol block in the north and the Ta-pieh block in the south. The surface characteristics of these three pieces of lowland are quite distinct. The northern most, the central Manchurian plain, is an erosional surface. It is therefore well drained for the most part, and gently rolling, not flat. The central piece, the North China plain, was built up by successive layers of alluvium. It is nearly flat. Gradient to the sea is so gentle that large areas, even in the recent past

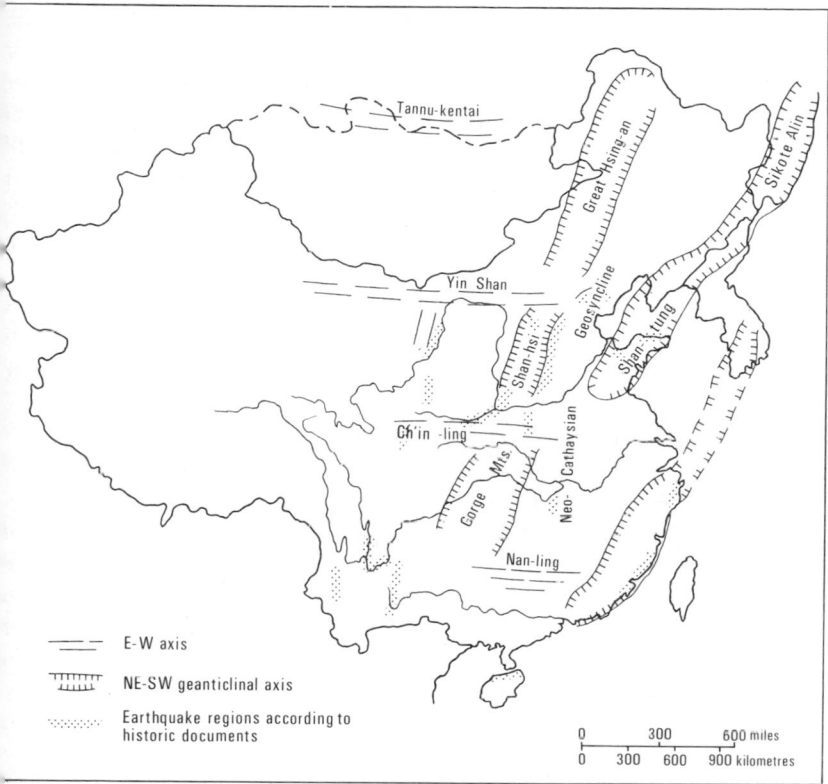

E-W axis

NE-SW geanticlinal axis

Earthquake regions according to
historic documents

| 0 | | 300 | | 600 miles |
| 0 | 300 | 600 | 900 kilometres |

. Chequerboard pattern and structural axes of China. (After Lee).

ere seasonally covered by sheets of water or were otherwise ill drained. One
eason why floods on the North China plain brought such prolonged economic
ardship to the peasants was the slowness with which the flood water could be
ed off. A bizarre though not exceptional scene in North China was to see a
valled city that rose out of a broad sheet of water, and to see farmers fishing
n their flooded fields outside the city walls. Yet normally the North China
·lain, especially on a windy, dust-laden day in winter, looks brown and parched.
ts summer rainfall is only just sufficient for its dry crops. The wettest and
1ost low-lying of the three segments of the lowland is the southernmost.
t is made up of the lake basins of the central Yangtze Valley, and has the
ppearance of a new earth recently born of a watery chaos. Standing on the
hores of either the Tung-t'ing or Po-yang lake one could well imagine oneself
 be at the edge of the ocean.

To the west of this sunken strip of lowland is the most prominent of the
ortheast to southwest geanticlinal axes. Its main units are the Great Hsing-an

Mountains in Manchuria, the Shan-hsi plateau, and the Gorge Mountains across the Yangtze Valley. The Great Hsing-an Mountains separate the two treads of a step-like structure: the higher tread is the Mongolian plateau, and the lower one the central Manchurian lowland. Seen from the lower tread the Hsing-an rises prominently as a scarp. But seen from the higher tread the crest of the scarp is merely a treelined swell on the horizon. The T'ai-hang Shan on the eastern border of the Shan-hsi plateau stands even more sharply above the alluvial surface of the North China plain. The plateau itself is made up of a series of folds complicated by faulting. One down-faulted strip finds topographic expression as the Fen Ho Valley.[2] The Gorge Mountains, too, are an accordion of folds, only here the Yangtze Chiang transects dramatically the northeast to southwest trend of the mountains to produce a series o stupendous defiles. The river emerges from the defiles at I-ch'ang. For a short distance downstream it remains confined between terraces but it eventually swings free in the watery landscape of the Tung-t'ing lake basin.

West of the axis of the Hsing-an and Gorge Mountains, three areas of relatively lower relief and elevation may be discerned: the Mongolian plateau, the Shen-hsi plateau with adjoining Wei Ho Valley, and the Red basin of Ssu-ch'uan. These are separated by two of the east to west axes that transect the more striking physiognomy of the northeast to southwest trends. The Yin Shan east–west axis appears as a low range separating the Gobi desert from the Ordos desert and Shen-hsi plateau to the south. The Ch'in-ling east–west axis however, is one of the sharpest boundaries (floristic, faunal, and human) in the geography of China. Where it separates the Shen-hsi plateau from the Red basin of Ssu-ch'uan its crest stands at about 7,000 feet. The northern flank of the range rises as a mountain wall above the Wei Ho Valley. The sharp physiographic contrast expresses a structural relationship, for the Ch'in-ling wall is a complex faultline scarp overlooking the sliver of earth crust, the Wei Ho trough, that has been let down.[3] The Red basin to the south lies encircled within a curtain of mountains. It is one of the more distinctive pieces within the Chinese chequerboard. In contrast to the North China plain and the central lake basins, the treads to the west of the Shan-hsi plateau and Gorge Mountain axis are not flat. Both the Shen-hsi plateau (which is structurally a basin) and the Red basin have high local relief. To their west the lineaments of structure become harder to decipher.

It will be noticed that the concentric belts of northeast to southwest upfold and depressions do not appear to continue into South China, except for th mountains of the southeast coast. Structure and topography lack the simpl relationship that they have in the central and northern parts of the country The Nan-ling east–west axis has no evident surface expression; and the mos distinctive landform in southwest China is the result of rock material rathe than structure. This is the landform of discrete mountain peaks and roc spires that have developed through the weathering and denudation of limestone.

The relief pattern of China has been characterized as chequerboard. It can also be described as having two distinct parts, West and East. The western part of China contains the Tibetan plateau, one of the highest in the world, as well as high mountain ranges, such as the Kun-lun, the T'ien Shan and the Altai, that have no match in the East. Among these elevated plateaux and mountains of the West are almond-shaped depressions or basins of east-west orientation; for example, the Dzungarian, the Tarim, and the Tsaidam. Eastern China is lower and descends to the sea through a series of giant steps separated by rises that trend from northeast to southwest. The overall gradient of China is from west to east, and this fact is emphasized by the direction of flow of the three main rivers, the Huang Ho, the Yangtze Chiang, and the Hsi Chiang.

The unstable earth

Tectonic and hydrologic changes in western China

The framework I have thus described is not set in rigidity. It is not an immobile stage on to which we can usher the human actors. Its components are subject to slow movements and sudden shifts. Such had been the case throughout the second half of the Pleistocene epoch when man appeared on the Chinese scene and added his capacity to alter to that of geophysical agents. But even in the period of recorded history, movements of rock and shifts in water course continue; together with human efforts they account for the persistent and changing aspects of the Chinese earth.

Sinanthropus pekinensis (H. erectus pekinensis) or Peking Man appeared on the Chinese stage sometime in the Middle Pleistocene epoch, probably some 300–500,000 years ago. Through his knowledge of the use of fire, Peking Man was the first hominid in China to have had the power to alter significantly the biotic cover of his homeland. Let us consider some of the natural changes in landscape that have taken place since Peking Man first appeared. A major change was the broad uplift of the Tibetan plateau. Its present height appears to be a late achievement. The last rise of some 8,000 feet may have taken place only in the second half of the Pleistocene.[4] One consequence of the rise was to cut off the moisture brought in from the Indian Ocean by monsoonal winds. The numerous lakes of the Tibetan plateau are all shadows of their former selves: some are surrounded by terraces that stand almost 200 feet above the present water-level. It is possible that the rise of the Himalayan barrier has contributed towards the desiccation of the plateau.[5] Another consequence of the uplift was that it increased the gradient of the rivers that flowed off the borders of the plateau, enabling them to incise into the plateau and produce gorges and canyons without parallel for length, depth and density in the world.

The canyons at the southeastern edge of Tibet, clothed in dense vegetation, provided an effective barrier between the Indian and Chinese civilizations. The rivers are still cutting down rapidly. The deepening of the canyons is not at an end. And indeed the Tibetan plateau has not yet achieved stability: seismic disturbances along the length of the Himalayas, capable of bringing disaster to foothill settlements, are indicative.

To the north of the Tibetan plateau is the Tarim basin. This is the driest area in the Chinese domain, the dryness being accounted for by its continental location but even more by the fact that, except for the opening to the east, the Tarim basin is rimmed by high mountains and plateaux. At the centre of the basin lies a great expanse of sterile sand, known as the Takla Makan desert. Yet, in the Ice Age, not sand but the waters of a large glacial lake occupied much of the basin floor. The western part of the lake was soon filled with sediments, but eastwards open water persisted long enough to produce a beach line on the flank of the Quruq Tagh (Dry Mountain). The beach line, however, is tilted. It slopes eastwards at an appreciable gradient. As a result of the tilt the lake was displaced to the east, forming a new lake in approximately the area of the present Lop Nor basin.[6] The precise dates for these major alterations of hydrography and topography are not known but they very probably took place towards the end of the Pleistocene. If this still sounds remote, we may add that changes in hydrography, of a kind to affect the fate of settlements and trade routes, were known to have occurred in historic times and are indeed a present possibility. The effect of changes in water course on settlement may be seen, for example, in the fate of Lou-lan, to the west of Lop Nor.[7] Lou-lan was at one time an important settlement on the trade route between China and Western Asia. Its solidly constructed fortresses, temples, stupas and houses were located along the distributaries of a delta that terminated in Lop Nor. The river that brought water to Lop Nor and served as the lifeline of the settlement was the Tarim. However, sometime during the second quarter of the fourth century A.D. the Tarim River changed its course; it swung to the south and fed into another lake. Lou-lan soon had to be abandoned. This is not the end of the story, for sometime in the early decades of the twentieth century, a branch of the Tarim River resumed its old course, and brought enough water to the Lop Nor basin to give it a new lease of life.[8]

Loess in the middle Huang Ho basin

In eastern China natural changes of landscape since the Middle Pleistocene were caused by phases of deposition and erosion, and by tectonic adjustments along the main structural axes. Deposition is clearly and widely recorded in North China. During the Middle Pleistocene the most common type of deposit consisted of red slope-wash clays and thick red loamy alluvium. Limestone caves, including those inhabited by Peking Man, were thus filled. After

5. Loess topography

a short phase of erosion, deposition was resumed. The material this time was a fine loamy silt laid by wind and known as *huang tu* (yellow earth) or loess.

Deposition of loess began sometime in the Upper Pleistocene, perhaps under the cool dry conditions that pertained in the interior of Asia during the last glaciation. Strong winds from the interior brought fine dust southwards and banked them against the mountain ranges and plateaux of western and northern China. Small patches of loess are known to occur on the high flanks of the Kun-lun Mountains. Dust from the floor of the Tarim basin is trapped there, and later returned to the basin by streams as pockets of loessical alluvium of great fertility.[9] Farther east, loess is banked against the northern slopes of the Nan Shan in Kan-su province; and when redeposited by streams in the adjacent lowlands they produce oases of rich soils. But the thickest and most widespread blanket of loess appears in North China roughly to the south of the line of the Great Wall. They drape over the hills and basins of eastern Kan-su, Shen-hsi and Shan-hsi provinces, forming here a thin veneer, there a thick cover that submerges an older, eroded topography.[10] In northern Shen-hsi province and in the valleys of southeastern Kan-su loess locally attains a thickness of more than 250 feet. Over the more rugged topography of Shan-hsi it is thinner. Everywhere it yields a distinctive landscape. Thin patches may be seen to cling precariously on mountain slopes. Their removal in the course of geological denudation is only a matter of time, measurable in thousands or perhaps in hundreds of years. Population pressure on the limited cultivable land in North China is such that even these small patches may be terraced and sown to crops. The farmer extracts what food he can from land that will soon be delivered by sheetwash and gullies to the Huang Ho, and eventually to the sea. The areas of thick loess in the valleys and basins have longer life but they too are ephemeral features on the time scale of human evolution in China.

Peking Man picked hackberries, roasted venison over his hearth and probably practised some kind of strongly flavoured religion long before the pall of dust settled over North China. In the last 5,000 years this dust, this loess, sustained continuously an agricultural way of life; and through the phases of peace in the historic period it enabled agriculture to support a remarkably high population density in a land that is climatically marginal for the more intensive forms of land use. But, according to one estimate, in less than 40,000 years nearly all this loess will be removed from the uplands.[11] The processes of removal are everywhere evident today. A characteristic of loessic topography is the element of surprise. One travels over a flat surface, over what seems a broad tableland, and suddenly finds one's path terminating in a vertical trench. Steepsided gullies, some of which may be several hundred feet deep, cut the uplands into fantastic relief. In areas of thick loess collapse depressions and natural bridges are not uncommon. They are caused by water that seeps into the loess through fissures and then undermines it by moving out to the side of a gully as a tongue of mud. Sheetwash, after heavy rain, also works to strip the uplands of their burden. Another process that contributes to the rapid disintegration and removal of the loess cover are the jolts given to it during periods of seismic activity.

The structural framework of China, however, is not set. The loess-draped uplands are one of the least stable areas in China. The Shan-hsi plateau, part of the loess upland, is also part of the updomed geanticlinal axis that extends from the Great Hsing-an scarp in Manchuria to the Gorge Mountains of the Yangtze. It responds to crustal tension by faulting. The Fen Ho Valley occupies a down-faulted piece of the Shan-hsi plateau; it continues westward as Shen-hsi's Wei Ho Valley, which, too, is bounded by faults. These and other faults in the loess region are occasionally reactivated. Severe earthquakes bring disaster, involving much loss of life, to the region because a high proportion of the people who live in areas of thick loess live in caves that are dug into the soft, easily collapsible material. An earthquake of the intensity of the one that affected eastern Kan-su in December 1921 resulted in the death of a quarter of a million people. It also caused extensive landslides: masses of loess shifted into the valleys, from there to be removed out of the uplands by swollen streams. The importance of the effect of earthquakes on man and on topography in North China may be gauged by the fact that, according to historical record, fifty destructive earthquakes occurred during the interval from A.D. 996 to 1920 in eastern Kan-su alone.[12] This corresponds to an average of one great earthquake in every eighteen and a half years.

In the historic period winds too have tended far more to erode and remove loess from the exposed slopes of the uplands than add to the thickness. A characteristic scene on a windy winter day in North China is one in which the colour yellow is pervasive. The world then seems to be made of one material – loess: the soil is loess; houses are made of pounded loess bricks or dug out of loess; roads are tracks sunken in loess; vegetation is coated with loess, and the blueness of the sky itself is compromised by yellow veils of loess.

Deposition and subsidence in eastern China
The loess is being removed from the uplands south of the Great Wall. Its final destination is the sea. But a wayside station is the North China plain. Much of the surface layer of the North China plain consists of loessic alluvium; that is, of silt from the uplands brought down to the plain by the Huang Ho and other rivers, and there deposited together with the coarser sands and pebbles. It is helpful to consider the twin processes of fluvial erosion and deposition in the context of the structural framework sketched earlier. The two longest rivers in China, the Huang Ho and the Yangtze Chiang, flow across the succession of great geanticlines and geosynclines that trend from northeast to southwest. Over the uplifted folds the rivers maintain their gradient by rapid incision, producing in the case of the Huang Ho the long deep canyon that separates Shan-hsi province from Shen-hsi, and in the case of the Yangtze Chiang the famous gorges. Over the depressed belts of the crust deposition takes place. The Yangtze Chiang emerges from the Gorge Mountains to meander freely on the flat plains of the central lake basins. The basins are an area of deposition, but they are also an area of slow downwarping.[13] Large but shallow bodies of water occupy the depressions. They are being maintained by contrary processes; subsidence, which tends to enlarge them, and sedimentation, which tends to work towards their demise. The Yangtze delta too is an area where the crust appears to be sinking. The alluvium there is rarely a veneer over bedrock; in places it is hundreds of feet thick. The coastline of the delta is advancing as a result of the vast amount of sediment brought down by the river. The progress seaward, however, is slower than what one might expect from the quantity of deposit available. Crustal downwarping checks the dry land's movement out to sea.

The Huang Ho emerges from the confines of Palaeozoic bedrock to the alluvium of the North China plain somewhere to the east of the San-men gorges. The North China plain used to be thought of as a shallow sea which had been filled with alluvium only in recent geologic times. However, it is now seen as part of a belt of subsidence the surface of which represents a fluctuating state

6. The Hsi Ling gorge of the Yangtze

of balance between the rate of downwarping and the rate of alluvial deposition. As with the Yangtze delta the migration of coastline seaward, north of the Shan-tung peninsula, is slower than the rate one might deduce from the sediment load of the rivers. Only at the mouth of the Huang Ho itself has the coastline shown quick advance. The North China plain then carries a thick burden of alluvium; and yet in spite of continuous deposition it has large, ill-drained swamps and lakes, such as the Ta Lu Tien (*c.* 60 miles south of Cheng-ting), the Hsi Tien (east of Pao-ting) and the Wan An Wah about 30 miles southwest of T'ientsin. It is possible that in early Chinese history these three depressions were connected marshes and that the ancient Huang Ho flowed northward along their eastern margins towards the location of T'ientsin and thence to the sea.[14]

Changes in the course of the Huang Ho

The Huang Ho has dramatically altered its course several times in recorded history. It has behaved in a way that is unique among rivers of comparable size. At one time or another it has debouched to the sea all the way between T'ientsin in the north and the mouth of the Huai Ho, even of the Yangtze, in the south. The general pattern of shift appears to have been southward. At various times it even maintained two branches, one on either side of the Shan-tung peninsula, as, for example, during the thirteenth century. The cause for these shifts is not certainly known except in the last three occasions, in 1855, 1937, and 1947. The first of these was brought about by man unintentionally, the last two intentionally. But what of the early shifts? The earliest recorded major change of course occurred as long ago as 602 B.C. It seems unlikely that man at that time had effected it. Certain, however, is the fact that the complete abandonment of an old course for a new one is not physically possible unless the *bed* of the river stands above the general level of the surrounding plains. This is the case at present and must have held also in the past. Short streams, especially in a dry climate, are known to flow through shallow and elevated channels but for a river of the length of the Huang Ho the raised bed is exceptional. It may be explained in part by the exceptionally heavy load of silt that the river carries from the loess-covered uplands, in part by the sharp drop in gradient after the emergence of the Huang Ho from the canyons, thus encouraging deposition; and in part by man's effort to confine the river within dykes so that the silt load, which normally would be spread over the adjoining land during the occasional flood, is in fact laid on the river bed as the flood water subsides. The one distinguishing mark of the Huang Ho remains its heavy load in relation to volume. No other river of comparable size comes close to it. The heavy load is the result of the easy erodibility of the loess in the uplands. Here the question may be raised: was the rate of loess erosion accelerated through the clearing of forests by hunters and farmers in the Late Neolithic and early historic times? If so, then man may have played an important, though indirect, role even in the earliest changes of the river course on the North China plain.

Climate of western and northwestern China

The part of China that has been most radically transformed by man is obviously the part that most readily responds to his needs. The primary need was, and remains, food. From the point of view of capacity for food production a three-fold climatic partition can be recognized. China is roughly divisable into two equal halves, if we trace a broad curve that begins along the crest of the Great Hsing-an Mountains in the north, swings southwestward across northern Shen-hsi to the city of Lan-chou, and then continues southwestward nearly as a straight line to the Tibetan plateau north of Lhasa. This curved line demarcates a fluctuating boundary between the dry northwestern half of China and the subhumid to humid southeastern half. The next division then is between the subhumid north and the humid south. It may be taken at the latitude of the Ch'in-ling Mountains. To the north mean annual precipitation drops sharply to the 20–30 inches characteristic of the Wei Ho Valley, the North China plain, and the Shan-tung peninsula. To the south the precipitation everywhere exceeds 40 inches; and south of the Yangtze River, in the highlands, large areas receive more than 60 inches annually.

Northwest of the curve rainfall over large areas is less than 5 inches a year. Agriculture cannot be sustained without irrigation. A belt of variable width along the curve itself receives sufficient rain in most years for extensive agriculture using dry-farming practices. Another sizeable area capable of being dry-farmed is the Dzungarian basin at the base of the T'ien Shan. Cyclones migrate eastward through this passage during spring, and yield sufficient moisture to support an original steppe vegetation. Historically, the Dzungarian basin provided an inviting corridor to the migrating Huns, Turks, and Mongols, in contrast to the Tarim basin, which was extremely dry and lacked pasture for the horses of the nomads. Little is known of rainfall distribution over Tibet. The high Chang-tang plateau probably receives only sparse precipitation. The eastern and southeastern parts of Tibet, however, are much wetter. The strength of the Indian monsoon is such that even the high Himalayan barrier can be vaulted, bringing in some years 60 inches or more of rain to the Lhasa basin and beyond.

As one can well imagine, very low temperatures have been recorded in Tibet in spite of its modest latitudinal position between 28° N and 36° N. At the western tip of the plateau Sven Hedin observed a reading of −40°C (−40°F) in December. However, under the strong sunlight one can easily feel uncomfortably hot in sheepskin clothes even in winter: at least this is true of the lower elevation at Lhasa. Summers may be surprisingly mild. At Lhasa mean daily maxima of more than 23°C (73°F) have been recorded for June and July. On the other hand, in northwestern Tibet temperature may drop to −7°C (19°F) in August and frost can be expected every night. Sven Hedin recorded a daytime shade temperature of 43°C (109°F) in mid-September.[15] Strong winds and dust storms in winter and early spring are a regular feature and add to the severity of the Tibetan climate. They commonly move in from the west and are of extraordinary force. The landscape is totally hidden by the driven dust. Street life in Lhasa comes to a stop. The Potola disappears. Strong winds and dust storms also afflict the Tarim basin, although they appear to come more frequently from a northeasterly direction and the winds are less bitingly cold. The elevation of the Tarim basin is only 3,000 to 4,500 feet above sea-level. The fortieth parallel north passes through it. Because of its interior location and aridity the basin experiences wide diurnal and annual temperature ranges. Within the twenty-four hours of a summer day temperature may change by 36 degrees C (65 degrees F), and this range is only slightly less in winter. January temperatures average around −8 to −7°C (17–18°F) and not infrequently plunge to −17.8°C (0°F). Summers may be extremely hot, with average readings in July above 32°C (90°F). The Turfan depression, some 900 feet below sea-level, may be the hottest place in China. A maximum of 48°C (118°F) has been recorded.[16] Temperature ranges are even more extreme on the Mongolian plateau. Naturally there are differences between Outer and Inner Mongolia. It is Outer Mongolia that experiences the most extraordinary annual fluctuations. In the years 1941 to 1960 the highest temperatures at

Ulan Bator have frequently reached 32°C (90°F); in winter temperature has plunged to −45°C (−50°F).[17] Inner Mongolia is only relatively milder. Average January temperature in the Ordos desert may be a few degrees above zero but a minimum of −33°C (−27·4°F) has been recorded.[18] Sharp changes in weather are another characteristic. Autumn is the pleasantest season with sunny days and cool nights, but there may be sudden snowstorms or, alternatively, a monsoonal downpour that momentarily converts the dry steppe into a land of shimmering lakes and rushing water. Icy blasts may occur in summer; and a herdboy of the Ordos can be seen to wear a heavy sheepskin coat in August.[19]

Climate of humid and subhumid China

The great curve that separates the dry northwest from the subhumid to humid part of China may be taken as the inner edge for the effective penetration of moisture-bearing onshore winds. The climate of China is largely governed by the prevailing wind systems that reverse themselves with the seasons. In winter the north monsoonal winds dominate nearly the whole of China. They sweep quickly southward from the Mongolian high-pressure area and cover most of the country in one month. This is the dry season, particularly in North China where, from November to March inclusive, each month receives on the average only 1 per cent of the year's total rainfall. The southeasterly summer monsoon is a much weaker current than the winter monsoon. It reaches the South China coast in April and does not penetrate into Manchuria until the end of June or the beginning of July. It brings rain in time to most of China southeast of the curve, and even far beyond it to the Mongolian plateau. But in comparison with India the onshore monsoon, when it hits the coast and the interior highlands of South China, yields only moderate precipitation. One reason is that the mountains of South China are not high enough to force the currents to reach the level necessary for copious condensation. Orographic rain seems significant only when the monsoon current runs into the high plateaux of Yun-nan and Kuei-chou, and into the mountains of Ssu-ch'uan. Thus the famous Omei Shan of Ssu-ch'uan is one of the wettest places in China, and receives on the average about 76 inches a year. Most of South China has far less. Rain is caused then not so much by orographic uplift as by frontal uplift and in cyclones where air masses of different densities meet. Over the Yangtze Valley warm moist air from the south and cold air from the north begin to converge in spring; cyclones there are especially frequent in April, May and June. North China, however, is not affected by many cyclones until later, in July and August, by which time visitations to the Yangtze Valley have begun to decline.[20] Precipitation over the Yangtze Valley is thus not only heavier than it is over North China but far more evenly distributed through the year.

Another characteristic of precipitation in eastern China is the rapid decrease in both total amount and frequency at about the latitude of the Ch'in-ling Mountains. The mountains themselves are not the full explanation, for the gradient remains steep over the flat coastal province of Chiang-su. Thus south of the Yangtze estuary mean annual precipitation is 43 inches and rain may be expected on 130 days of the year. Less than 300 miles to the north, precipitation declines to 27 inches and the number of rainy days to 50.[21] The very modest precipitation in North China, its high variability from year to year, and the delay in the onset of summer rains until (too often) early July are some of the factors that add to the uncertainty of agriculture.

Temperature pattern in eastern China as a whole is dominated by latitude and locally by relief. The effect of latitude is especially pronounced in winter. Temperature then decreases rapidly polewards. Roughly speaking, average January temperature along the South China coast and in the Hsi Chiang Valley is of the order of 13 to 15°C (55 to 60°F). Frost is rare and the region can be said to have no winter. In the Yangtze Valley January temperatures range from 3°C (38°F) near the coast to 5 to 6°C (42 to 44°F) in the interior. The fact that winter becomes perceptibly milder and shorter as one moves up valley into the depth of the continent is rather unexpected. It appears to be related to the nature of the topographic barrier along the northern rim of the Yangtze Valley. The Red basin of Ssu-ch'uan province lies sheltered behind the Ch'in-ling and Tapa Mountains. Their crest is only about 6,500 feet high, but the mountains nevertheless succeed in keeping out some of the weaker cold waves. In contrast, the lower Yangtze Valley is completely open to the icy blasts.[22] The freezing line for January falls on the latitude of the Ch'in-ling range. Over much of the North China plain average January temperature lies between −8° and −1°C (18° and 30°F). At Peking average temperatures fall below freezing for three months, and minimum temperatures drop to −18°C (0°F). It is in winter that the greatest contrast is seen between North and South China. North China is almost wholly the colour of yellow earth. The few poplars, elms and willows are leafless; the arable lands lie fallow or carry in them the seedlings of winter crops. Dust storms are common and taint everything, even the sky, a pale yellow. South China and the Ssu-ch'uan basin, in contrast, remain green; the green of vegetation on the hillslopes and of growing winter crops in the valleys. In summer the control of latitude weakens. The temperature gradient polewards is very gentle, and in fact average July temperature (28°C; 82°F) in the lower reaches of the Huang Ho is the same as that of the Canton delta, and probably a little higher than that along the exposed coasts of southeast China. Aside from the Turfan depression in Hsin-chiang (Sinkiang) province, the hottest part of China lies in the middle and lower Yangtze Valley. Maximum temperatures of 43°–44°C (110°–112°F) have been recorded in Ch'ang-sha and Nan-ching.[23] The great heat combined with high humidity and the numerous mosquitoes from the numerous lakes, irrigation ditches and ponds all make the Yangtze plain in summer a rather uncomfortable place for human beings.

The appearance of the landscape changes with the seasons: this elementary fact has perhaps been taken too much for granted, for we have no careful description of how the colouring of the land alters seasonally in various parts of China. The live sand-dune deserts and the high arid plateaux presumably undergo little visible change during the yearly cycle despite the extreme variations in temperature. Except for the snow the appearance of the great coniferous forests of Manchuria is affected only in small degree by the seasons. Tropical South China remains green throughout the year. In the Yangtze Valley of central China notable differences exist on the two sides of the Gorges. While the land east of the Gorges may lie in the grip of frost and snow, in the Ssu-ch'uan basin to the west wild grass does not turn yellow, trees shed their leaves but slightly and wheat fields are like the leek in greenness.[24] Undoubtedly the most strikingly seasonal transformations of landscape occur on the North China plain and in the loess-covered valleys of the uplands. Here the shading of green to yellow and yellow to green is an annual pageant.

Climatic fluctuations

Climate also fluctuates from year to year and through time spans much longer than the year. During the Ice Age major changes in climate have occurred in China as in other extra-equatorial parts of the world. In the west the high ranges of Kun-lun and T'ien Shan bore large ice caps which sent tongues of ice to the floor of the Tarim basin. But far more surprising are the evidences of glaciation and intense frost action on the low mountain ranges bordering the central Yangtze Valley at latitudes between 29° and 32° N, and even in such subtropical regions as Kuei-chou and northern Kuang-hsi.[25] During the Ice Age cold spells alternated with periods of warmth. Peking Man lived in North China through one of the longer warm and moist periods that nevertheless had cool and dry intercalations. The end of the Ice Age was marked in North China by a cool and dry phase, a time of strong winds from the interior and the deposition of loess. The environment then appears to have been unattractive to man. Human artifacts in the loess are scanty in comparison with what has been found in the gravel lenses at the base and on the surface. The end of loess accumulation was initiated by a tilting of the uplands and by a change in climate to one of greater warmth and humidity. Erosion set in. The most notable change in the landscape, however, was probably in the vegetation. Much of the loessic uplands became wooded or covered with grass. The steppe bordering the Gobi desert contained many shallow lakes; along their shores lived hunters and fishermen. We need to visualize an altogether richer and better watered scene then than we can see today.

Sometime early in Chinese history desiccation began to affect northern China, and it is still a moot point whether this was brought about primarily by a worsening of climate or primarily by man. Some scholars argue that the climate of the lower Huang Ho basin was warmer and more humid during the Shang dynasty (*c*. 1500–1000 B.C.) than now. Several lines of evidence appear to support this view; for example, Shang sites reveal wild indigenous as well as domesticated animals that have become extinct; and more pertinent, such warmth- and water-loving animals as the elephant, the water deer, the tapir, the rhinoceros, and the bamboo rat have migrated southward.[26] Divinations concerning the weather as recorded on oracle bones also appear to bear witness to a warmer and, in particular, more humid climate during Shang times.[27] However, none of the arguments are conclusive. We simply do not know enough to build a convincing case for climatic change from animal ecology and oracle bones. The gap in knowledge is regrettable for it prevents us from making any confident appraisal of man's role in transforming the Chinese landscape in these early times.

As the number of documents increased in the later historic periods, a more reliable picture can be drawn on the nature of climatic fluctuations.[28] Data concerning the time when certain plants begin to bloom and certain migrating birds appear are recorded in such texts as the *Li Chi*, the *Huai Nan-tzu*, the Annals of Lu and the Book of Chou Kung. They suggest that the lower Huang Ho basin was warmer and more humid in the centuries 250–50 B.C. than now. Records of damaging frosts and colds indicate that the number of severe winters declined from the sixth to the eighth century A.D.; it became exceptionally large in the period A.D. 1100 to 1400, and declined again in the fifteenth century. Chinese chroniclers were especially diligent in recording droughts and floods for the obvious reason that their impact on the welfare of the people was hard and immediate. The ratio of droughts to floods varies significantly from century to century. The fourth century A.D., the period A.D. 500 to 700, and the fifteenth century were notably dry. And during at least two of the dry periods, in the seventh and fifteenth centuries, extensive migration took place.

Natural vegetation

Landforms and climate may be treated simply as natural setting, as the given and stable facts of the physical environment to which human beings adapt themselves. They also have active roles. Earthquakes, changes in river course, floods and droughts act on the Chinese people in no uncertain ways. Natural vegetation has no such role; it is the most vulnerable part of nature. The vegetation cover of China has been drastically altered by man. The precise extent of this alteration is difficult to evaluate, for man has been on the Chinese scene for so long that over large areas all signs of the primeval vegetation have been removed. Recent work suggests that the natural plant cover of China has the following characteristics.[29]

First, there is the basic distinction between woodland on the one hand and grassland and desert on the other. About half of the Chinese domain was originally wooded; the other half was covered with steppe and desert vegetation. The line that separates these two halves is approximately the great curve that lies along the boundary between the arid and the subhumid–humid parts of China (Fig. 7). The curve follows the Great Hsing-an Mountains in the north, swings southwestward to the northern edge of the Wei Ho Valley in central Shen-hsi and to southeastern Kan-su, and continues southwestward to Tibet east and southeast of Lhasa. China east and southeast of this line was originally covered with woodlands. Again, as with climate it is more accurate to think of this curved line as a fluctuating belt of variable width. Between the forest

. Natural vegetation of China. (After Wang)

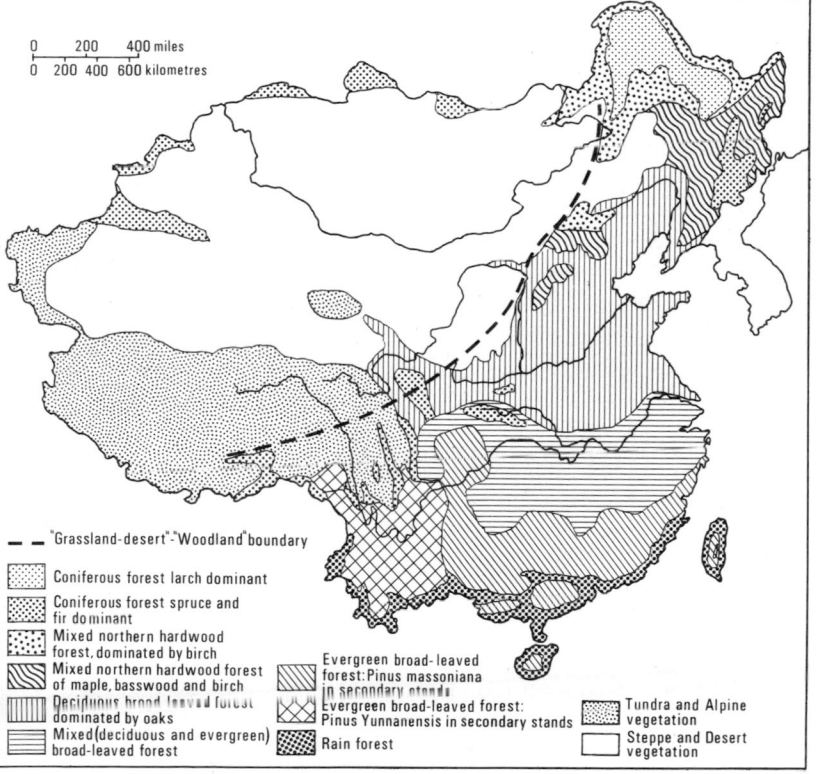

— — "Grassland-desert"-"Woodland" boundary

- Coniferous forest larch dominant
- Coniferous forest spruce and fir dominant
- Mixed northern hardwood forest, dominated by birch
- Mixed northern hardwood forest of maple, basswood and birch
- Deciduous broad-leaved forest dominated by oaks
- Mixed (deciduous and evergreen) broad-leaved forest
- Evergreen broad-leaved forest: Pinus massoniana in secondary stands
- Evergreen broad-leaved forest: Pinus Yunnanensis in secondary stands
- Rain forest
- Tundra and Alpine vegetation
- Steppe and Desert vegetation

and the steppe there usually exists a transitional zone of woodland-steppe. Moreover, patches of forest grow on the well-watered mountain slopes far to the west of the curve. Thus dense forests of tall spruce clothe the cool wet flanks of the T'ien Shan and the Altai Mountains. On the other hand tongues of steppe protrude into the woodland region. The most conspicuous tongue is the one that extends eastward into the upper Liao Ho (Hsi Liao) basin. West of the curve vegetation tends to segregate into concentric rings that reflect the underlying pattern of soil and the rings of increasing humidity away from the dry core. From the centre (a salt lake or a dried lake basin) outwards, the successive rings are alkaline–saline plant communities, desert scrub, steppe and the transitional zone of woodland steppe. On the high Tibetan plateau, too, one can discern concentric patterns focused on the inland lakes and marshes the sequence is from meadows and marsh plants at the centre to the desert shrubs and alpine plants of the rocky plains and slopes beyond. The most common shrub of the cold desert is the white burtsa (*Eurotia ceratoides*) which provides the only vegetable fuel in some parts of the country. It should be added that west of the great woodland-steppe boundary large tracts exist that have practically no vegetation. These are the great sand-dune deserts including, for example, the sand piles of the Ordos and the Takla Makan.

East of the great curve a vast expanse of unbroken forest communities once extended over China in roughly latitudinal belts, from the coniferous forest of northern Manchuria to the rainforest along the South China coast. The Manchurian coniferous forest is strongly reminiscent of those in North America and in Europe; and shares with them many common closely related species. The main trees are: *Larix dahurica, Pinus sylvestris, Picea abovata, P. microsperma, Pinus pumila, Juniperus dahurica.*[30] Composition varies with differences in climatic and soil conditions. On the high Great and Lesser Hsing-an Mountains larch dominates the coniferous forest. On the mountains east of the central Manchurian plain, that is, the Chang-kuang-tsai range and the Chang-pai Mountains, spruce and fir are the most common trees. Below the mountain rim, over the foothills and extending to the northern part of the central Manchurian plain, is a broad semicircle of mixed hardwoods, composed mostly of maple, birch and basswood, with open oak forest in the drier areas. Within the semicircle is the western section of the central Manchurian plain and adjoining hills. In at least the last 200 years or so this has been a broad grassland area with scattered elms *(Ulmus pumila)*, and, to a less extent poplars and oak *(Quercus mongolica)*. It is probable, however, that trees were far more numerous in earlier times. Climate clearly places no barrier to a woodland vegetation over much of this area.

South of the mixed hardwood forest of Manchuria the land has been occupied by man, and – in large areas – intensely exploited by him, for some 2,000 years. The natural vegetation has been almost entirely removed, and in its place we find a deeply humanized landscape. The region includes the North China plain, the Wei Ho basin of Shen-hsi, the lower Liao Ho Valley of Man-churia, and the adjoining uplands such as the lower slopes of the Liao-tung peninsula and the Jehol Mountains, the Shan-hsi plateau and the Shan-tung peninsula. On the basis of vegetation relics, odd bits of literary evidence, and the nature of the environment, it seems possible that the greater part of this region was once wooded, and that the major exceptions were the special plant communities that flourished in the marshes and such salt-impregnated areas as the low coasts and certain interior depressions. The original vegetation was probably a deciduous broadleaved forest dominated by oaks. The several species of the *Quercus (Q. aliena, Q. dentata, Q. variabilis)* were admixed with small stands of ash, elm, and the Chinese hackberry.[31] Along the river courses of the North China plain there grew in the distant past, as now, tall willows *(Salix matsudana* and *S. babylonica)*, and some poplars, though in the past these were not confined to the river courses. If there remains some doubt as to whether the North China plain was originally forested, there is little doubt that its humid southern margin, the Huai River basin, was. At present, not only deciduous, but evergreen broadleaved trees can grow in the basin.

Farther south, in the Yangtze Valley we enter a humid region of mild winters and very hot summers. The original vegetation was a mixed forest formation of deciduous and evergreen broadleaved trees. The zone may therefore be regarded as transitional between two types of broadleaved forests, deciduous in the north and evergreen in the south. In the middle Yangtze Valley itself, elevation differentiated the two types. Deciduous broadleaved trees dominated the moderate elevations, whereas the foothills and the adjoin-ing plains probably had more evergreens including evergreen oaks and the banyan *(Ficus lacor, Ficus* spp.).[32] The upper Yangtze Valley, from western Hu-pei upstream into the Ssu-ch'uan basin, has long been famous for the rich-ness of its flora. The floristic wealth is far from being catalogued, and only in recent years were plants of such singular interest as the *Metasequoia* and the *Taiwania* discovered. In Ssu-ch'uan province the great range in elevation and climate is paralleled by the plant life. The warm valley floors support tropical plants, including useful specimens like the Litchi *(Litchi chinensis)*, the Lung-yen *(Euphoria longana)* and the Chinese olive *(Canarium album)*. The high peaks, on the other hand, reach into zones of permanent snow and support an Alpine vegetation. Between these extremities are broad bands of montane conifers, deciduous broadleaved trees mixed with conifers, and evergreen broadleaved trees.[33] At moderate elevations the entire region, which includes Kuei-chou, Ssu-ch'uan, Hu-pei and parts of Hu-nan, was once covered with a broadleaved forest.

The original vegetation of South China, from southeastern Chê-chiang in the east to southwestern Ssu-ch'uan and Yun-nan in the west, was an evergreen broadleaved forest. In remote areas, much of it still exists. The forest consists mainly of evergreen trees belonging to the genera *Castanopsis*, *Pasania*, and *Quercus*.[34] Though dominated by a few genera, the forest is very rich in species. And in spite of the fact that the constituents are derived from remotely related natural stocks, the forest is remarkably uniform in physiognomy, having the same life-form of rounded, evergreen canopies with glossy, leathery leaves. The trunks are straight and clear, and lacking in plank buttresses. The forest crown reaches a height of over 100 feet. Understoreys of small trees and shrubs exist but are not dense. Lianes and epiphytes are common though not as common as in the rainforest.[35] Thickets of bamboo are locally conspicuous in the evergreen broadleaved forest. They vary greatly in height, from dwarfs (*Arundinaria*) of the upper elevation to the giants (*Dendrocalamus*, *Bambusa*) in the warm, humid valleys.

Along the coast of South China and in some of the interior valleys are narrow strips of a tropical rainforest. It is a part of the evergreen broadleaved formation but it is distinctive physiognomically and generically. The rainforest canopy is solidly packed, with the spreading crowns of large trees and palms protruding above the general level. These may attain heights of 130 to 170 feet. The rainforest is almost entirely evergreen and has a wealth of epiphytes, lianes, climbing palms, and other parasitic plants. The interior of the forest is often open; its floor usually has only a scanty grass cover.[36]

Chapter 2
Man's role in nature

With the appearance of the fire-using *Homo erectus*, man in China must increasingly be counted as a potent force in altering the details of earth's surface. However, it is important to add that from the time of Peking Man, major physiographic changes have taken place in China irrespective of man; that the tectonic forces which shaped the chequerboard physiography remain totally unaffected by human feats; that areas of geologic erosion remain areas of geologic erosion, and the major areas of geologic deposition, such as the North China plain, the central lake basins of the Yangtze Valley and the coastal deltas, remain the major areas of geologic deposition. For all his power, man has thus far affected only the rate, not the direction, of geologic change. Only in small areas and for a limited time can it be said that through human agency the physical processes were checked or reversed. Thus the farmer may be responsible for initiating erosion in small alluviated basins; and by ponding streams he temporarily reverses the process from erosion to deposition in the quiet waters behind the dams. From the air the intricate gullies that seam the loess uplands look very impressive indeed. The farmer has certainly played a part in the multiplication of these gullies but the process of loess erosion began independently of him; and the entire loess layer, even without human interference, would in short geologic time be washed on to the plains and eventually into the sea – unless a major change of climate occurs that once more favours deposition.

Soil processes: natural and man-induced

In North China the total effect of human interference was to accelerate the processes of erosion and deposition, and this had taken place despite the Chinese farmer's strenuous attempts to check erosion by building elaborate tiers of sod and stone walls on the hillsides. The effect of erosion, however, is not always bad, for the concomitant process of deposition enriches the soil in the valleys. On the North China plain, a farm can be completely ruined by alluvium laid down during flood. The silt may be several feet thick. It not only submerges the crops but half buries the farmstead. For a time the land looks utterly derelict. Yet, within two years a new crop will rise out of the new silt and farm life goes on – at a slightly higher level – as though no disaster has occurred. Floods cause more permanent damage when, instead of silt, coarse sand and gravels are laid down. This happens with increasing frequency as gullies cut below the surface cover of loess in the uplands to the underlying clays, coarse sands and bedrock. Slow geologic erosion and deposition may in fact be interpreted as the steady transference of soil fertility from the uplands to the lowlands, a process which, apart from the inconvenience of floods that distribute the silt, is a long-range blessing to the lowland farmer.

The Ssu-ch'uan basin has long acquired fame for its fertility and productivity despite prolonged human use. The Ch'eng-tu plain at the foot of the Tibetan plateau is especially fertile. It appears to owe much of its enduring fertility to the large quantity of rich silt delivered to the plain by the Min Ho. And the source of this rich silt is the thin black or dark brown soil of northeastern Tibet. A dense mat of grass roots normally binds the highland soil but periodically the sod is broken by rodent burrowing and freeze-thaw action so that running water can easily remove large sheets of it and deliver them eventually to the Ch'eng-tu plain.[1] Elsewhere the fertility of hilly Ssu-ch'uan is maintained by the quick weathering and steady erosion of a purplish-brown soil from the underlying bedrock of silty sandstone and shale. In a humid climate immobile soils tend to be leached of their nutrients. A hilly topography, on the other hand, encourages high soil mobility and erosion. In Ssu-ch'uan rice terraces prevent excessive erosion, and yet downhill migration of soil particles occurs at a rate sufficient to prevent excessive leaching. However, in some parts of Ssu-ch'uan sheet erosion does become excessive. These are the areas of steeply dipping sandstone. The soil on them was originally very shallow. When such lands were cleared for cultivation sheetwash quickly removed the sandy soil so that large areas of bedrock are now exposed.[2] The Ssu-ch'uanese farmer's response to erosion is heroic. He gathers up what small patches of soil he can still find and builds them into narrow crescentic strips or terraces. These are only 20 to 30 feet wide and are surrounded by bare rock.

In central and South China, wherever elaborate rice terraces have been built, soil erosion is practically nil. But it would appear that farmers have achieved this erosion control largely by accident. Farmers construct level terraces, supported by walls, in order to hold back water for rice; and, as a byproduct of their efforts, they manage to produce an effective system for erosion control.[3] The proof of this belief lies in the fact that the farmer's sense for soil conservation totally deserts him when he plants upland crops on unirrigated fields near the rice terraces; he does this in neat rows up and down the cleared hillside, and erosion is immediate. Extensive forests in South China have been cleared for upland crops and other reasons, with the inevitable accompaniment of excessive erosion on the hillsides and deposition in the valleys. During the early stages of this process the effect was not always bad. For example, in South China many valleys were of the V-shaped type with bottoms too narrow and stony for extensive farming. Soils washed from the hills were deposited in the alleys which thus became flat-floored and well suited to rice cultivation. But the blessing was temporary; further erosion on the hillsides brought the leached and impoverished tropical soils of the hills into the valleys, covering their floors with a more or less sterile layer. This layer the farmers must remove in order to reach the fertile soil underneath.

The effect of man on the soil has also a constructive side. In the long-occupied and densely settled valleys and plains the nutrient level of the alluvium is largely a human achievement. The intensity with which the Chinese farmer fertilizes his land – using almost every conceivable source that can be locally obtained – is well known.[4] However, since an important proportion of the fertilizer occurs in the form of night soil, there is always a larger amount available near the big cities and towns than in the remote country districts. Large cities are therefore surrounded by irregular rings of fertile soil which extend at least as far as a man can walk and return in one day with a load. From the air, the city appears to be the centre of a green oasis which fades gradually to the brown of the distant countryside. This distinctive pattern is produced by the flow of nitrogen and other plant foods in the form of agricultural produce from the farms to the city and the return flow of faeces from the city to the farms; but only to farms within easy walking distance of the city, for greater distance would raise transportation charges sufficiently to make it uneconomical to transport night soil.[5] In the delta regions of eastern and southeastern China, however, these fertility rings are less noticeable because the farmers there are able to transport night soil and other fertilizers to far greater distances in canal boats.[6] Another practice characteristic of farmers on the low-lying deltas is the use of canal mud to fertilize the fields. Canal mud is spread over the fields in the course of natural flooding but farmers are contributing to the process so that the level of the land is rising somewhat faster than it would if it depended entirely on natural deposition.

Effect on vegetation cover

Although man's impact on large physical features and on geologic processes is modest, his impact on the vegetation cover and the related systems of soil, run-off and microclimate is profound. About half of the Chinese domain could have been forested at one time. Now, only a small fraction of the country is forested, and an even smaller fraction retains anything like a primitive cover. As a recent visitor, S. D. Richardson, has said, the shortage of forest produce must be experienced to be believed. Bamboo, bagasse, straw and grass are frequently used in building construction and paper manufacture. Jointed transmission poles are a regular feature of the landscape; and it would seem that in some districts used toilet paper is collected and returned to the mill for repulping.[7]

Significant areas of relatively little disturbed forest still exist in the remote parts of Yun-nan, in western Ssu-ch'uan, on the edge of the Tibetan plateau in the Ch'in-ling Mountains, in Kuang-hsi, Kuang-tung (particularly the interior of Hai-nan island), Kuei-chou and Chiang-hsi. But by far the largest and most accessible virgin forest lies in northern Manchuria, in a horseshoe area formed of the eastern margin of the Mongolian plateau, the Great and Lesser Hsing-an Mountains and the Chang-pai Mountain complex. This northern coniferous forest now contains about 60 per cent of China's total reserves.[8] Until the beginning of the twentieth century it was, as one naturalist puts it, a 'sea of green' with 'no gap visible', and it 'just rolled on and on seemingly without end'.[9] When the Manchus ruled China northern Manchuria was reserved for themselves and forbidden territory to Chinese settlers. But the beginning of the twentieth century saw the opening of this land to Chinese farmers, who at the crest of migration in the early 1930s, moved in at the rate of almost half a million a year. It is true that most of them settled on the woodland steppe of the central plains and on the rich forest soils of the lower foothills, but many migrated into the zone of the conifers. In the drainage basin of the Mutan Ho (a tributary of the Sungari) and on the slopes of the Chang-pai Mountains, farmers have noticeably altered the composition of the spruce-fir forest. Extensive areas of conifers were cut, and the space tended to be filled by hardwood species.[10] Below the horseshoe of coniferous forest, a vast mixed coniferous forest once covered the foothills of the mountain rim and extended to the eastern part of the central Manchurian plain. Farmers, however, have reduced it to a shadow of its former self. The drier western part of the central plain is also being rapidly transformed into large state farms, but there is less certainty as to the nature of its original vegetation. In the nineteenth century, when the plain was very sparsely settled, the drier western edge was an open steppe country with scattered trees, mostly elms. Trees do reproduce themselves in this semi-arid and subhumid belt; it seems likely therefore that they were once far more prominent in the landscape than they are today or in the last 200 years. Although population on the central plain has made rapid gains only since the beginning of the present century, nevertheless the plain has been the home of Tungusic peoples for much longer; perhaps for more than twenty centuries. In that time the Tungus were at first hunters and fishermen, later pastoralists and farmers, having picked up farming techniques from the Chinese who had established themselves at the southern end of the lowland prior to the Ch'in dynasty (222–207 B.C.). The plain may owe its grass cover more to man, his use of fire and his livestock, than to a climate that is hostile to tree growth. Since 1951 the Chinese government has attempted to plant a vast belt of trees, covering some 11,500 square miles, at the dry edge of the plain. Among the species used in the planting is the native elm (*Ulmus pumila*), as well as drought-resistant poplars and willows.[11] It is of great interest to see whether the planted trees will survive and reproduce themselves.

The part of China that has supported a dense population for the longest period of time is a large territory: it includes the Wei Ho basin and Shan-hsi plateau in the west, the Shan-tung peninsula in the east and the North China plain in between. To this region, in winter, we can suitably apply the term 'Yellow Earth'. In summer it has a green carpet of grass and crops, but very few trees can be seen; and these occur in clusters around temples in the mountains, around villages on the plains, and in thin rows along a few roads. All are protected or planted by man. The exposed slopes of Shan-hsi plateau and the hills of Shan-tung receive more rain than the North China plain. Although the greater part of these uplands now look sadly barren they were undoubtedly well wooded in an earlier period of Chinese history. The Japanese monk, Ennin, for example, crossed both the Shan-tung peninsula and the Shan-hsi plateau in the ninth century, and his descriptions of a wooded and, in part, wet, poorly drained landscape are in striking contrast to what can be seen in these uplands in the nineteenth and early twentieth century.[12] There seems little doubt also that where the soil cover has not been wholly washed off, reforestation is easily possible. Thus the strip of land north of the port of Ch'ing-tao in Shantung province is forested, in sharp distinction to the barren hills beyond. The forest was planted under German supervision, at a time when Ch'ing-tao came under their judicial control. If the port bears unhappy witness to Germany's imperialistic ambition, the green belt is a tribute to that country's attitude towards land.

But what was the nature of the primary vegetation on the North China plain? Opinions vary. Steppe, woodland steppe, and woodland have all been suggested. C. W. Wang favours the woodland.[13] He believes that the plain was once covered extensively by a deciduous broadleaved forest, in which the *Quercus* dominated, and that it was similar in composition to the upland forests of Shan-hsi and Shan-tung. This image of a well-wooded North China plain is hard to conjure up today. The willows, poplars and elms along the watercourses may be in their proper ecological niches. However, a great many other species can also be found. Wang lists forty, including *Ailanthus altissima*, *Albizzia julibrissin*, *Koelreuteria paniculata*, Chinese hackberry (*Celtis sinensis*), 'Red cedar' (*Cedrela sinensis*), ash, English walnut, Chinese juniper, elms, poplars, oaks, willows, pine (*Pinus tabulaeformis*), *Thuja orientalis*, and *Zizyphus vulgaris*. On the hills these trees may grow wild but on the alluvial plain they exist in plantations and in seminatural stands under human protection. The vegetation type owes much to man. Thus Wang thinks it likely that the common *Zizyphus vulgaris*, which grows semiwild but is also planted for its fruits, is a domesticated form of the common thorny shrub *Zizyphus vulgaris* var. *spinosa* of the hills. There is the fact that certain trees would be negligible in a dense forest but prosper in the present open fields; for example, *Ailanthus*, *Koelreuteria*, pine and *Thuja*. The composition of trees on the alluvial plain has also been altered because man has favoured certain species, either because they are fast-growing and have evident economic value or because they have acquired religious sanction.

Forestry has old roots in China. In the *Chou Li* or *Rites of Chou* (3rd century B.C.?) we find two classes of officials whose duties were concerned with conservation. One was the *Shan-yu*, inspectorate of mountains, and the other the *Lin-heng*, inspectorate of forests. The inspectors of mountains were charged with the care of forests in the mountains. They saw to it that certain species were preserved, and in other ways enforced conservation practices. Thus trees could only be cut by the common people at certain times; those on the south side in the middle of winter and those on the north side in the middle of summer. At other seasons the people were permitted to cut wood in times of urgent need, such as when coffins had to be made or dykes strengthened, but even then certain areas could not be touched. The *Lin-heng* or inspectors of forests had similar duties. Their authority extended over forests that spread below the mountains.[14] Another ancient literary reference to conservation practice was in the *Mencius*. The sage advised King Huai of Liang that he would not lack for wood if he allowed the people to cut trees only at the proper time.[15]

There existed then an ancient tradition of forest care, and this tradition has persisted into the present century. It received official encouragement but was practised by the people on their own initiative when forest care did not conflict with the urgent needs of the moment. Nearly forty years ago, the American conservationist W. C. Lowdermilk noted how thousands of acres in An-hui and Ho-nan were planted to pine from local nurseries, a practice he recognized as ancient and independent of the modern forestry movement.[16] Lowdermilk also found that the North China plain 'actually exports considerable quantities of logs of *Paulownia tomentosa* to Japan and poplar (*Populus tomentosa*) to match factories. It is true that no forests are to be found in this plain, but each village has its trees, which are grown according to a system.'[17]

Roadside planting is an ancient practice in China and dates back to the Eastern Chou (722–222 B.C.) and Ch'in (222–207 B.C.) periods. Common species traditionally used for roadsides include the poplar (*Populus simonii*), pines (especially *Pinus tabulaeformis*), willows (*Salix babylonica, S. matsudana*), chestnut (*Aesculus chinensis*), elm (*Ulmus parvifolia*), and the Chinese scholar tree (*Sophora japonica*).[18]

The best-known illustration of Chinese knowledge of forestry and of their desire for forest aesthetics and products is the tree grove in the temple compounds. Almost every large village has a temple with its well-managed cluster of trees, and in particular is this true of temples and monasteries located in the mountains.[19] Certain trees appear to have special religious significance and receive special care as, for example, the maidenhair tree (*Ginkgo biloba*), the white-barked pine (*Pinus bungeana*), and the peacock pine (*Cryptomeria*

8. Pijun Temple in the Western Mountains of Peking (Peiping)

japonica). These are rarely seen in the wild state. Other trees of religious significance are the chestnut (*Aesculus chinensis*) for the Taoists, and later the Buddhists, and the linden (*Tilia mandshurica*) for the Buddhists, to replace the tropical peepul tree (*Ficus religiosa*) of India.

In Communist China trees are extensively planted in answer to dire economic need but also for aesthetic reasons. Roadside plantings use the 'traditional' trees, in particular the poplars. Afforestation proceeds in villages, and most conspicuously, in cities, new suburbs and industrial districts where trees hide a great deal of the raw ugliness of new construction. As Richardson says:

> Their variety, the extent of the planting and the flowering shrubs which are often grown with them are serving to put new developments in China's city suburbs among the most attractive in the world. The millions of trees which have been planted in Peking make a memorable sight, while the avenue plantings of Kunming, Sian, Hangchow, and Kwangchow are almost as impressive; even the industrial slums of Harbin and Shanghai are being systematically blotted out by greenery.[20]

Except for the mountain rim, the lower slopes and the alluvial basins of the Yangtze Valley are as denuded of their forest cover and as intensely transformed by man as the North China plain. The original vegetation was probably a mixed (evergreen and deciduous) broadleaved forest at moderate elevations, changing to a predominantly evergreen forest on the valley floor. However, the valley lands and a large part of the surrounding hills have been under cultivation for a long time. The vegetation that is to be found in modern times reflect strongly human influence. E. H. Wilson, the naturalist who explored western China in the early part of this century, has indeed expressed the view that man has lived in the Ssu-ch'uan basin for so long that no part of the remaining forest can be regarded as natural.[21] Evergreen oaks, the evergreen *nanmu* of the *Lauraceae* family, and the common banyan (*Ficus* spp.) occur in small clusters and suggest that the primary vegetation might have been an evergreen broad-leaved forest. However, the banyans, which are very noticeable in Ssu-ch'uan appear to owe their conspicuousness to human protection. Thorp says that 'They are used for ornamentation and shade and as objects of worship. It is very common to see one of these broad-spreading trees capping the top of an otherwise bare hill.'[22] By far the most important and widespread of the planted trees in the Yangtze Valley is the Chinese fir (*Cunninghamia lanceolata*). It is now the most useful general-purpose timber outside Manchuria. Though once it might have formed an important element in the mixed broadleaved forest of the Yangtze Valley, it is now, in the lower part of the valley, rarely found outside the plantations. From the mountains of western Hu-pei upstream, *Cunninghamia* begins to reappear as a constituent of the natural forest.

Within the drainage basin of the Upper Yangtze and on the limestone areas of the Kuei-chou plateau are great expanses of tall grass. Small patches of broadleaved forest with a scattering of pine still surround temples and can also be seen at the base of steepsided limestone hills where deep soils accumulate. The natural vegetation of broadleaved trees has been largely cleared, in part for cultivation but even more for raising cattle, which happens to be an important occupation in Kuei-chou.[23] Repeated burning, in places annual, perpetuates the grass cover. A secondary growth of pine and oaks may appear in the burned-over areas. In western Kuei-chou conifers now dominate the landscape.[24]

South China's natural vegetation cover is an evergreen broadleaved forest. Along the coast it assumes the physiognomy of a rainforest, with its characteristically dense, uneven canopy, and great wealth of lianes and epiphytes. Extensive tracts of the little-touched rainforest still exist in Yun-nan, Kuang-hsi, and in the interior of Hai-nan island. Much of the lowland has been cleared. North of the coastal rainforest the wide belt of shorter, broadleaved evergreens, dominated by the genera *Quercus*, *Castanopsis* and *Pasania*, has been transformed by fire and cultivation to an impressive degree. Whole mountains in northeastern Kuang-hsi are nearly treeless and covered with tall, coarse grasses (*cogonals*). Over vast areas throughout the southern uplands, fire and cultivation have reduced the original vegetation to secondary growth of bushes, tall grasses and ferns (*Gleichenia* and *Pteridium*), and secondary forests of hardwoods and pines (*Pinus Massoniana* and, in Yunnan, the longeedled *Pinus yunnanensis*).[25] In the southern uplands, as in the Yangtze alley, the most popular planted tree is the *Cunninghamia*. Bamboo thickets e a conspicuous element of the natural vegetation. They have also been ostered by farmers. Certain trees are protected in the villages of South China. he camphor tree (*Cinnamomum camphora*), for example, is a prominent ilhouette in the landscape as one approaches a village surrounded by cultivated elds. The camphor is also commonly found on grave plots.

Causes of deforestation

What forces, under human direction, brought about these enormous changes in the plant cover, and hence in the character of the Chinese landscape? Of my long-settled, intensely humanized region in the world, we can draw up a st of forces and the motives for their use that are capable of explaining the transformation of the biotic mantle; and it would not be very different from any list such as we may compile for China. Thus fire is almost universally used y man to clear forests. The forest is cleared to create more grazing land. Close grazing by livestock hinders the regrowth of forest, and may indeed cause the complete destruction of the vegetal cover. Forest is cleared to extend rable land. Its timber is needed for the construction of palaces, houses and hips; for domestic and industrial fuel, and as raw material for pulp mills. Then again the forest is pushed back because it may harbour dangerous wild nimals, or because it is simply rather merry to see the trees and grass go up n flame. But there are naturally differences of means and motives. In contrast o the Mediterranean world, for example, China's vegetation suffered less rom depredations by sheep and goats, and from the enormous demand on imber made by the shipbuilding industry of the maritime powers. China's orests, on the other hand, suffered more from the exigencies of a dense farm-ng population, from the demands of house construction and the need for domestic fuel.

Consider some of the conditions distinctive to China that help one to under-tand the deforestation of so much of the country. Peking Man has already been mentioned, and this is a good place to reintroduce him, for of the hominid ncestors of modern man he is one of the earliest to whom knowledge of fire an be attributed with certainty. The Chou-kou-tien site bears abundant evidence of hearths, suggestive of family groups that gathered at the same place or extended stays. The people at the site made use of plants in the area, in particular the hackberry, but to judge from the prevalence of deer bones among he animal remains it would seem that their favourite food was venison.[26] This raises an interesting problem, for the deer is a swiftfooted, elusive animal, not one that the people of Chou-kou-tien, with their very primitive weapons of clubs, axe and spear, can hunt down or entrap with ease. C. O. Sauer asked

3

'whether the tool that early man managed best, namely fire, was not also t
device by which he drove this fleet and timid game to destruction at his hands
In what ways can the earliest hunters and gatherers, using Peking Man as
model, transform the landscape by making significant alterations in the pla:
cover? C. O. Sauer says:

> The glimpse into a remote past afforded by the Peking finds is sufficient f
> us to ascribe to man an ancient role in the modification of vegetation. He h:
> habitual camp sites; he wore paths out from them that became bordered l
> trailside weeds that took advantage of the added sunlight and tolerat«
> trampling and other disturbance. Seeds and roots were dropped along tl
> trails and at the camps, and some of them grew and reproduced themselve
> Kitchen refuse, thrown out about the camps, enriched the soil with ash«
> and nitrogenous matter, and new combinations of plants found advanta;
> in the altered soil. Collecting grounds were disturbed by the digging f«
> food, from roots and grubs to rodents. Dug ground is always open to veg«
> tation changes. If fires were set primordially, at first to facilitate collectin
> and then as a hunting device, a most potent aid to vegetative modificatio
> was assured, . . . [Burning] was the best simple device for driving fleet an
> big game so that it could be destroyed in mass. Where it was used, it affecte
> the reproduction of plants and altered the composition of vegetation.[27]

Hunting was a necessity to the people of Chou-kou-tien; fire may have bee
used as a principal device. By the time of the early Chou period in Chines
history (c. 1000–700 B.C.) hunting became a sport – at least for the nobles
and evidence exists in the Shi Ching that fire was used to drive out the wil
animals.[28] In an agricultural civilization the commonest reason for setting o
fires was undoubtedly to extend cultivable land. The grand historian of Chin:
Ssu-ma Ch'ien (145?–90? B.C.), in his monumental Shi Chi, described th
sparsely settled Yangtze Valley as a country where land is 'tilled with fir
and hoed with water'.[29] The ambiguous expression translated as 'tilled wit
fire' probably referred to the clearing of the land with fire. That it is a com
mon practice in modern times and in the more sparsely settled areas has ofte
been observed. Sowerby in 1913 was impressed by the vast and seemingl
virgin forest of northern Manchuria. However, even then he could see trail
of smoke rising out of it where men had settled. Flying over the rugged part
of South China today, it is easy enough to observe the severely deforested an«
eroded nature of the country, and to recognize the continuation of this proces
in the large number of smoke plumes, which mark, in all likelihood, the tem
porary clearings of the slash-and-burn agriculturists.

Chinese farmers have also engaged in the immemorial practice of setting th
forest on fire in order to deprive dangerous animals of their hiding places. Ther
exists an interesting account in the Mencius of how in ancient times the luxuri

nt vegetation sheltered so many wild beasts that men were endangered. The great minister Shun of legendary repute ordered Yih to use fire, and 'Yih set fire to, and consumed, the forests and vegetation on the mountains and in the marshes, so that the birds and beasts fled away to hide themselves.'[30] In modern times Shaw reported that non-Chinese tribes in Kuang-hsi and Kuei-chou provinces burnt forests to drive away tigers and leopards, and Thorp noted in 1924 numerous fires in central Shen-hsi which were started ostensibly for no other purpose.[31] It is not always easy to establish the real reason for setting fire to forest. When asked the farmers may say that it is to clear land for cultivation, although the extent of burning far exceeds the needs for this purpose; or it is to leave fewer places in which bandits may hide; or to encourage the growth of small-sized sprouts in the burnt-over area, which then would save the farmers the labour of splitting wood! And even more shocking, there is the possibility that people may enjoy a big blaze.[32] A fire can of course be started accidentally. A risk that is special to the Chinese is the forest fire caused by the burning of paper money at the grave mounds, which, in the rugged parts of the South, are commonly located beyond the fields and at the edge of the forested hills.

The need for fuel has made, and still makes, a heavy toll on Chinese forests. An enormous amount of wood is consumed for cooking and for heating, particularly in North China where the winters can be bitterly cold. Farm children are regularly employed to gather household fuel; and in the badly denuded parts of the country such as Shan-tung, this means scavenging among the stunted shrubs, picking up odd twigs, dried leaves and grass. A persistent problem in modern afforestation programmes is to discourage farmers from breaking off branches and twigs of young trees during cold spells, when immediate needs overcome their recognition that it is desirable to build up supplies for the future. Forests in North China were ravaged in the past for the making of charcoal as an industrial fuel. From the tenth century onwards the expanding metal industries swallowed up many hundreds of thousands of tons of charcoal each year, as did the manufacture of salt, alum, bricks, tiles, and liquor. Robert Hartwell calculates that in 1080, if only charcoal had been used, a forest of 22,000 medium-sized trees would have been needed to mint iron and copper cash alone.[33] Brick became a common construction material in China since the Later Han times. It was used for building houses, facing tombs, and for dressing the faces of the earthen walls of great cities. The demand for wood and charcoal as both household and industrial fuel had reached such a pitch by the Sung dynasty (A.D. 960–1279) that the timber resources of the country could no longer meet it, and this probably led to the increasing substitution, since the Sung period, of coal for wood and charcoal. It is of interest to note that cremation also required wood as fuel. The fact may seem unimportant because the normal Chinese response (certainly the official response) to cremation was one of horror. However, under the influence of Buddhism and the pressure of the shortage of land for burial, the burning of corpses was a fairly common practice from the tenth to the fourteenth century in the coastal provinces of Shan-tung, Chiang-su, and Chê-chiang, as well as in some inland districts.[34]

An enormous amount of timber was needed in the construction of the Chinese city, more than was needed in a Western city of comparable size. The reason for this lies in the dependence of traditional Chinese architecture on timber as the basic structural material. The *Shi Ching*, a collection of poems that includes some of the oldest pieces of Chinese literature, describes in one poem how a temple is built.

> We ascended the Ching mountain
> Where the pines and cypresses grew symmetrical.
> We cut them down, and conveyed them here;
> We reverently hewed them square.
> Long are the projecting beams of pine;
> Large are the many pillars.

The temple was completed – a resting place (for his spirit).[35]

A large palace of the sort that the first Ch'in emperor was said to have begun constructing in 212 B.C. would require a far greater quantity of fine timber than the sort of temple described in the *Shi Ching*. A whole mountain may be denuded of its trees for the purpose. At least this was how one poet put it.

> When the Six Kingdoms came to an end
> When the Four Seas were unified
> When the mountains of Ssu-ch'uan were denuded
> Then the A-p'ang palace appeared.[36]

And if a large palace required much timber, a whole city would require much more, especially if it were of the size of Ch'ang-an, capital of the T'ang dynasty, and Hang-chou, capital of the Southern Sung dynasty. Both had populations of over a million people. The great expansion in the size of Hang-chou in the thirteenth century caused the neighbouring hills to be stripped of much of their forest for construction timber. The demand for timber was such that some farmers gave up rice cultivation for forestry.[37] Cities in which houses were largely made of wood ran the constant danger of demolition by fire and this was especially true of southern metropolises where the streets tended to be narrow. The necessity to rebuild after fire put further strain on timber resources. But of far greater consequence than the accidental burning of parts of cities was the deliberate devastation of whole cities in times of disorder, as rebels or nomadic invaders toppled a dynasty. The succeeding phase of reonstruction was normally achieved in remarkably short time, by armies of men who made ruthless inroads on the forest to acquire building materials.

In contrast to maritime civilizations, shipbuilding in China played a relatively minor role in deforestation compared with the needs of other types of construction. Beginning in the Southern Sung dynasty, however, China entered a phase – lasting some two or three centuries – in which she became the dominant maritime power of Asia. It was during the Southern Sung dynasty that, for the first time, China acquired a national navy and in short time built up a sizeable fleet. In 1130 the Sung had eleven squadrons with 3,000 men; in 1237, twenty squadrons with 52,000 men. The Mongols who followed the Sung in ruling China further enlarged the navy. They embarked on a gigantic programme of shipbuilding, with shipyards at Ch'ang-sha, Canton, Lung-hu (in northeastern Ho-pei), the Korean provinces of Cholla-do and other places. The northern shipyards made severe demands on the northern forests, those in the mountains of Jehol and on Quelpart island. It is recorded that on one occasion an army of 17,000 men was sent to fell trees in Jehol.[38]

This section may suitably close with the observation of a phenomenon that is uniquely Chinese. E. H. Schafer has recently said that the most civilized of all arts was responsible for the deforestation of much of North China. The art was the art of writing, which required soot for the making of black ink. The soot came from the burnt pine. 'Even before T'ang times, the ancient pines of the mountains of Shan-tung had been reduced to carbon, and now the busy brushes of the vast T'ang bureacracy were rapidly bringing baldness to the T'a-hang Mountains between Shansi and Hopei.'[39]

Part Two
Landscape and Life in Chinese Antiquity

Chapter 3
Prehistoric scenes

A cool and dry phase prevailed over North China towards the end of the Pleistocene. Loess was being deposited. North China and Inner Mongolia appear to have been very sparsely settled at this time, perhaps more so than the Ssu-ch'uan basin and South China. The end of the loess stage was marked by a series of changes the effect of which was to introduce an environment much more congenial to man than had been the case during the immediate past. In the Huang Ho basin the climate became warmer and more humid; the vegetation cover expanded; animal life was more abundant and showed a change from such Pleistocene forms as mammoth and the woolly rhinoceros to a modern faunal group that included many southern species. The land had risen, and this, together with the fact that streams were better fed in a moister climate, caused the Huang Ho and its tributaries to begin a new phase of erosion.[1]

In this attractive and diversified setting population gained rapidly: fishermen and hunters established themselves over a vast territory including Manchuria, the middle Huang Ho Valley and Inner Mongolia. With the appearance of agriculture and village life population increased even more rapidly, if we can judge from the thousands of sites thus far identified and from the size of some of the villages.[2] However, the area of occupation seems to have experienced no further growth in the northern regions; instead there was a tendency for settlements to be concentrated in a narrower band centred on the middle Huang Ho basin. Somewhat later, the area occupied by Neolithic villages spread eastward and southward to the North China plain and the coastal regions of southeast China. If the changes in settlement pattern are traced to early historic times one gains the impression that the dry margins of northern China were gradually abandoned by farmers and taken over by nomads. In still later periods documented evidence of the desiccation of landscape begins to appear. Not only the plains of Inner Mongolia but the core area of Chinese civilization was affected. How does one explain this apparent trend? The explanation that most readily comes to mind is that climate had become progressively dry since the wet phase that followed the laying down of loess. But the explanation is not satisfactory for general climatological reasons. Moreover, in marshalling evidence for this view it is all too easy to misread the evidence of landscape: one tends to identify a wooded land with humid climate and a sparsely vegetated land with dry climate, when the difference in vegetation may simply have been caused by the farmers' axes. An alternative interpretation is that there has been no progressive change in climate since the end of the Pleistocene, only fluctuations, and that the striking evidences of desiccation in various parts of North China and Inner Mongolia were man-induced. There is much to support this view, especially in the historic period. But we can be less certain of what happened in Mesolithic and Neolithic times. It seems incontrovertible that, following loess deposition, the climate turned significantly warmer and more humid. The difficulty is to evaluate the extent to which the subsequent drying up of the land was initiated by a return to more arid climate. Human agency alone seems insufficient to explain the phenomenon. As the landscapes of North China from prehistoric to early historic times are being described, this unresolved problem should be borne in mind.

The well-watered landscape of the prehistoric North

In recent history – that is, within the last several hundred years – Inner Mongolia, the upper Liao basin and parts of the central Manchurian plain have been a semi-arid steppe country, just as they are today. Dry-farming techniques allow pioneer farmers to grow crops, but yields are uncertain. For more than 2,000 years pastoral nomadism was the dominant way of life. The landscapes of Inner Mongolia, in particular, are dry and flat, the flat surfaces punctuated here and there by large and small hollows. Around the rims of these hollows and partly embedded in wind-blown sand, archaeologists have found with surprising frequency cultural remains that indicate the presence of hunters and fishermen; people who were not merely passing through but found temporary homes there. Obviously the environment then was quite different from what we can see today.[3] The dry river beds, the dry basins and hollows that now contain salt pools then had fresh water, well stocked with fish and molluscs. The surrounding country was not a poor steppe but had rich grass and scattered trees. The favoured game appears to have been the ostrich. Fragments of ostrich egg shells are preserved at the camp sites. Hunting – at least of large game – was subordinate to collecting and fishing, and this suggests that the settlements grouped around the lakes and streams had some degree of permanence. Farther north, in the vicinity of the Djalai-nor the climate was cooler and more humid. Pleistocene fauna, such as the *Elephas nomadicus* and *Rhinoceros tichorhinus*, survived there to a later date than in Europe. It is curious to find a fragment of a basket made with willow sticks together with remains of a Pleistocene animal. The basket might have been a fish trap. The dweller of Djalai-nor was a fisherman who also hunted. A similar culture and environment existed on the central Manchurian plain, which at that time was ell wooded. North China too was well wooded. On the edge of the North China plain, men lived in dry limestone caves.

Nearby there were woods in which tigers, leopards, bears, and wolves dwelt; there were steppes on which the Chinese deer, the red deer, and gazelle roamed about; and plains and lakes in which gigantic fish swam. The man hunted in the woods and fished by the lakes, and made abundant bone and shell artifacts.[4]

The appearance of agriculture

t was in some such wooded, well-watered and diversified environment that he fishermen and hunters in North China turned to agriculture, and introduced the arts, the skills, and the large communal style of living characteristic of Neolithic cultures. There had been no decisive break with the past. The skills of the lake-dwellers and woodland hunters were continued to the later Neolithic stage. In Mongolia the sites remained the same, near to areas of water. Desiccation had not yet set in. Pottery fragments and spindle whorls indicate that the lake-dwellers of Inner Mongolia had come under the influence of farmers to the south, but their way of life probably saw few major changes. It still depended on fishing, food-gathering, and hunting, although the appearance of hoes and digging weights suggests that some sort of agriculture was eventually practised.[5]

In the Huang Ho basin, though certain traditions from an earlier time lingered on, the innovations were numerous and fundamental. Most important of all was the great increase in available food through the acquisition of domesticated plants and livestock. Archaeologists have determined the presence of such cereals as foxtail millet (*Setaria italica*), common millet (*Panicum miliaceum*), kaoliang (*Andropogon miliaceum*), rice (*Oryza sativa*) and possibly wheat. Among domesticated animals dogs and pigs were by far the most numerous and most widespread in distribution. Less common were cattle, sheep and goats. Industries included the weaving of hemp, which was probably cultivated, and perhaps even the weaving of silk.[6]

Some thousands of Neolithic sites have thus far been identified in the Huang Ho valley and plain. Most of them belong to two stages, the earlier one known as Yang-shao and the later one known as Lung-shan. The nucleus of the Yang-shao culture corresponds to a topographic basin that has been known traditionally as the nuclear area of the Chinese civilization. The area is drained by the Huang Ho and two confluents, the Wei and the Fen, which together assume the shape of a crescent. At a later date the cultural complex of the nuclear area sent an extension to the west, to the neighbourhood of the confluence of the T'ao Ho with the upper Huang Ho. The nuclear area of the

Lung-shan culture is less well defined but remains of the Lung-shan stage occur typically on the North China plain, on Shan-tung peninsula and in southeastern China.

Late Neolithic landscapes

Yang-shao

What was the natural environment of the Yang-shao farmer and how had he transformed it? We may begin by noting some of the present characteristics of the landscape, and from available evidence infer the condition of the distant past. The Swedish geologist, J. G. Andersson, was the first person to recognize and excavate a late Neolithic village in China. The site he more or less stumbled upon in 1921 lay on a strip of eroded land between the Huang Ho in the north and a tributary, the Lo Ho, in the south.[7] This is the inner edge of the North China plain, not far from the place where the Huang Ho emerges from its hardrock bed. The material underlying the area is loess and red clay, the loess forming an irregular mantle over the eroded surface of the clay. The strip had been severely dissected. Some ravines are more than 150 feet deep and have cut through not only the loess but the clay underneath, into the bedrock itself. Irrigation on any scale is clearly impossible on the deeply trenched topography. Crops depend on the normally light rainfall, and if it should fail there is no reserve of moisture in the subsoil. Yang-shao ts'un was an insignificant village on the loess plateau, until its present fame in the archaeological world. It is built partly above ground but part of it consists of cave dwellings dug into the sides of the ravines. In the neighbourhood of this village Andersson discovered potsherds in a grey cultural layer topping the loess plateaux and pillars. The potsherds were taken to belong to a Neolithic village that occupied the present site of Yang-shao ts'un some four or five thousand years ago. But the site then looked totally different from what it is today. It had a level surface, with a scattering of ponds and streams, and was well wooded. Several lines of evidence support this rather sylvan picture of the Neolithic past. For one thing, the cultural stratum was once obviously continuous whereas now it caps narrow ridges and pillars on which settlement is impossible. For another, gravel accumulations as much as 20 feet thick occur on the surface of the loess and indicate that in the Neolithic age deposition rather than erosion was the dominant process in at least some localities. There is also indication that the Yang-shao farmers dug wells; if so the water-table of those times must have been much higher than it is today for the wells nowhere reach the present deep water-table.[8] Evidence of a well-wooded landscape lies in the great abundance of ash and charcoal in the Neolithic cultural stratum and in the frequency with which bones of wild game may be found, suggesting the proximity of forests. The dependence on wooden pillars and poles in the construction of numerous

Neolithic villages implies that there was no lack of this raw material. Andersson conjectured that the Yang-shao farmers might have cleared the forest with fire and axe. The stoneless loess soil then offered no resistance to their limestone hoes.[9] This disruption of the natural vegetation would certainly have modified the character of surface run-off leading, perhaps, to gullying, a process that is proceeding very rapidly in the treeless landscapes of modern times.

Yang-shao culture spread into the upper Huang Ho basin, where the Huang Ho is joined by the T'ao Ho. Settlement in this region was later than in the nuclear area downstream, and the Neolithic style of life appears to have continued here long after the nuclear area had moved on to the use of metal and the development of cities. In modern times the broad and flat floor of the T'ao Ho is a well-irrigated, intensively cultivated and densely settled plain. On both sides terraces rise to 170 feet, and the small villages established there depend on the cultivation of wheat and other crops that do not require artificial watering. In late Neolithic times the flat floor was a marshy and well-wooded area, infested by big game like the deer, and also by beasts of prey. Neolithic farmers shunned it and sought out instead the dry surface of the terraces on which to build their villages. Another advantage of the terraces was that they had been dissected into lobes and islands, which provided natural fortification against wild animals.[10] Thus, in contrast to the Yang-shao ts'un area the Neolithic settlers of the T'ao Ho Valley did not initiate erosion but they deliberately selected surfaces that were already eroded, and were therefore much drier than the bottomland and less vulnerable to surprise attacks.

During the Yang-shao stage of the Chinese Neolithic, a remarkable number of village communities sprang up in the Huang Ho basin and also beyond it, as, for example, in the middle Han Chiang Valley to the south. In a well-wooded environment, the Yang-shao settlers would have to clear at least some of the vegetation for their villages and small fields. Although farming was the primary occupation, hunting, fishing and wild grain collecting continued to be practised and were apparently necessary. At the Pan-po ts'un site in the Wei Ho Valley, Shen-hsi province, remains of chestnuts, hazelnuts, and pine seeds have been found. Wild animals brought to the settlement included bamboo rats, water deer and sika deer. Bones found in other Yang-shao sites would extend the list of wild animals to include the horse, wild cattle, rhinoceros, hare and marmot. Fishing was very important, as indicated by the variety and number of fishing gear, the abundance of fish bones, and the prominence of the fish motif in the decoration of pottery. These activities were rooted in the Mesolithic past. Radically new were the cultivation of crops, such as millet; the care of domesticated animals, in particular, the pig and the dog; and the communal life of large, permanent villages. As to the size of the villages, it has been suggested that the ancient Pan-po ts'un at its height of settlement had more than 200 houses with a population of between 500 and 600 people.[11] On the question of

permanence there are differences of interpretation. Undebatable is the fac
that some sites were persistently occupied. At Pan-po ts'un, for example, fiv
superimposed layers of floor have been unearthed. But was the occupatio
continuous? At Hsi-yin ts'un, a Neolithic site in southwestern Shan-hs
province, no barren layer was found in the entire cultural stratum althoug
some sections were dug to a depth of 13 feet. This implies continuous occupa
tion perhaps to the order of several hundred years. The site was occupied lon
enough for small evolutionary changes in pottery and house-construction t
take place, and in this respect the Hsi-yin ts'un site was not unique. On th
other hand, K. C. Chang has recently argued for a distinction between 're
peated' and 'continuous' occupation. Chang saw the farmers of Yang-sha
stage as shifting cultivators, who cleared land by the slash-and-burn technique
extracted crops from it for a time, and then moved to another locale, frequentl
returning to the favoured site after a temporary absence.[12] The reason fo
making these changes is not clear, but presumably it was to allow the wil
game and fish to regain their normal populations in the woods and in th
streams. Soil exhaustion might also have been a factor, though perhaps
minor one for the loess or loessic alluvium on which many of the villages wer
located did not deplete so easily from the simple demands of the Yang-sha
farmers.

On the appearance of these Yang-shao villages, much can be learnt from the
example of Pan-po ts'un, which is among the more thoroughly excavated o
archaeologic sites in China. First, the site was occupied on and off for a long
time and at least two stages can be distinguished: an earlier stage, in which the
houses were either squarish or circular in outline and were all subterranean in
structure, and a later stage in which the houses were larger, often oblong in
outline; some were partitioned into several rooms. Population had evidently
increased. Not only the greater size of the later houses bears witness to this
but also the fact that storage pits, of which a great number had been dug, were
nearly twice as large in the later stage of settlement. A typical house of Pan-po
ts'un might be 10 to 17 feet in diameter, of square, round or rectangular shape;
its walls were made of wattle and daub filling the spaces between wooden
pillars which supported a conical or pyramidal roof of wooden beams plastered
with layers of clay and straw. The village compound was ringed by a ditch; its
purpose might have been defence, or to keep the livestock in, and wild beasts
out, at night. The smaller ditches inside the compound were probably used
for drainage. The houses were grouped around a plaza in the middle of which
was a large communal house, measuring some 66 feet in length and 41 feet in
width. House doors faced southwards or towards the centre of the plaza. The
east side of the village had an area for pottery kilns and the north side, beyond
the ditch, a village cemetery.[13] As the villages grew larger and established
satellite communities it would seem that the practice of setting up a communal

burial ground some distance away for the use of several settlements was adopted. A striking example of this may be seen in the late Yang-shao villages of the T'ao Ho Valley. The villages were built on terraces above the floodplain. The cemetery shared by the villages lay some distance away on the upland, which rises more than 1,300 feet above the level of the terraces.[14]

Lung-shan

Succeeding the Yang-shao stage of Neolithic China was the more advanced Lung-shan stage. One remarkable change was in geographical area: from an essentially upland setting of the middle Huang Ho basin to the great alluvial plains of the lower Huang Ho and the lower Yangtze Chiang, as well as northwards to southern Manchuria and southwards to the coastal regions of South China, and across the Taiwan Strait to Taiwan. Can we speak of a core area from which the elements of Lung-shan culture spread outwards? Too little is known to give a confident answer. It would seem, however, that the Lung-shan culture developed out of the Yang-shao in the general locality where the Huang Ho makes its way from the upland to the plain (western Ho-nan), and that from there it spread westwards into Shen-hsi and eastwards to the alluvial lowland. The villages of the Lung-shan stage in the core area were larger than the Yang-shao villages, which could often be found stratigraphically below them. In the new environment of the wet alluvial plain, however, the Lung-shan settlements were in general smaller than the Yang-shao sites.[15] On the upland the characteristic site of the Lung-shan village was the river terrace, as had been the case for the Yan-shao village. On the lowland it was a low rise next to a stream. The rise was in part natural but more the result of prolonged human occupation. At one site nine successive floors were found, and it could have been occupied for hundreds of years. Where possible the settlement was built within sight of a hill which provided refuge in times of flood.[16] This was not difficult on the lower Yangtze plain where islands of bedrock not infrequently surface above the mud, nor in the small deltaic plains of southeast China. On the broad flat surface of the North China plain safe sites were, and are, more difficult to come by.

The Lung-shan people were more sophisticated than their Yang-shao predecessors. Their artifacts were better made. Their potters knew the use of the wheel; they knew how to prepare a fine black paste from the local clay of the plains and make from it a fine lustrous black ware. At the Yang-shao site of Pan-po ts'un six kilns were found in one part of the village, suggesting the importance of pottery making and its differentiation as a separate activity. The Lung-shan people had carried this a step further in the use of the wheel and in achieving a certain degree of standardization of the product. Stone industry remained basically the same as that of Yang-shao. But knives and sickles of a semi-lunar and rectangular shape began to appear, and this type of implement – later made of iron – persisted into modern times. As we may expect from the wet lowland and coastal environment, bone artifacts were more abundant and better made than those of the Yang-shao stage. Things made of mollusc shells appeared. The Lung-shan people hunted and fished in varying intensity, depending on the nature of the site, but their economy was based primarily on hoe agriculture. Farming implements comprised not only polished stone but also shell, bone and wooden tools. Among domesticated animals pigs and dogs still predominated but the number of cattle, sheep and goats increased. Some sites have yielded horses and chicken as well. Of crops, millet probably remained dominant in the north; wheat has been discovered in northern An-hui and rice more frequently in river valleys and plains such as that of Han Chiang, Huai Ho (An-hui) and the lower Yangtze Chiang (Chiang-su). As to the appearance of the villages there were no striking changes in the structure of dwellings. The most significant architectural addition was perhaps the wall. A number of Lung-shan villages were surrounded by walls of stamped earth.[17] Only a sort of defensive ditch has so far been found in Yang-shao villages, and it could have been used more to keep out wild beasts than men. The massive Lung-shan walls have a more militant air.

Lung-shan culture takes us to the dawn of recorded history, metallurgy, of rituals involving human sacrifice, of wars, and of a society that was to become increasingly stratified – in other words, to the doorstep of civilization.

Chapter 4
Early regional development

Lung-shan culture extended beyond the uplands to the North China plain and coast. It ventured into a broad, floodplain environment which offered many more challenges to man than the river terraces and plateaux of the middle Huang Ho basin. Below the place where the Huang Ho emerges from the confines of bedrock the river's gradient drops sharply, and over the flat surface of the North China plain it is, and has been since early historic time, subject to violent overflows, bringing disaster to the peopled countryside. It may be, as I have already suggested, that even at the dawn of China's recorded history the Huang Ho was already carrying an abnormally heavy load of silt, which encouraged it to build up its channel and to break into branches in times of flood run-off. In view of the fact that the loess upland had long been settled by Neolithic farmers who probably made significant inroads on the forest cover, it is not difficult to see how erosion might have set in on the susceptible loess, washing it into the Huang Ho and greatly adding to the river's burden of sediments. In any case, 'flood' is an important element of Chinese legendary history. The Great Yu, founder of the Hsia dynasty (the existence of which has yet to be proved), was canonized by the Chinese as a culture-hero for his role in taming the waters. To him was attributed the prescient observation that, 'since the (Yellow) river was descending from high ground and the flow of the water was rapid and fierce, it would be difficult to guide it over level ground without frequent disastrous breakthroughs'.[1]

The wet environment of the North China plain

In early Chinese history the lower Huang Ho flowed north-northeastwards over the plain and debouched into the sea near the site of T''ientsin. At some point the river subdivided into branches which rejoined before reaching the coast. This, at least, is how one could interpret the passage in the *Shi Chi* in which Yu is credited with the performance of this feat. The pattern of drainage suggests a flat, marshy landscape where the river broke into multiple channels, and it was difficult to tell land from water. In the section 'Tribute of Yu' of *Shu Ching*, marsh lands receive frequent mention. Ssu-ma Ch'ien, author of *Shi Chi*, interpolated the 'Tribute of Yu' and gave Yu the credit of 'opening up the rivers of the nine provinces, and fixing the outlets of the nine marshes', so that peace and order were brought to the lands of the Hsia and his achievements continued to benefit succeeding dynasties. Yu became known as the founder of Hsia only during the eastern Chou dynasty. Earlier he was thought of more as a god who separated land from water. All these beliefs and descriptions add up to an image of a poorly drained and difficult environment over which man had to expend much energy to gain a measure of control.

Faunal remains also throw some light on the environment of the North China plain at the beginning of Chinese history and civilization. Some twenty-nine mammalian species have been recognized at An-yang. Among the more surprising finds were whale bones. Clearly they were taken from the coast. Such animals as the bear, the tiger and the panther could well have been indigenous to the area, and disappeared through man's destruction of their natural habitat and through hunting. Others, such as the water buffalo, the tapir, and the elephant present something of a problem; if they are regarded as indigenous or at least well adapted to the northerly setting of the latitude of An-yang then they suggest a warmer and moister environment than that of modern times.[2] Or they could have strayed or been brought in from the south. Unfortunately, too little is known of the ecology of these animals to make safe inferences as to the nature of either the vegetation or the climate.

We are on safer ground in attributing a far more thickly wooded and wetter landscape to those ancient times. The great variety of mammalian species found at An-yang, even if some were not native, suggests variety in the environment, ranging perhaps from broad reed swamps and grasslands in areas of alkaline soil and low water-table to forests. The history of the *Mi* deer (*Elaphurus davidianus*) indicates the sort of change in natural environment that can take place through human agency. The essence of the change was towards the creation of a more uniform and drier landscape by modifying the natural vegetation and draining the swamps. The natural habitat of the *Mi* deer is the marsh. As late as 1877 herds of deer could be seen in the imperial hunting grounds to the south of Peking. There they grazed with several other kinds of wild game among marshes and streams.[3] But, in fact, except for such preserves the deer had migrated out of the region long ago. During the two earliest periods of Chinese history, the Shang and the Chou, the deer was very common on the North China plain. The wealth of elaphure antlers found in deposits of Shang age attests to their number, and they may indeed have been the most common cervine animal in the lower Huang Ho basin at that time. They maintained their number to the middle Chou period (seventh to fifth century B.C.), but by the Han dynasty the elaphure was more characteristic of the Yangtze basin than of the North China plain.[4] In the year A.D. 2 by far the most common mammal on the North China plain was man, of whom there were some 35 million.

Shang culture

The cities

Having sketched the natural setting at the beginning of the Chinese historical period, we may now turn to what man has made of it. Until modern archaeology, in field sessions carried out between 1928 and 1937, established the existence of the Shang, there was widespread doubt among Chinese scholars trained in the methods of Western textual criticism that Chinese history could be authenticated beyond the middle Chou period. A good historical work like Ssu-ma Ch'ien's *Shi Chi* may have a section on ancient China that reaches back to the third millennium B.C., a section in which one could find the rough chronicle of Hsia and Shang rulers; however, the few sources on which it was based could not claim great antiquity. Of the Shang dynasty (*c.* 1630–1520 B.C.) the *Shi Chi* claims that it lasted seventeen generations, with periods of prosperity and chaos. The capital of Shang moved six times and finally settled on the banks of the Huan Ho, a tributary of the ancient course of the Yellow (Huang) River. In 1928, close to An-yang and at a bend in the Huan Ho, archaeologists discovered the last Shang capital of literary tradition, with the result that what had verged on myth acquired the status of substantial history. Later, another and earlier capital of the Shangs was excavated near the modern city of Cheng-chou. Both sites occur in northern Ho-nan, that is, along the inner edge of the North China plain. It seems probable that northern Ho-nan was the nuclear area of the Shang culture and that from there it spread eastwards to southern Ho-pei and western Shan-tung of the North China plain, and that eventually its influence, if not the whole configuration of the cultural complex, permeated the Yangtze Valley.

The distinguishing elements of the Shang way of life are best exemplified by the two sites of Cheng-chou and An-yang. Of cultural innovations the most significant were the development of a sophisticated bronze metallurgy and writing. Architecturally the ancient Shang capitals were much larger and more complex than anything that was put up by the prehistoric Lung-shan people. There existed, however, distinct links between the two traditions. The town wall of pounded earth first appeared around Lung-shan settlements. It became more massive, and enclosed a much larger compound in Shang times. The Lung-shan walled settlement of Cheng-tzu-yai had an area of approximately 43 acres; the Shang capital at Cheng-chou was bounded by a wall of some 23,600 feet in perimeter. Its enclosed area of about 1·3 square miles was more than twice the size of the modern city of Cheng-chou.[5] The rectangular shape of the walled Shang capital is also of great interest; for the rectangular city, its sides more or less aligned with the cardinal directions, had eventually come to be the characteristic form of the major political centre in North China. The stratified and specialized nature of Shang society was reflected in the spatial and architectural arrangement of the city and its satellite villages. This was a distinctive innovation of the Shang, though again we could see roots and fore-shadowings in the Neolithic past. Even the Yang-shao village of Pan-po ts'un displayed a recognizable spatial pattern in locating the large communal house at the centre of the plaza, in having one quarter set aside for pottery kilns and another for the cemetery. Lung-shan settlements carried the differentiation a step further: the walled villages probably had ceremonial and political functions that the open villages had not. Another feature was the clustering of settlements in one area, suggesting the possibility that each unit, though largely self-sufficient, had a somewhat different role from the other. But these were shadows of the pattern that came into full being during the Shang period.

At the Cheng-chou site the enclosed area was the administrative and cere-monial centre. Here the large buildings were located, as well as a platform of compressed earth which was probably an altar. Outside the city walls lay a number of residential quarters and handicraft workshops. There were bone factories, pottery kilns and bronze foundries. The dwellings of the common folk showed little advance beyond the type enjoyed by Neolithic farmers. They were semisubterranean, and circular or rectangular in shape. However, the metal workers appear to have been a privileged group for they lived in stamped-earth houses. At the An-yang site, no wall has yet been discovered around the last capital of the Shang kings. But there was a distinct ceremonial and ad-ministrative centre, which consisted in a large number of rectangular or square houses built on foundations of stamped earth, and arranged roughly in parallel rows and columns. The largest of these measured 47·6 by 278·8 feet. Pre-sumably some of the houses were official residences, some were royal temples and archives (suggested by the concentration of inscribed oracle bones), and most of them had ceremonial significance. One square platform of stamped earth might have been an altar. The houses were all above ground, raised on platforms, and their pitched roofs supported by hefty pillars and beams that were cut, probably, from the well-wooded mountains only 20 miles to the west. Many sacrifices, human and animal, were offered at the consecration of the buildings. The Royal City was a curious amalgam of human aspirations. Associated with the elevated architecture, the mastery over bronze and the elaboration of ceremonials of divination and worship was an exalted view of a man as a force – at least, as a transmitter of force – of some consequence in the universe. On the other hand, the life of the common people was extremely debased. Along with the domesticated sheep, oxen and dogs, humans had their uses – including use as sacrificial victim. Human bones served, though rarely, as raw material for artifacts. It is curious to reflect on the population of the city; one group was alive and above ground, the other dead and below ground. In a sense the Royal City was also a necropolis, composed of human sacrificial victims. At the consecration of an important building, not only would a human victim be necessary to ensure the soundness of the foundation but also one was needed at the base of every pillar, at the door, and then, when the entire building was completed, several hundred more people had to lose their lives.[6] Outside the royal centre were specialized quarters for the different industries, and residential areas and villages that were more or less self-sufficient in subsistence but dependent on the royal centre for administration, and for religious and ceremonial affairs. The dwelling of ordinary folk was the same type of semisubterranean pit house, some 13 to 15 feet wide and as many feet deep, as that which can be found at the earlier Shang site of Cheng-chou; and indeed the underground dwelling continued to be built even after the fall of the Shang dynasty.

The countryside

Archaeology enables us to visualize roughly how Shang capitals may have looked, but we are much in the dark concerning the appearance of the countryside. It is possible to infer. Thus, although Shang culture, in its half a millennium of existence, had expanded over the greater part of the North China plain, only a very small portion of the area could in any sense be called a manmade landscape. If the figure of 4 or 5 million is taken as roughly the population of Shang China at the time it was conquered by the Chou,[7] this would yield a modest average density of twenty to thirty persons per square mile; in other words, the sort of density one associates with the better settled parts of Europe in medieval times. The abundance of game alone suggests the prevalence of forest and marsh wildernesses. The Shang nobles were great hunters. Oracle bones frequently recorded inquiries about hunts. One piece noted that two tigers were captured and 162 deer shot in a single chase. Other animals that were captured and perhaps kept in royal preserves included foxes, boars, rhinoceroses and elephants. Interestingly enough, the highest figure given in the oracle inscriptions as taken in any one chase was 348 *Mi* deer.[8] And the *Mi* deer was an animal that flourished in a wet marshy environment. The king and nobles hunted not only with bows and arrows, but also with the aid of horse-drawn chariots, hounds, nets and traps and fire. Fire, as emphasized earlier, is singularly effective in altering the composition of the vegetation cover. The following poem from the *Shi Ching* provides us with a glimpse of the hunting scene:

> Shu has gone hunting
> Mounted in his chariot and four.
> The reins are in his grasp like ribbons,
> While the two outside horses move
>   (with regular steps) as dancers do,
> Shu is at the marshy ground.
> The fire flames out all at once,

And with bare arms he seizes a tiger
And presents it before the Duke.[9]

Fishing remained important, to judge from the presence of fish bones in refuse heaps in the underground pits, the presence of fish hooks, and of scripts for fish nets and tangles, and the fact that pictures of the fish were widely used as decorative motifs in Shang arts and crafts. Although China developed as a 'continental' civilization poised on the edge of the desert, the fish has had persistent importance, both as food and as symbol, to the Chinese. Notice the frequency of the fish motif on Yang-shao pottery, and the wealth of meaning that the fish has acquired through the long course of history.

In domesticated animals the Shang inherited from the Neolithic farmers, pigs, dogs, cattle, sheep, horses and chickens. There were, however, far more of them. The Shang nobles did not stint themselves in using the animals for sacrifice. A poem in the *Shi Ching* tells of a flock of 300 sheep and a herd of ninety cattle kept for sacrificial purposes.[10] One large pit in the An-yang site contained the nearly complete skeletons of thirty oxen and three sheep.[11] It is reasonable to assume the existence of some pasture land in which these sizeable flocks were kept. Among the newly acquired domesticated animals were the water buffalo and, possibly, the elephant.

Hunting was an aristocratic occupation carried on largely for pleasure and as part of the military ethos with which the upper class Shang was imbued. Most domesticated animals served as food. Game and fish supplemented the meat diet, which was ample for the nobles. But the basis of the Shang economy was farming. This is suggested even by the oracle records which show persistent concern about the harvesting of crops, but neglect the condition of livestock – except in so far as the animals were to be sacrificed in the interest of better harvests. Domesticated plants included two kinds of millet, barley, wheat and sorghum, and probably rice.[12] Agricultural implements showed little evidence of improvements from Neolithic types. The field was prepared with a stone hoe or a forked wooden digging stick. One innovation was the appearance of a more efficient harvesting tool, the *lien*, a semi-lunar sickle made of slate.

Although it has been suggested that the Shang practised irrigation and used fertilizers the evidence is thin. Yet, food production must have greatly exceeded that of Neolithic times to feed the far larger population, a population that included industrial workers and rulers who did not produce food. The Shang, moreover, must have had sufficient surplus of food and leisure to engage in wars. What made this possible? The answer appears to lie in the organizing ability of the Shang rulers. They made powerful machines of men. It has been estimated, for example, that to build the walls of the Shang city at Cheng-chou, some 10,000 workers must have been commandeered to work 330 days a year for eighteen years.[13] And, of course, warfare implies organization in that it requires the disciplining of large bodies of men. It would seem that farm labour was also organized; that farmers were sent into the fields in groups under a superintendent. The ruler kept control of the tools, a fact suggested by a storage pit in the An-yang site which contained no fewer than 400 used stone sickles. The development of a complex calendar system in late Shang times may be seen in the context of a need to centralize agricultural activities. Greater food production was also made possible by double cropping in some fields; that is, by producing two crops, either millet and wheat or millet and rice, in one year. But we should be careful not to exaggerate the geographical extent of organized agriculture. Perhaps it was characteristic only of the royal domains. The majority of villagers, spread more or less in isolation over the North China plain, could well have remained free farmers, and carried on a way of life little different from that of their Neolithic forebears.

Western Chou: landscape and life

Some time after 1150 B.C., the Shang rulers of the North China plain were overthrown by the Chou, who established a dynastic house that lasted some 800 years. In this long period, which is traditionally subdivided into Western Chou (1127–723 B.C.), Ch'un-ch'iu (722–463 B.C.), and Chan-kuo (462–222 B.C.), a great many changes took place. Population may have increased from perhaps 10 million at the beginning to possibly as many as 50 million towards the end of the period; and related to this great demographic gain were innovations in agricultural techniques, in technology (the use of iron, for example), and in the burgeoning of commerce and cities.[14] Landscapes, rural and urban, naturally reflected these gains in population and changes in economy. We shall attempt to reconstruct some of the scenes, although often they can only be envisaged hazily and by implication, through the little that we know of Chou society and livelihood.

The original homeland of the Chou people lay to the west of the Shang domain, in the Wei Ho basin of Shen-hsi province. Practically nothing is known of the state of Chou civilization before the conquest of Shang. The Chou were descended from the Neolithic settlers of northern China like the Shang, and like them they were fundamentally an agricultural people. After the conquest the Chou took over and propagated the Shang civilization, modifying it in minor ways. This suggests that culturally they were less advanced than the people they subdued. Too little is known about Shang society to tag it with a general label. Chou society, once its rulers extended their sway from the Wei-Fen valleys in the interior to the coast, developed traits which may be characterized as feudal. Thus the Chou king invested the leaders of his clansmen and allied tribes with sovereign rights over land. In return these leaders (vassals or lords) gave military aid and tribute to the king.

The total number of domains during the Western Chou period was very large, more than a thousand; most of them were modest in size. On the North China plain the lord probably established his city next to a stream somewhere near the middle of his estate, whereas in the uplands of the Wei and Fen drainage system a prominence was favoured.[15] Again, on the featureless plain a clump of trees growing on a rise in the ground may have been the deciding factor in the location of the city. The eminence was moulded into a square and became the earth altar. Around it a wall was constructed in short order, though with due ceremony. Before 600 B.C., the average seat of a Chou lord had little that was architecturally grandiose. The residences of the lord and his relations were modest, partially fortified structures packed close together. Nobles lived cheek-by-jowl with their retinue of followers who manned shops, arsenals, granaries, stables and temples. Markets and suburbs huddled outside the walls.[16] Common folk in the countryside probably still lived in subterranean dwellings, or in loess caves, as the following lines in the *Shi Ching* suggest:

> Of old Tan-fu the duke
> Scraped shelters, scraped holes;
> As yet they had no houses.[17]

Poems in the *Shi Ching* give us a glimpse into the livelihood of ordinary people. It was hard, and seems to revolve much of the time around the many needs of the lord. In the course of a year, girls collected mulberry leaves and the men ploughed; they made 'a robe for the lord'; they gathered in the harvest; in winter they hunted the racoon, foxes and wild cats 'to make furs for our lord'; they also hunted boar, keeping the one-year-old and offering the three-year-old to the lord; they made millet wine, worked on the house, gathered thatch reeds, and twisted ropes. Domesticated animals received little attention in the literature except in sacrifice. Ox, sheep, pig, and dog were all used for food on occasion, but there is no evidence that they were raised in large numbers. Only the rulers and officials ate meat to any extent.

Farming was by far the most important activity. New ground was prepared by felling trees, tearing out bushes, and setting fire to the debris. In the *Shi Ching* there exists no mention of manure other than ash. New agricultural land was divided up into plots and separated by balks upon which vegetables were grown. A field consisted in numerous strips or plots of land scattered over a wide area. Part of each field was cultivated by the common people for the benefit of their lord, who owned the land, and part was cultivated by them for their own use.[18] In the upland home territory of the Chou, topography is varied; fields had different aspects. In the *Shi Ching* south-facing or east-facing fields receive frequent mention and they appear to have been the preferred land. On the flats of the North China plain a more geometric division of the fields became possible. Early in spring farmers left the fortified city to clear a piece of ground, and then subdivided it into nine units by drawing up boundaries and footpaths that crossed each other at right angles. Each family group had assigned to it some 4 acres of land, the size of which varied with the quality of the soil, but the work of cultivation and harvesting was performed by all family groups working together. The farmers also worked on the so-called 'public land' for the benefit of the lord, or it may be that the lord had teams of slaves to labour on his plot.[19] After harvest the farmers returned to the city and took up other occupations, such as repairing houses and tools, making clothes and performing sundry services for the aristocrats.

Life for most people was divided into two parts: one in the city during winter and the other out in the fields during summer. This dual aspect of life may have stimulated the articulation of a philosophy that saw nature in terms of *yang* and *ying*, of brightness and shade, summer and winter, masculine and feminine.

In appearance, the landscape probably showed a rectangular bias: the walled city was a rectangle, the plots of the field were rectangles, the field boundaries in turn predisposed the roads and footpaths to be rectilinear and aligned in a north to south or east to west direction. On the other hand we should not envisage a 'fixed' landscape of persistent patterns. The fields themselves were abandoned after a few years of cultivation, and new ones were cleared. Cultivated land intermingled with old fields in process of acquiring a cover of secondary vegetation, and with wildernesses as yet untouched. The following pieces from the *Shi Ching* give us an idea of farming activity:

> They clear away the grass, the trees;
> Their ploughs open up the ground.
> In a thousand pairs they tug at weeds and roots,
> Along the low ground, along the ridges
> There is the master and his eldest son,
> There the headman and overseer.
> They mark out, they plough.[20]
>
> Truly those southern hills –
> It was Yü who fashioned them;
> Those level spaces, upland and lowland –
> The descendant tills them.
> We draw boundaries, we divide the plots,
> On southern slopes and eastern we set out acres.
> . . .
>
> The boundaries and balks are strictly drawn;
> The wine-millet and cooking-millet give good yield,

To be harvested by the descendant;
That he may have wine and food
To supply the Dead One and the guests
And so get life long-lasting.

In the midst of the fields are the huts;
Along the boundaries and balks are gourds.
He dries them, pickles them,
And offers them to his great forefathers.
So shall the descendant live long
Receiving Heaven's favour.[21]

Eastern Chou

Irrigation works and agricultural techniques

In the Ch'un-ch'iu period of the Chou dynasty, the power of the Royal House, after the transference of the capital from the Wei Ho Valley in the west to Lo-yang in the east, suffered continuous decline. Simultaneously, the vassal lords gained power and increasing autonomy within their fiefs. There were also fewer fiefs and their more powerful rulers acquired such ascendancy over the Chou kings that the fiefs could be regarded as independent states. Within the states the old feudal system of landownership, obligations and services underwent steady change. For example, the introduction of tax by the sixth century B.C. can probably be taken to mean that the peasant farmers acquired greater control over their own destiny. There was much waste land to be reclaimed, and during the Ch'un-ch'iu period farmers were able to undertake the reclamation on their own initiative and with the understanding that the new land would not belong to specific manors. For a time they probably did not have to pay tax on it.[22] In the Chan-kuo period, some officials made deliberate effort towards reclaiming waste territory in order to enrich the coffers of their rulers, and thus ingratiate themselves. This practice was condemned by Mencius.[23] As more and more land came under the plough timber grew scarce. Mencius found it necessary to counsel King Huai of Liang: 'If the axes and bills enter the hills and forests only at the proper time, the wood will be more than can be used.'[24]

It has been suggested that population in China may have increased fivefold during the Chou period to something in the neighbourhood of 50 million. This increase was made possible by the extension of cultivable land, but also by certain important changes in agricultural practice, most of which took place since the end of the Ch'un-ch'iu period. The *Chien Han Shu* contains a passage in which Li K'uei was credited with having worked out for Duke Wen (403–387 B.C.) of Wei a policy for the utmost use of the strength of the land.

Wei state in the Chan-kuo period occupied an area that corresponded roughly to southern Shan-hsi and northern Ho-nan provinces, north of the Huang Ho. Li K'uei reckoned that:

A territory of one hundred square *li* held totally 90,000 *ching* [*c.* 427,140 English acres]. Deducting one-third for mountains and marshes, settlements and cottages-in-fields, there was left for cultivation six million *mou* [*c.* 284,760 acres]. If the land was diligently and carefully managed, then each acre would yield an increase of three pecks *tou* of grain. If it was not diligently cultivated, then the decrease would in that case be the same.[25]

As a result of adopting Li K'uei's policy the yield of grain per acre was increased to about 43 bushels.

The practice of irrigation has been postulated for the Shang dynasty. Drainage ditches of some kind certainly existed at the An-yang and Cheng-chou sites but one cannot be certain of irrigation. The earliest literary documentation on the artificial watering of fields dates back to about the sixth century B.C., and it applies to the small city-state of Cheng.[26] But the credit for developing large-scale irrigation works belongs to the powerful western state of Ch'in. This state was centred on the Wei Ho Valley: from that base of ancient Chinese civilization it eventually acquired sufficient wealth and power to conquer the other Chan-kuo states, and thus establish the first unified empire of China. The economic power of Ch'in was greatly enhanced when in 329 B.C. it extended control over the rich Ssu-ch'uan basin. Its power was further confirmed when, not long after the conquest, Li Ping became the Prefect of Shu (as the Ssu-ch'uan territory was then known), and he and his son achieved lasting fame by perfecting the irrigation system of the Ch'eng-tu plain. Before Li Ping, the kings of Shu had probably already established water-works and canals, but the flow of water into the fields was still irregular and undependable. Large areas of the Ch'eng-tu plain were dry, inaccessible to the normal overflows of the Min Ho and its distributaries, whereas other areas were permanently waterlogged. Floods were common and wrought such disaster that they were attributed in popular legend to the anger of a dragon who had to be placated with human sacrifices. Li Ping tamed the floods and brought permanent wealth to the region by repairing the waterways of thirty-six streams, beginning at Kuan-hsien where the Min Ho emerges from the plateau, to as far south as Sui Fu on the Yangtze River.[27]

The power of Ch'in was explained by Ssu-ma Ch'ien in *Shi Chi* as the result of the construction of an irrigation canal that connected the Ching Ho with the Lo Ho on the north side of the Wei Ho Valley sometime in the middle of the third century B.C.

When [the canal] was finished, it was used for leading away stagnant waters and for irrigating the alkali fields, the whole amounting to 40,000 *ching* (456,000 acres). Within the entire territory there ensued harvests amounting to one *chung* per *mou*. Thereupon the land within the passes became a fertile plain and there were no more bad years. Ch'in in this way became rich and powerful, and ended by conquering the feudal lords.[28]

Crop yields increased five times after irrigation. Another cause of greater yield was the more widespread application of fertilizers to the fields during the Chan-kuo period. In Western Chou times the fields probably depended solely on the ash that was introduced to the soil after burning. At least the *Shi Ching* mentioned no other source. In Eastern Chou times, however, fertilizers were mentioned in several works, including the *Mencius*, where it was referred to casually as though manuring was a common practice; and in the *Chou Li*, where a passage indicated that different kinds of fertilizers were used on different soils.[29] In farming implements iron ploughshares began to appear by the beginning of the Chan-kuo period, and were probably in common usage by Mencius's time. The iron ploughshares, however, were rather small and wide and could not have made deep furrows in the soil. They may have been drawn by cattle, but there exists no archaeological evidence for heavy ox-drawn ploughs until the Former Han period.

In spite of these improvements in agriculture it should be said that crops still suffered very much from the vagaries of nature. In North China natural hazards consisted primarily of visitations by drought and flood. Yield fluctuated widely in the Chan-kuo period: it could be four times the average in the best years and one-fifth the average in the worst.[30]

Commerce and transportation

The course of Chou history saw the transformation of a large number of small fiefs in a feudal economy to a small number of large or wealthy states. The self-sufficiency of Western Chou times gave way to an economy that was increasingly based on specialization, interdependence, and trade. The farmer in *Shi Ching* provided for nearly all the needs of his household; the farmer in *Mencius* could no longer do so.

In the Western Chou period merchants were retainers of noble households who procured goods not available in the local areas and, at the same time, sold local products. The self-sufficiency of the farmer's household applied, at a much higher level, to that of the feudal domain. In the early part of the Ch'un-ch'iu period there were still hundreds of more or less compartmentalized states. The existence of trade, however, was signified by the custom of maintaining toll-gates at the capitals and tariff collection at the state border. The difficulty of maintaining good roads, and of communication in general, encouraged self-sufficiency and discouraged commerce on any scale. The alluvium of the North China plain lacked the sort of material needed for surfacing roads, and even in modern times travelling on roads that have been rutted by ox-carts presents special difficulties both after heavy rain, when they turn into mud, and during drought, when they become a banded surface of hard interwoven ribs. Nevertheless the Chou rulers built highways, with perhaps military and political rather than commercial intentions. Trees were supposedly planted along road-sides and watchmen were appointed to maintain the roads.[31] It would seem also that throughout the Ch'un-ch'iu period official contacts among states were frequent. Embassies travelled with gifts that filled 'one hundred chariots', and movements of goods and dignitaries on such a scale implied adequate roads. Travelling by both officials and private persons – itinerant teachers like Mencius, and merchants – became far more frequent in Chan-kuo times, and roads were no doubt improved and multiplied to meet the need.[32] Waterways developed throughout the Eastern Chou period, particularly in the southern states of the Yangtze Valley, the states of Ch'u, Wu, and Yüeh. Wu and Yüeh were centred on the lowlands of the lower Yangtze Valley; both were drawn into the political world of the Chou during the Ch'un-ch'iu period. Wu con-solidated its power by connecting its lakes and rivers with waterways, and crowned its achievement with the construction of the Han-kou Canal which joined the Yangtze delta with the Huai River system. The *Shi Chi* records another long canal which joined the Ssu River, a tributary of the Huai Ho, with the Huang Ho, so that it was possible to go by water all the way from the mouth of the Yangtze delta to the mouth of the Huang Ho at the northern end of the North China plain.[33]

The development of cities (Fig. 9)

Important changes during the Eastern Chou period include increase in culti-vated land, improvement in agricultural techniques, increase in population, the decline of economic self-sufficiency and the rise of commerce, and the amalgamation of states so that by Chan-kuo times there were only seven large states and a few small ones. Naturally, the urban scene also underwent trans-formation, both in the number of cities and in their function and form. The Ch'un-ch'iu period was a time when the number of cities increased rapidly throughout northern China. No fewer than seventy-eight cities were recorded as having been built: the largest number in the state of Lu (southern Shan-tung province), followed by Ch'u in the Han and Yangtze valleys. The northern state of Chin could boast of ten, whereas the small but prosperous and cen-trally located state of Cheng added four.[34] The capital of Wei was destroyed by Ti tribes in 658 B.C. A new one had to be built in what is now southern Ho-pei. A poem in the *Shi Ching* records the construction. Of particular interest is the procedure for city building in the middle Chou period: notice

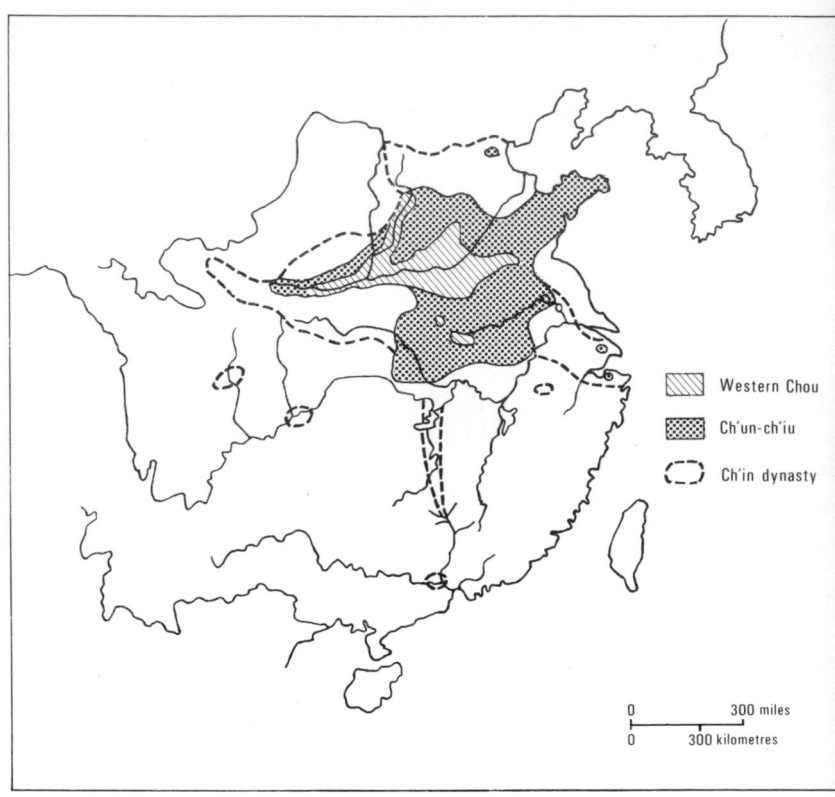

Western Chou
Ch'un-ch'iu
Ch'in dynasty

0   300 miles
0   300 kilometres

*9. Expansion of areas with walled cities, from Western Chou to Ch'in dynasty.
(After Chang)*

the role of astronomy, the importance of directions, and the early planting of trees.

> The Ting-star is in the middle of the sky;
> We begin to build the palace at Ch'u.
> Orientating them by the rays of the sun
> We set to work on the houses at Ch'u,
> By the side of them planting hazels and chestnut trees
> That we may make the zithers great and small.[35]

Reflecting the breakdown of the limited, feudal economy, a new urban form found expression towards the end of the Ch'un-ch'iu period. In addition to the enclosed and fortified aristocratic centre, a much larger rampart was constructed to enclose the industrial quarters, the commercial streets and suburbs. The resultant plan became a fundamental type of the Chinese city, one which

66

remained in evidence among cities in northern China until well into the twentieth century. The type consisted of at least three contrasting spatial units: a small enclosure which was the aristocratic and administrative centre, mixed (in early times) with dependent tradesmen and artisans; industrial and commercial quarters, with residences, in a large enclosure; farm lands immediately beyond the city walls. In the Chan-kuo period sometimes three successive ramparts were built, suggesting a need to extend protection to increasingly large areas of commercial activity. Another change lay in the strengthening of the outer walls at the expense of the walls of the inner citadel, which were allowed to go into decay. One consequence of this trend towards the commercialization of cities was that their shape tended to depart more and more from the rectangle and from orientation to the cardinal directions. Where there were three sets of walls, the inner walls that surrounded the administrative core tended to be rectangular whereas the outer walls deviated increasingly from any simple shape. Moreover, since Ch'un-ch'iu times towns were founded and grew without any political function. One illustration of this was the rise of six towns on a piece of no-man's-land between the borders of the states of Sung and Cheng. A dispute arose as to which state had sovereignty over the towns and war had to be waged to settle it.[36]

Some of the enclosed settlements of the Eastern Chou period were surprisingly large. The official capital of the Chou kings, Wang-ch'eng (located on the site of modern Lo-yang), boasted an area of more than 3 square miles. Capitals of vassal states were probably smaller. City sites excavated in Shen-hsi and Shan-hsi provinces reveal dimensions of less than 1 square mile. In this respect it is interesting to note the urban size order that the *Tso chuan* attributed to Ch'un-ch'iu cities. The circumference of a large city would be approximately 15,100 feet, enclosing an area one-third the size of the capital. (This opinion seems to be supported by archaeologic evidence.) A medium city is one-fifth, and a small city one-ninth the size of the capital. According to the *Mencius*, the dimensions of a typical Chan-kuo city were seven *li* (*c*. 9,550 feet) for the outer wall and three *li* (*c*. 4,100 feet) for the inner wall.[37] Archaeologic evidence, however, suggests that some of the Chan-kuo cities were very much larger. Han-tan, capital of Chao, had a roughly square shape and each side measured *c*. 4,590 feet. A Lu city had more than twice the area of Han-tan; another, in the state of Ch'i, was bigger by five-and-a-half times. The largest of all appears to have been the Yen Hsia-tu. Its north–south dimension was 16,400 feet, and east–west dimension 21,320 feet. The irregular area within the city walls probably approximated 10 square miles. Population in these cities appears to have been large. Lin-tzu in the state of Ch'i, for example, may have had 70,000 households. Its streets were crowded with shops and people, its roads jammed with traffic.[38]

In the Eastern Chou period large parts of the Huang Ho basin were deeply

transformed by man. Irrigated agriculture and urbanization produced artificial landscapes. Forests receded before human demands for more agricultural
land and for more fuel, both domestic and industrial. From the Eastern Chou
period onwards brick came into increasing use for construction, and the firing
of bricks required wood. The value of trees was appreciated.

> On the hill were lovely trees,
> Both chestnut-trees and plum-trees.
> Cruel brigands tore them up;
> But no one knew of their crime.

Trees were a blessing:

> So thick grow those oaks
> That the people never look for firewood.
> Happiness to our lord!
> May the spirits always have rewards for him.

On the other hand, wild life seems to have existed even in some of the long-
settled parts of Chou China. The state of Han, centred on the lower Fen Ho of
southwestern Shan-hsi, was described as a very pleasant land:

> Its rivers and pools so large,
> Its bream and tench so fat,
> Its deer so plentiful,
> And black bears and brown,
> Wildcats and tigers.[39]

It would also seem that within the core area of Eastern Chou civilization
there lived non-Chinese tribes who could muster sufficient force to become
a serious threat to an established state. Thus in 658 B.C. the people of Wei,
under continual harassment by the Ti tribes, had to abandon their capital
north of the Huang Ho in northern Ho-nan. Yet, notwithstanding the persistent presence of non-Chinese, perhaps nomadic, enclaves in the core area
of Chou civilization, its boundaries expanded greatly both to the north and to
the south during the Eastern Chou period. In Western Chou times the northern
limit of Huang Ho civilization permeated into southern Shan-hsi and southern
Ho-pei, while a Neolithic way of life persisted in small pockets among forests
and wooded steppe. Small clusters of people farmed and supplemented their
food supplies with game and fish as they had done for at least a thousand years in
the past. By Eastern Chou times the edge of Huang Ho civilization had pushed
much farther to the north. Clear evidence of its extension into Inner Mongolia
and Jehol lies in the iron foundries that had been established there during the
Chan-kuo period.[40]

ontemporaneous with the northward spread of Chou civilization was the
stward expansion of the steppe nomads. From about 700 B.C. onwards the
omadic way of life, based on herding, hunting and fishing, came to displace
creasingly the sedentary farmers. Desiccation also appears to have set in,
ough slowly. Large permanent agricultural settlements were still in ex-
tence during the Eastern Chou period around the small streams and lakes
' Inner Mongolia. These sources of water had since dried up. From prehis-
ric times to the Western Chou period the broad zone between the Mongolian
lateau and North China was a zone of cultural transition, in which subsis-
nce rested fundamentally on agriculture supplemented by game and fish.
ut during the Eastern Chou period, and increasingly thereafter, this zone
ame to be a zone of conflict between farmers who engaged in more and more
tensive forms of land use and nomads who progressively abandoned their
gricultural heritage in favour of mobility and dependence on livestock. The
onflict intensified after the nomads had learned how to fight on horseback,
id thus negate to a large extent the Chinese superiority in numbers, armoury,
id in that swift but rather undependable machinery, the horsedrawn chariot.[41]
  The wall was the architectural expression of the existence of conflict, and
ie need to define the limits of a cultural region. In China the first walls were
uilt to define and protect the orderly life within a city against the chaos and
reats of an unreclaimed world beyond. In the Ch'un-ch'iu period walls were
uilt within the borders of the Huang Ho civilization to define the limits of
ates. In the Chan-kuo period they were built at the confines to separate the
ivilized world within from the barbarous world without (see Fig. 10, p. 76).

ultures of Central and South China

n the Ch'un-ch'iu period powerful states arose in the middle and lower
angtze Valley. Shang influence in this area had been marginal but the ex-
ansion of the Huang Ho civilization into the lower Yangtze basin during
Western Chou times is well established by archaeologic evidence.[42] Three
ew states came into being: Ch'u, centred on the middle Yangtze Valley, and
Vu and Yüeh, centred on the lower reaches of the river basin. By Ch'un-ch'iu
imes, Ch'u was the most powerful state in central China; it dominated not
nly Wu and Yüeh but exercised considerable sway over the northern states.
o possess such power it must have had an economy, technology and urban
fe comparable to that of the northern neighbours. The discovery of elaborate
ombs in the Ch'ang-sha area gives cause for believing that the Ch'u state
ossessed a stratified society and a fairly well-developed economy. Its metal-
urgy was advanced and it excelled in a variety of handicrafts, including

4

ceramics, wood-carving, carpentry, bamboo crafts, leather-work, lacquer-wor
silk and hemp weaving and stone and jade crafts. Nonetheless, the great
part of the Ch'u territory was a forested wilderness in which large timbers an
wildlife, such as rhinoceros, elephant and deer, abounded. Exports from Ch
were raw materials including ivory, hides and feathers.[43] Agriculture w
based on rice cultivation. Farmers cleaned the land by burning: they irrigate
their fields and had hoes and spades made of iron. Rice and fish were the stapl
of their diet.

In delineating the changing landscapes of China we shall, in the main, cor
centrate on the evolution of civilization in the Huang Ho basin and then tra
its spread to Central and South China. The main movement of people throug
out historic time has been from north to south, and these migrations natural
diffused the cultural traits of the North. However, we need to add two caves
to this generalization: one is that the Huang Ho civilization itself had bee
strongly influenced by the cultures of the South since at least Neolithic time
the other is that we must beware of slighting those aspects of landscape ar
life in humid and maritime China that were not derived from the North.

The domesticated animals of the northern Yang-shao culture were dog
pigs, cattle, sheep and goats. In the Lung-shan phase of the late Neolithi
chickens and horses were added to the list. The later historic Shang cultu
had, in addition, the water buffalo and possibly the elephant. It is a revealir
fact that among these animals, cattle, sheep, goats, and horses came from tl
subhumid regions of western Asia. There they first attracted the attention
man and were domesticated by him. During Neolithic times and probably als
during the Shang, these animals were subordinate in number to the dog and tl
pig, and there are reasons for believing that the dog and the pig (*Sus vittatus*
as also the fowl, were woodland animals whose native habitat was souther
Asia. The water buffalo and the elephant certainly came from warmer ar
moister regions than the North China plain. So, at the beginning of agricultur
life in the Huang Ho basin, we find not merely the presence but the dominanc
of southern elements in livestock. Other southern or maritime introduction
include rice (*Oryza sativa*, probably native to the less wet margins of the Ba
of Bengal) and cowrie shells.

It is important to point out that these southern traits did not enter into rel:
tion with the Huang Ho culture simply as discrete units but rather as part of
cultural complex. Animals like dog, pig, and fowl were domesticated in pr
historic times in southern Asia primarily for ceremonial uses, as in sacrifi
and divination, and secondarily for food. The dog, in particular, was the foc
of an ancient cult.[44] Its ancient significance to the Huang Ho civilization
testified in several ways. Thus dogs were commonly buried in tombs and in tl
foundation of buildings of the late Shang period. There are records concernir
dog sacrifice in Chinese classics such as *Chou Li*, *Yi Li*, and *Li Chi*. The *Ch*

i refers to the appointment of an officer, the Dog-man (*ch'uan-jen*), whose duty lay in ensuring that the dog of a proper colour was selected, and the proper procedures followed, in sacrifice. While the custom slowly declined in North China, as indicated by the replacement of straw dogs for real ones since the first centuries B.C., it persisted in the remoter parts of South China down to modern times. In the twentieth century, dog sacrifices were still practised in Kuei-chou, and a stone dog and cock could still be seen guarding a village gate.

The significance of the dog, and to a less extent the chicken and the pig, in rituals is only part of a southern maritime cultural complex that includes other elements such as female shamans, traces of a matriarchate society, tattooing, shifting rice cultivation, pile-built granaries, dug-out canoes, and the long house.[45] Some of these elements have not completely disappeared: for example, shifting cultivation, as practised in the remoter areas, still calls for the removal of villages to new sites every few years. Semi-pile dwellings are fairly common along stream banks in modern China. Houses built completely on piles are less common, though they have been reported among the Miaos of Kuei-chou. No prehistoric pit-dwelling has been found in Central and South China on low-lying sites for obvious environmental reasons. Even in North China drainage ditches were a necessary amenity of certain Yang-shao villages, and they were common in the Shang sites of An-yang and Cheng-chou. The village built on a mound or on wooden piles thus seems to be a response to the special problems of a wet, low-lying environment.

Another distinctive architectural feature of South and, in particular, coastal China is the long house. Its modern representative is a structure, several hundred feet in length, made of wood and bamboo, and raised above ground on piles. It has a gabled roof, and a continuous gallery covered by the projecting edge of the roof. A row of rooms, each the abode of one family, opens on this gallery. Below the house, among the piles, is space that serves to shelter dogs, pigs, and chickens, canoes and fish nets.

A ceremony of great antiquity in South China is the dragon-boat festival, held sometime in early summer. Originally it probably centred on a human sacrifice by drowning, as part of a magical ceremony to control the seasons and secure bountiful crops. The boat itself is a long narrow canoe manned by a crew that varies from twenty to a hundred members. Besides its role in ritual, the long canoe also had a major function in wars which were fought over water.

In the Eastern Chou period, as we have noted, powerful states arose in the Yangtze Valley. To what extent were they a part of the southern maritime complex we have sketched? The most powerful of the southern states, Ch'u, was strongly influenced by the Chou civilization of North China. Yet there were many distinctive local features, such as its special deities and ceremonies, the highly developed wood and bamboo crafts, boat burials, and the tattooing

of faces. Of the kingdoms in the lower Yangtze Valley, Wu and Yüeh, ol
Chinese records tell of natives who tattooed themselves, wore their hair shor
and had few domestic animals other than dogs, pigs and fowls. Also, unlik
northern states which waged wars against each other in horse-drawn chariot
the peoples of Wu and Yüeh fought on water in fleets of canoes. And as a re
flection of their knowledge of the ways of water, in the fifth century B.C. it wa
a king of Wu who ordered the digging of the ancient canal that connected th
Yangtze and Huai rivers. The canal was dug in an effort to extend Wu's powe
to the north.

Part Three
Landscape and Life in Imperial China

Chapter 5
From the Ch'in to the T'ang dynasty

China was unified for the first time into a powerful, centrally administered empire in 221 B.C. by the western state of Ch'in. The large number of states in the early years of the Eastern Chou period was steadily reduced so that by the Chan-kuo phase only a dozen or so remained. These fought each other until one, Ch'in, achieved military ascendancy. Political disunity during the last two-and-a-half centuries of the Eastern Chou period was a superficial phenomenon that veiled the underlying cultural unity of China. This cultural unity, and the beginning of its conscious acceptance by the sedentary Chinese *vis-à-vis* the barbarians to the north, made it easier for the ruler of the Ch'in state to unify China politically, and for the succeeding Han dynasty to maintain that unity for some 400 years.

The Ch'in Empire and Landscape

What enabled the Ch'in, long regarded as an outsider by the inner core of Chou states, to achieve supremacy? Historians since the Former Han dynasty have given various reasons. One was that the state of Ch'in, based on the Wei Ho Valley, enjoyed certain geographical advantages. Chia I (198–165 B.C.), for example, was less willing to give credit to Ch'in rulers than to the fact that the country was protected by mountains and girdled by the Huang Ho; it had barriers on four sides.[1] The weakest side was the north, which opened to the Ordos desert and was subject – since at least 771 B.C. – to barbarian attacks. In the first part of the third century B.C., Ch'in constructed a wall along its north flank to ensure extra protection. Another reason offered for the power of Ch'in was that in having to deal with barbarian tribes along its vulnerable flank it acquired military experience and new techniques, especially the technique of conducting warfare on horseback. But the favoured explanation was that Ch'in had greatly expanded the economic basis of its power after it gained control of the fertile and already well-developed plains and valleys of the Ssu-ch'uan basin. The extension of irrigation works on the Ch'eng-tu plain under Li Ping made the region even wealthier. As we have already noted, in the Wei Ho Valley itself the construction of the Ch'eng-Kuo canal reclaimed some 450,000 acres of wasteland and increased the valley's productivity fivefold.

Thus, in the century or so before the Ch'in state became an empire, its

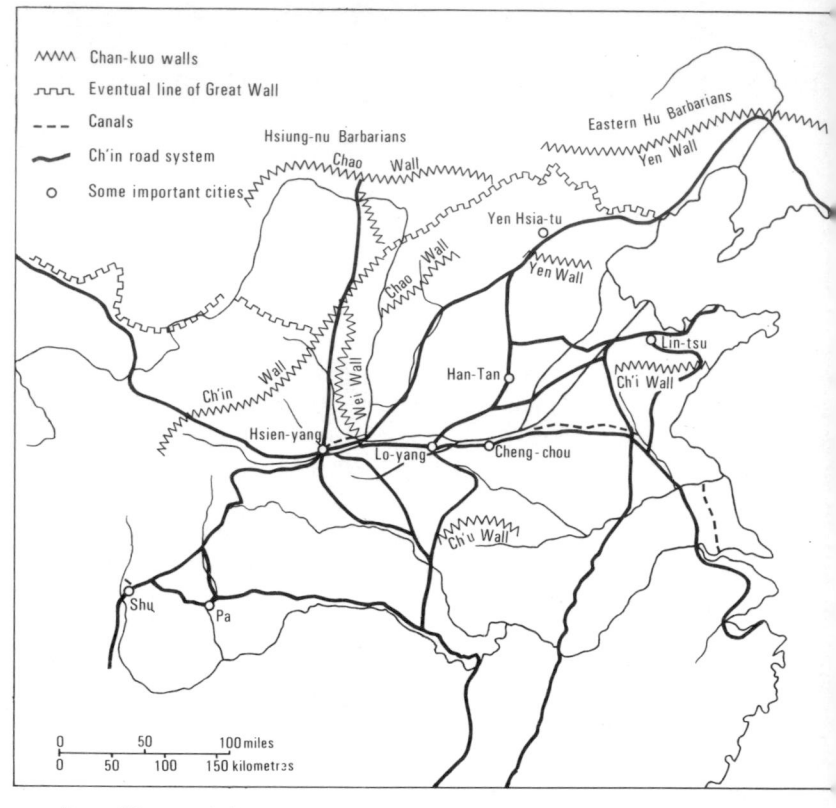

Hsiung-nu Barbarians

Eastern Hu Barbarians

Chao Wall

Yen Wall

Yen Hsia-tu

Chao Wall

Yen Wall

Lin-tsu

Ch'in Wall

Han-Tan

Ch'i Wall

Ch'in

Wall

Wei Wall

Hsien-yang

Lo-yang

Cheng-chou

Ch'u Wall

Shu

Pa

0   50   100 miles

0   50   100   150 kilometres

10. Late Chou and Ch'in major constructions

rulers undertook to secure Ch'in's frontier against the barbarians by buildin
a wall; the state acquired the resources of a fertile basin to the south, engage
in large irrigation works, and in addition induced settlers to move in b
breaking down the feudal system of land tenure. As an empire under Shih
huang-ti (the 'First Emperor'), Ch'in sought to achieve unification an
centralization, but succeeded in these ends at the expense of economic welfare
The northern boundary of the empire was physically defined by piecing to
gether the fragmented ramparts of the Chan-kuo states (Fig. 10). Except fo
the wall built beyond the great northern loop of the Huang Ho, which was new
the Ch'in empire made no attempt to extend its territory into the steppe to th
north. There would have been little point in doing so, for the walls of the Chan-
kuo states already approached the environmental limit for the kind of intensiv
land use that the Chinese farmers engaged in, and which distinguished then
from the nomads. By contrast China, south of the Yangtze Valley, was a forestec
wilderness that offered unlimited possibilities for colonization and the agri-

ultural way of life. The Ch'in emperor was tempted and in a series of cam-
paigns during 221–214 B.C. his armies reached beyond the partially sinicized
Yangtze basin to conquer the non-Chinese regions of Fu-chien, Kuang-tung,
Kuang-hsi, and lands as far south as Tonking. The conquest was accompanied
by a remarkable engineering achievement: a canal of some 20 miles in length
was dug to link the Yangtze River with the Hsi River and the Canton (Hsi)
delta of South China. Colonists, consisting mostly of merchants, convicts,
political exiles and riff-raff, were dispatched to consolidate the new holdings.
They met with little success in the extreme South, having had to face both the
challenges of a tropical, probably malarial, environment, and the hostility of
well-organized natives. Military agricultural settlements could only establish
footholds in the more northerly region of modern Hu-nan and Chiang-hsi.[2]

Within the basins of the Huang Ho and Yangtze Chiang, unification and
centralization required that the units of weights and measures be standardized,
as well as language, currency, and the gauge of cartwheels. The last rule suggests
that over much of the country the routes between cities were little better than
rutted cart-tracks. Ch'in Shih-huang-ti sought to remedy the situation by
having a network of roads constructed throughout the empire. These roads
radiated outwards from the capital in the Wei Ho Valley; they were said to be
fifty paces broad and treelined.[3] One reason for these roads was probably the
practical one of conveying enough food to feed the greatly swelled capital of
the new, centralized empire. Another was for the efficient dispatch of troops
and to facilitate the far-ranging tours of the emperor (Fig. 10). In any case,
commerce appears not to have been an important factor.

Ch'in's policy discouraged trade. The burgeoning of cities during the Chan-
kuo period under the stimulus of trade came to an end under Ch'in's policy of
control and centralization. Some cities no doubt declined, especially since the
emperor took to the notion of getting a large number of the powerful and rich
people of the empire to abandon their feudal strongholds and move to his
capital of Hsien-yang. A visible sign of extreme political centralization was the
enrichment of a parasitic capital at the expense of the countryside. No statistics of population are available but we catch a glimpse of the architectural
extravagance of the Ch'in capital from certain passages in the *Shi Chi*. It is
said, for example, that within 200 *li* around Hsien-yang the 270 palaces of the
nobles should be connected by covered roads and wall-lined roads;[4] and that
when the imperial palaces were captured and burnt by rebels in 206 B.C. the
flames of the conflagration lasted three months.[5]

The Ch'in empire was shortlived: it barely survived the death of the First
Emperor. Its impact on Chinese culture and history has been nonetheless
profound. Among the lasting influences were, on the one hand, the disappearance of the remaining vestiges of feudal domains, and on the other the development of what the anthropologists would call a 'We-group' feeling among the

11. Mountains on the west side of the Nan K'ou Pass, some forty miles from Peking, with part of the Great Wall.

sedentary farmers south of the Great Wall. The roads symbolized unity within the Great Wall the existence of an 'outside', of something non-Chinese and threatening.

One can point to palaces, roads, canals, and walls as additions to the landscape; but of the general appearance of the countryside and types of land use very little is known. It is probable that despite military ventures into the South and ambitious attempts at colonization the landscapes there remained a vast forested wilderness. The population centre remained in North China and was to do so for several more centuries. The Wei Ho Valley and certain parts of Ssu-ch'uan basin perhaps supported more people than they had ever done before. The construction of Hsien-yang made great demands on timber, and denuded some hills even in Ssu-ch'uan. The massive public works undertaken by Ch'in Shih-huang-ti did not benefit, in fact exhausted, the state. The benefits were inherited by the succeeding Han empire which lasted some 400 years.

To consider some of the changes in land use and landscape that had taken place during China's first extended imperial age, the Han, and during the later imperial age of comparable splendour, the T'ang, we need to look briefly at the agents of change – at population numbers and patterns, and at the territorial expansion of Chinese civilization.

78

The Former Han empire: population and land use

Before the Han dynasty, we can at best only make guesses as to the population of China. It has been suggested, for example, that during the Chan-kuo period the total might have reached 50 million. From the Former Han dynasty (202 B.C. – A.D. 9) onward, however, censuses have been taken periodically, and these, though often difficult to assess, nevertheless give us a far sounder basis for judging both the total number of people and their distribution at different times.

The first reliable census was taken in the year A.D. 2, towards the end of the Former Han dynasty. The total population then appears to have been about 58 million. The great majority of Chinese, some 43 million, lived in North China, north of a line extending from the Ch'in-ling Mountains to the Yangtze delta.[6] Outside the Huang Ho basin, only the Ssu-ch'uan basin in the Yangtze Valley had dense population clusters; one on the Ch'eng-tu plain and the other along the Chia-ling River. Both areas had sophisticated cultures by Chan-kuo times as the abundant remains of bronze and iron artifacts, and the specimens of writing indicate. The middle and lower Yangtze Valley, on the other hand, remained sparsely populated during the Former Han dynasty despite its long period of development under the Eastern Chou states. The great Han historian Ssu-ma Ch'ien's well-known characterization of the valley is worth quoting at length. Note, also, how he explains the easy-going ways of the inhabitants by the mildness and wealth of the natural environment.

> To sum up, the region of Ch'u and Yüeh is broad and sparsely populated and the people live on rice and fish soups. They burn off the fields and flood them to kill the weeds, and are able to gather all the fruit, berries, and univalve and bivalve shellfish they want without waiting for merchants to come around selling them. Since the land is so rich in edible products, there is no fear of famine, and therefore the people are content to live along from day to day; they do not lay away stores of goods, and many of them are poor. As a result, in the region south of the Yangtze and Huai rivers no one ever freezes or starves to death, but on the other hand, there are no very wealthy families.[7]

In North China, census data for A.D. 2 suggest that the densely settled parts were the great alluvial plain of the lower Huang Ho and the Fen-Wei valleys in the loessic uplands. Probably as many as 35 million out of the total of 43 million people in North China were concentrated on the alluvial plain. Large desolate areas existed within it, such as the broad strip along the northward course of the Huang Ho and the sand tracts and salt swamps of the entire low coast.[8] But an important fact of the Han dynasty was the shift of the population and economic centre from the Wei-Fen valleys eastward; from the upland basins west of the defiles through which the Huang Ho passes to the great alluvial plain, that is, to Ho-tung, the region east of the River. At the time of Wang Mang's short reign (A.D. 9–23), of the five densely populated metropolises – Lo-yang, Lin-tzu, Wan, Han-tan, and Ch'eng-tu – all but Ch'eng-tu were located to the east of the Shan-hsi uplands.[9]

However, through much of the Former Han period the Wei Ho basin remained the economic centre of China, and the densest agglomeration of people was to be found in the vicinity of the capital, Ch'ang-an. This was the ancient core area of Chinese civilization: on its fertile alluvium agricultural knowledge and tradition reached back for some 1,000 years to the time of the Western Chou. It had known peace: at least, from the time of the Warring States (Chan-kuo) to the fall of Ch'in it was always the base for troops and never a battlefield itself. Under the Ch'in the construction of the Ch'eng-kuo canal north of the Wei River had greatly extended the productivity of the basin

The fall of Ch'in must have affected the farmers in the countryside adversely, although the extent of the disturbance has yet to be determined. Peace was restored with the establishment of the Han dynasty and the wounds of war were healed during the reign of the third and fourth emperors. Population and productivity increased, the former at a faster rate than the latter.

During the reign of Emperor Wu (140–87 B.C.) a canal was constructed along the south side of the Wei River. It led from Ch'ang-an eastward to the Huang Ho, and thereby reduced the distance of travel along the Wei Ho by 300 *li* and avoided some of the worst dangers of that course. The canal not only made it far easier to transport grain from the plain east of the Pass (the Huang Ho defiles), but increased the irrigable farmland of the Wei basin by 10,000 *ch'ing*.[10]

The existence of at least two sharply delimited natural environments in North China, the loessic uplands and the great alluvial plain, has already been emphasized. Of the two the uplands were the easier to develop, since their small river basins did not harbour vast swamps, nor did the rivers in them indulge in the sort of violent, uncontrollable rampages characteristic of the Huang Ho. Chinese culture was nurtured in the upland basins and ventured on the low plains only after it had acquired greater confidence in mastering nature. It is interesting to note how even during the Han dynasty, the Wei Ho Valley was so much easier to develop than the Huang Ho plain east of the Pass. The Wei canal, with its dual purpose of transportation and irrigation, was completed in six months and proved a success. This inspired the governor of Ho-tung to say to the emperor:

Every year over a million piculs of grain are transported to the capital from the area east of the mountains. Since it is brought up the Yellow River, it must be shipped through the dangerous narrows at Ti-chu Mountain,

80

where much of it is lost. . . . Now if we were to dig canals from the Fen River to irrigate the region of P'i-shih and parts of Fen-yin, and other canals from the Yellow River to irrigate P'u-p'o and the rest of Fen-yin, I believe we could bring five thousand ch'ing of land under cultivation. At present this region is nothing more than a strip of uncultivated land along the Yellow River where the people graze their flocks but, if it were turned into irrigated fields, I think it could be made to yield over two million piculs of grain.[11]

Here then we have a worthy project, which, if successful, would transform land that was good only for grazing into irrigated fields. The emperor considered the idea sound and called up twenty or thirty thousand labourers, who spent several years digging canals and opening up the fields. But all to little purpose, for the Huang Ho changed its course so that the water did not flow into the canals properly, and the farmers who worked the newly opened fields could not produce enough to repay the cost of planting.

Agricultural techniques and landscapes

What kinds of crop did the farmers of the Former Han dynasty plant? What was the agricultural practice of 2,000 years ago? It is possible to essay tentative answers to these questions, thanks to the preservation of scattered comments made by an eminent agriculturist, Fan Shêng-chih, who lived in the later half of the first century B.C. Fan's comments provide us with a brief summary of the kind of agriculture practised in the sub-humid and semi-arid basins of the middle Huang Ho Valley: they give special emphasis to dry-farming techniques and say relatively little about farming methods on the flood-plain environments of the lower Huang Ho and Yangtze basins. Fan Shêng-chih, from what has been preserved of his work, gave more or less detailed directions on the cultivation of thirteen kinds of crop, namely: spiked millet, glutinous millet, winter wheat, spring wheat, rice, soya bean, lesser bean, hemp, gourd, melon, taro, water-darnels and mulberry tree.[12]

To envisage the agricultural landscape of Han times in the loessic uplands, we have to depend on the description of agricultural practice and on the ecological needs of the different crops that were known to be grown. The extension of farming to climatically marginal lands is indicated by Fan's persistent advice on how to conserve moisture. To begin with, one must watch sharply for any rainfall in the dry spring and dry and hot summer. Again and again we read in his directions, 'plough . . . after a drizzle', and 'plough when it rains'.[13] Adaptation to the hard winters of the north was indicated by the first mention of spring wheat in oriental writing. Land use was intense. Among the methods for maintaining soil fertility were the use of silkworm excrement (which implies the existence of a widespread silk industry), well-ripened night soil, compost, and the technique of ploughing down grass and weeds in spring so

that they would rot and become green manure.[14] Intercultivation was prac
tised. Plots of glutinous millet grew in the midst of mulberry trees. Fan als
discussed an ancient method of making use of infertile lands such as mountains
cliffs, steep places near villages and even the inside slopes of the walls. Thi
method was known as the *ou-t'ien* system or 'shallow-pit' system.

In spite of a fairly full account given by Fan, it is not clear what he reall
meant. One thing is clear: the method required extra human labour and th
concentrated application of water and manure to small plots. It implied th
availability of labour and the need to make use of all kinds of marginal land.[1]
Fan claimed great antiquity for the *ou-t'ien* system, although this may simpl
have been a way of giving it the sanction of tradition.

Similarly, according to the *Ch'ien Han Shu*, the agricultural technique knowr
as the *tai-t'ien* system was of ancient origin. In the Former Han dynasty th
agricultural minister Chao Kuo (*c.* 85 B.C.) was skilled in it. Again we are no
clear as to the precise nature of the practice. N. L. Swann suggests that it is a
type of rotation system in which shallow trenches are separated by ridges
Each acre of land has three such trenches so that in an allotment of 100 acre:
there will be 300 of them. Seeds are sown in the shallow trenches. Grass i:
weeded over the raised ridges so as to allow the soil to be washed into th
trenches as the plants grow. By summertime the fields will be levelled. Th
soil that is washed into the trench gives support to the growing plants and en
ables them to withstand wind and drought.[16]

The *tai-t'ien* system thus seems to be another adaptation to the semi-aric
conditions of the middle Huang Ho Valley. It is therefore curious that humid
subtropical crops like taro and rice should be included in Fan Shêng-chih's
list. Indeed botanical geographers have suggested that rice was originally a
weed in taro fields; that in the course of weeding, it established itself elsewhere.
and that it eventually came under human care and selection after its own virtue
had been recognized.[17] Neither crop can be expected to prosper in northwestern
China without human care. Here is how the taro ought to be planted, according
to Fan:

> Pits are made 3 *ch'ih* [7·2 feet] across and deep. Fill the pit with dried bean
> stalks, and tramp down firmly. . . . Mix the moist loose earth from the pit
> with manure, and lay the mixture on top of the tramped bean stalks to a
> thickness of 2 *ch'ih*. Water, tramp firm to retain moisture. Place five taro
> seed tubers in the four corners and the centre of the pit. Tramp down again.
> Apply water whenever it is dry. The bean stalks soon rot underneath the
> germinating taro-tubers, and a new taro 3 *ch'ih* long may be obtained.[18]

Fan also gave detailed instructions on the cultivation of wet-rice, suggesting
that it was, even in his time, a traditional crop. Apart from suitable temperature,
which the hot summer of North China provides, the basic requirement of rice

standing water during certain phases of its growth. Two instructions given by Fan suggest that the paddy fields were terraced. One is: 'Rice fields should not be too large; in too large a rice field it is difficult to adjust the height of standing water.' The other is: 'At earlier stages of growth the rice plants must needs be kept warm. To keep warm, one should make the inlet and outlet gaps on the mud ridges directly opposite to each other. After summer solstice, it becomes intensely hot, then make the gaps distantly across.'[19] It is possible to envisage from these instructions the existence of small paddy fields, and clearly the greater the slope of the land the smaller the fields must be. In such small fields, forming perhaps narrow bands in a contoured landscape, temperature of the water is quickly sensitive to air temperature and needs to be controlled by regulating the volume of water moving across the field. By the first century B.C., and probably very much earlier, this regulation of water temperature was achieved through the proper spacing of the inlets and outlets on the mud ridges that separate the different levels.

Perhaps one should refrain from reading too much into these instructions of Fan Shêng-chih. Throughout the lower parts of the Ssu-ch'uan basin and over much of South China the elaborately terraced rice fields are – and have been for the last few hundred years – by far the most striking feature of the Chinese rural landscape. It is frustrating that their origins cannot be traced to any distant or precise time in the past. Fan Shêng-chih's evidence at least permits us to date the existence of paddyfields, probably terraced, to some time beyond the first century B.C. – and this in North China.

The new and improved methods of agriculture mentioned by such experts as Fan Shêng-chih and Chao Kuo of the Former Han dynasty were either in use or were meant to be put into practice. It has been a Han policy to appoint experts to teach the people, especially those in underdeveloped frontier areas, how to use the new methods. Advances in technique and their official propagation must have enhanced agricultural productivity in China, especially from Emperor Wu's time on. Wastelands were being opened up for cultivation, and abundant harvests were repeatedly reported during the reigns of both Emperors Chao and Hsüan (86–49 B.C.).[20] On the other hand, we should also stress the fact that ordinary farmers, despite the agricultural advances, remained very much at the mercy of nature. 'No matter how diligently they have worked, or how bitterly they have suffered, they yet have again and again to bear calamities of floods and droughts.' It was taken for granted that in every generation there were years of famine and years of plenty. Even the exemplary rulers Yü and T'ang could not shield the country from natural calamities. The life of the peasant farmer was hard. 'In spring they ploughed, in summer they weeded; in autumn they reaped; and in winter they stored up supplies, cut undergrowth for wood and fuel; they repaired government buildings and performed other labour services.'[21]

Territorial expansion: new products and scenes

Under the reign of Emperor Wu the Han empire expanded territorially in several directions. Southwards, in 111 B.C., one of Emperor Wu's expeditionary forces reconquered the southern kingdom of Nan Yüeh, the centre of which was Canton. As with Ch'in Shih-huang-ti's ventures to the south, military conquest was not successfully followed by colonization. The Han court ruled the southern kingdoms through local tribes. One result of Emperor Wu's conquest was the introduction of southern products such as oranges, areca and litchi nuts to the North.

Territorial aggrandizement along the northern frontier met with more evident success. Northeastwards Emperor Wu's forces conquered northern Korea in 108 B.C. and established four command headquarters there. The chief of them, Lo-lang, had a Chinese colony of approximately 315,000 people.[22] Northward, 100,000 men were dispatched to the great loop of the Huang Ho to build defence works. But the most important expansion was to the west, to the oases at the base of the mountain backbone of modern Kan-su, and beyond them to the Tarim basin. The expansion followed the victory of the Han army over the forces of the Hsiung-nu in battles fought between 121 and 119 B.C., and further military successes over the kingdoms of the Tarim basin and of western Asia. Military agricultural colonies were established. Some 600,000 garrison soldiers moved in during this period of conquest and many of them became farmers and permanent settlers.[23]

The Great Wall was extended westwards to protect the settlements and the caravans of traders and emissaries that passed through them to the world beyond the Pamirs. By 118 B.C. the wall had been prolonged to Chiu-ch'üan (Su-chou), and by 108 B.C. to the Tun-huang oasis.

Several new elements entered the Chinese culture as a consequence of this westward expansion. For the first time a trade connection, however circuitous, spanned the 4,500 difficult miles that separated the Mediterranean world from China. Products and skills of western Asia trickled across the interior deserts into the Han empire. From lands west of the Pamirs Chang Ch'ien, Emperor Wu's intrepid emissary, brought back knowledge of a special breed of horse, grape-vine (*Vitis vinifera*) and alfalfa (*Medicago sativa*). The Bactrian mandolin became the Chinese *p'i-pa*. Skins, cinnamon bark and rhubarb found their way into the Huang Ho basin. The Mediterranean region had little to offer to China except glass, though 'wool and linen textiles seem also to have travelled east to some extent'.[24]

A new scene was added to the panorama of Chinese landscapes; that of an irrigated and fortified oasis surrounded by sterile deserts. The tension between the steppe and the sown in China proper was vastly increased in these frontier outposts. A new sentiment appeared in the Chinese poetry of the Former Han dynasty, a melancholic sentiment that drew on images of frontier wars, deserts, immense distances and cold north winds.

The Later Han Empire: population changes and migrations

If the population of the Han empire in A.D. 2 was 58 million, in A.D. 57 it was reported to be only 21 million. This figure is commonly thought to be a gross underestimation; it seems improbable that the Later Han empire at that time could have had less than 40 or 45 million people.[25] Population had undoubtedly declined, for between these two censuses there occurred civil war, rebellion (Red Eyebrow), wars with the Huns and other steppe peoples, floods, famines and plagues. Nature, in the form of floods, played an active role in the civil unrest, migrations of people, famine and death. During the reign of P'ing-ti (1 B.C. – A.D. 6), the Huang Ho flooded parts of the great plain and sent a branch to the south of the Shan-tung peninsula into the Huai River. In A.D. 11 new breaks occurred and the northern branch of the Huang Ho shifted southeastwards, thus abandoning its ancient mouth near T'ientsin. The southern branch flooded the old P'ien canal which followed a depressed belt in the great plain. Gradient to the sea was so gentle that flood water remained on the land for a long time. Water that inundated both sides of the P'ien canal was put under control only in A.D. 70.[26]

The floods brought disaster to millions of people, for the great plain south of the Huang Ho, before the change in river course, supported almost half of the total population of China. As a result of the inundations, large movements of people took place. They were mainly in two directions: one was to the east, into the uplands of Shan-tung peninsula which lay embraced, as it were, between the two soggy arms of the Huang Ho. The other was to the south in three streams: towards the Yangtze delta, towards the Po-yang lake basin and then up the Kan River; and towards the Han River Valley, into the Tung-t'ing lake basin and then up the Hsiang River.

By A.D. 40, though large parts of the North China plain were still under water, politically the unification of the empire under the Later Han dynasty was complete. From then on, population probably increased gradually until it reached a maximum of about 50 to 55 million between A.D. 140 and 160. The population of the Later Han empire in A.D. 140 was still less by some 8 million people than that of the Former Han Empire in A.D. 2, but the change in geographical distribution was even more significant from the point of view of the future development of the country. In A.D. 2 the population of China was overwhelmingly in the north. In A.D. 140 it appeared much less so. The Wei-Fen valleys of the loessic uplands lost some 6·5 million people during that period, the great plain about 11 million. But China south of the line from the Ch'in-ling Mountains to the Yangtze delta gained some 9 million people.

Population in Hu-nan, Chiang-hsi and Kuang-tung quadrupled.[27] South-western China entered the Chinese orbit, and a trade route was established through Yun-nan that reached into India. The southern boundary of the empire in fact reached as far south as Annam.

But within South China there were large areas of very sparse population: the southeast coast, for example, and the swamp lands around the great lakes of the middle Yangtze Valley. The mountains were thickly forested, wild and inaccessible, presenting a scene that the Chinese had not yet learnt to appreciate. A poem written during the Former Han dynasty conveyed a poet's horror of rugged and untamed nature, in which 'cassia trees grow thick', their branches 'twisting and snaking'.

> In the deep wood's tangle
> Tigers and leopard spring.
> Towering and rugged,
> The craggy rocks, frowning.
> Crooked and interlocked
> The woods' gnarled trees.
> Green cyperus grass grows in between
> And the rush grass rustles and sways.[28]

Land use on the great estates

The life of the peasant farmer during the Han dynasty was extremely hard. As Ch'ao Ts'o reported (c. 178 B.C.), 'in summer they cannot avoid sultry heat, . . . in winter they cannot shun cold and ice. During the four seasons not a day can they stop and rest.' In the Later Han period the small farmer's life remained hard. Although theoretically he was honoured, in fact he was held in contempt and has been likened to a plant or beast. Whence the plight of the small farmer? Apparently the root goes back to the breakdown of the feudal system during the Chan-kuo period of Chou dynasty. At first the peasant gained a measure of freedom. He was able to till land that he could more or less regard as his own. But this state of affairs did not last. The feudal lords were displaced by great landowners who were able to expand their estates, reclaim new territory and withstand the vagaries of nature and man far better than the small farmer.

Throughout the Han dynasty the rich landowners gained power. They became the 'great families', the new nobility displacing the old feudal hierarchy. A great family was centred around an extended patrilineal family, but it included many other families and individuals appended to it through political or economic relations. More and more peasant farmers, unable to produce enough to meet their own needs, found it expedient to become dependants of the great families who acquired not only economic but political power.

What kind of landscape can we associate with these great estates, many of which were several thousand acres in area by the Later Han period? In the first place, these large holdings had abundant resources. There was no lack of labour supply, of ploughing oxen, livestock in general, and seeds. On the estate of a great landlord:

Aside from such crops as glutinous millet, ordinary millet, rice, and wheat, some scores of other crops were also planted, including linseed, large and small varieties of onions and garlic, clover, turnips, melons, squash, celery, mallow, legumes, waterpepper, mustard, indigo plant, chives, and so forth. Among the trees were bamboo, varnish tree, tung, *Catalpa ovata*, pine, cedar, and various others.[29]

What we may envisage from this is the existence of highly diversified land use involving grain crops, an extraordinary variety of vegetables, as well as fruit and ornamental trees. The large landowners were able to experiment with new agricultural methods, such as the rotation method of Chao Kuo and the block planting method of Fan Shêng-chih; and they were able to make use of new machinery, such as the water-mill for grinding. The head of such an estate lived in princely style. His mansion

contains hundreds of rooms. His rich fields extend across the land. His slaves are counted by the thousands. He trades by land and by water in all parts of the country. His bulging warehouses fill the city, his huge dwellings overflow with treasure, his horses, cattle, sheep, and pigs are too numerous to be contained in the mountain valleys.[30]

It is worth noting in the above description, which is from a contemporary source, that the great family engaged not only in farming but also in commerce, and that it had large herds of livestock 'too numerous to be contained in mountain valleys'. If our experience is of Europe, we may be tempted to visualize a sumptuous country house or even palace set in the midst of landscaped gardens and surrounded by farms and farming villages. But such a picture would not suit China. The country home might have been large and prosperous; as a rule it was also architecturally modest. The less educated and ambitious members of the family lived there and ruled the estate. The well-educated and successful members lived in the city house as officials in the capital.

The city house was very likely magnificent. Recall that Ch'in Shih-huang, in order to break up feudal power, made the nobles move their palaces to the capital. This policy was continued during the Han dynasty; only then it was the heads of great families who had to move to the capital where they came under the imperial surveillance, and where in any case the ambitious would flock for therein lay all sources of prestige and affluence. In the city house the well-educated and wealthy gentry could lead a life of scholarly leisure, but more frequently they became officials and engaged in the rewarding though hazardous game of politics. In the sad event of having incurred imperial displeasure the official could beg leave to retire to his country house and assume there the dignified life of a Taoist scholar. In times of civil unrest too, the scholar-official's thought turned naturally to a Taoist landscape in the countryside. T'ung Chung-chang's (A.D. 180–220) daydream, in this respect, was not untypical:

> All I ask is good lands and a spacious house, with hills behind and a flowing stream in front, ringed in with ponds or pools, set about with bamboos and trees, a vegetable garden to the south, an orchard to the north. . . . Then with two or three companions of philosophic bent discuss the Way or study some book, . . . and so ramble through life at ease, with a cursory glance at Heaven and Earth and all that lies between, free from the censure of my fellow-men.[31]

The Period of Disunion

The year of T'ung's death was, coincidentally, the year when the Later Han dynasty came to an end, and China was subdivided into a number of local kingdoms. For the next three-and-a-half centuries China remained, except for brief periods, divided and seldom at peace. Unity was re-established under the Sui dynasty in A.D. 589, and although the Sui rule itself lasted only a short time, China may nevertheless be regarded as a powerfully unified empire from that time until the collapse of the T'ang dynasty towards the end of the ninth century.

The Period of Disunion between the end of the Later Han and the beginning of Sui is extremely important in the context of historical and geographical change. It was a time of vast movements of people which resulted in the settlement of remote and difficult lands in South China; and it was a time of cultural innovations made possible through the weakening of traditional structures in the periods of turbulence.

In A.D. 157 an official census put the population of China at 56 million people. This was probably the peak for the Later Han dynasty. It is astonishing to note that in A.D. 280, when the Western Chin empire reached its shortlived apogee, the population was reported at only 16 million. The nadir was plumbed earlier in the dying decades of the Later Han dynasty when people at the time believed that only one-tenth of the Han population was left.[32] Under-reporting during periods of great unrest no doubt accounted for part of the decline, but death and migration were also major causes.

Life had little worth around the end of the second and third centuries. Besides the slaughter during the wars, plagues and poor harvests added to the toll of death. Cannibalism appeared again and again. Towards the end of the second century, because of disturbances in the central provinces, people migrated in groups of hundreds and thousands southwards; but also south-westwards to Ssu-ch'uan and Yun-nan and northeastwards to Ho-pei and Liao-ning. The greatest exodus to the south, however, was propelled by internal political chaos and border conflicts with the nomadic tribes which eventually led to their occupation of the whole of North China. Even during the first years of unrest (A.D. 298–307) the number of migrants involved was around 2 million. For about two decades after the revolt of the Hsiung-nu in Shan-hsi (A.D. 304) migrations reached a floodtide. According to the *Chin Shu*, from the fall of the imperial capital of Lo-yang in A.D. 311 to about 325, 60 to 70 per cent of the upper classes had moved from the central provinces to south of the Yangtze River. And by the middle of the fourth century about a million northerners had settled in their new homes in the south.[33] Between A.D. 280 and 464 the population of the Yangtze Valley and south China increased five-fold, swelled mainly by refugees from the Huang Ho basin.[34]

A major consequence of this great influx of people to the south was the settlement and development of areas that had hitherto been avoided because of inaccessibility or because of the difficulties of the environment. The mountainous southeast coast (Fu-chien) was incorporated into the Chinese sphere of influence and the swamps of the Hu-pei lake basin were settled by refugees. As population increased the older methods of cultivation were found to be unsuitable. Tu Yu, for example, criticized the ancient 'till the land with fire and hoe it with water' approach. 'Fire farming' was all right, he said, when the land was sparsely settled but it led to the misuse of land and the ruin of pasturage under the pressure of rapidly increasing population.[35]

Agricultural inventions of the Huang Ho basin spread to the south with the migrants; for example, irrigation projects, the ox-drawn sow-plough machine (the *lou*-plough), and the water-mill. In 321 two great reservoirs were built and a lake was deepened near modern Chin-chiang in Chiang-su province, and a little later the Yangtze was connected with another fertile valley, the Huai, by two canals.[36] Irrigation was practised in central China as early as the fifth century B.C. but it did not become important or widely practised in the hill lands of South China until the late third century A.D. onward. Dams and reservoirs were built so rapidly that their construction was faulty. They were liable to break during times of exceptionally heavy run-off and bring disaster to the plains below.

From the *Ch'i Min Yao Shu*, a book on botany and agriculture compiled in the first part of the sixth century A.D., we learn that new agricultural methods were being developed and put into use during the Period of Disunion. There was mention, for example, of a plough with a share that turned up the earth and a mould-board that turned it over; there was also a kind of spiked harrowing machine known as *pa-lao*. Millet and wheat remained the staple grains of North China. By the sixth century they were graded into an extraordinarily large number of varieties on the basis of growth and yield characteristics in slightly different local environments. A special 'three-fields-in-two-years' rotation system was introduced. In this system, late millet was planted after the wheat harvest or wheat was planted after the seeding of the early millet was complete. The *Ch'i Min Yao Shu*, beside giving directions for the management of living hedges, devotes one full chapter to the transplantation of trees and six chapters to the cultivation of trees for timber. The aim was apparently to provide subsidiary income for the farmers.[37]

In South China one beneficent result of the penetration of settlements into the subtropical regions was the discovery of tea. The habit of tea drinking may indeed be very old but the earliest reference to it was in the biography of an official who died in A.D. 273.[38] Tea drinking, moreover, was limited to central and South China for many centuries before it found wide favour in the North and in Tibet. The plant requires a heavy rainfall, for preference evenly distributed through the year, and a well-drained soil. In China it is grown almost exclusively on the valley sides.

The hill slopes of Chê-chiang and Chiang-hsi were the earliest centres of production. The tea plant apparently was never cultivated on large plantations but each household raised its own supply. Until the eighteenth century the Chinese left the forested hillsides largely alone, and when they did pull out

12. Tea Caravan on the Djesi La Pass near Tachienlu

the trees and clean till the slopes the result was disastrous erosion. Perhaps one of the earliest attempts to make use of the hillsides was in the cultivation of tea. Fortunately for this experiment, the tea bushes themselves formed a protective cover against the impact of rain and minimized the hazards of heavy run-off.

Buddhist contributions to the landscape

The Period of Disunion was also a time of cultural innovation. The fabric of Confucian ideals as well as the bureaucratic structure of state had been shaken by civil strife and the successful occupation of North China by non-Chinese peoples. The most important innovation at this time, one which left a permanent mark on Chinese culture and the Chinese landscape, was Buddhism. The earliest ascertainable community of Buddhist monks in China was in A.D. 65, a community that lived near the estuary of the Yangtze River. The earliest description of a Buddhist shrine and pavilion dates back to *c.* A.D. 190. The structure consisted of a two-storeyed pavilion topped by nine tiers of bronze discs. The covered galleries could hold about 3,000 persons.[39] It was in the third century that Buddhism began to capture the popular imagination in China and spread with great rapidity through the strife-torn country. By the beginning of the fourth century A.D. Lo-yang, capital of the Western Chin empire, boasted forty-two pagoda temples. Under the Turkic Northern Wei dynasty (386–535) the total number of clerics in North China reached 2 million. In South China the growth of Buddhism may be gauged by the number of temples extant during the succession of shortlived Chinese dynasties.[40]

DYNASTY	NUMBER OF TEMPLES
Eastern Chin (317–420)	1,768
Liu Sung (420–479)	1,913
Ch'i (479–502)	2,015
Liang (502–557)	2,846

The bare facts indicate the successful grafting of a new and foreign religion to the traditional and native, Confucian and Taoist, systems of China. To what extent, and in what ways, did this cultural innovation add new elements to the Chinese landscape? The extent may be judged by numbers; thus in the southern Chinese Liang empire there were 2,846 temples housing 82,700 monks. In the Northern Wei empire some 500 temples were scattered in and around Lo-yang and they took up two-thirds of the available land.[41]

Once Buddhism became an officially recognized religion its edifices assumed the traditional style of Chinese architecture, including such elements as the wall, high gate-houses, courtyards, galleries and monumental halls. By the

T'ang dynasty (A.D. 618–907), some of them, especially those in the capital Ch'ang-an, were huge and sumptuously appointed establishments. Thus the Chang-ching temple at the east gate of Ch'ang-an contained forty-eight courts and 4,130 cells. Of even greater magnitude was the Hsin-ming temple (completed in A.D. 656) although it had only ten courts and more than 4,000 cells. 'Trees bordered the outskirts and streams criss-crossed the grounds. Within the precincts, pavilions and halls reached toward the clouds, and the pillars covered with gold leaves dazzled the eyes.'[42]

Outside the cities Buddhist establishments such as temples, hostels or common cloisters dotted the landscape during the T'ang period. They served frequently as lodgings, not only for travelling monks but also for travelling functionaries, military officials and merchants. In certain parts of China religious hostels were only 3 to 10 miles apart. Some of them at least were fairly large, for in one hostel over a hundred travellers found shelter. A number of sumptuous monasteries were located in the mountains or at the foot of the mountains in the midst of their great estates which included forests, scrub-covered hillsides, pastures and arable land. They may be seen as areas of peace and beauty, made possible by a combination of religious fervour, worldly wealth, and the sweat of a large number of temple slaves.

A question that remains is, to what extent were these Buddhist establishments architecturally distinctive so that one can speak of Buddhist elements in the Chinese landscape? The answer seems to be that at first the Buddhist temples were barely distinguishable from any other Chinese structure of a certain size. The description of a monastery in Chiang-su of the Later Han period revealed, as we have seen, a characteristic two-storeyed pavilion. The novel element was the mast with its tiers of symbolic parasols on top of the pavilion. In the ensuing centuries of Buddhist expansion the monasteries and temples assumed increasing magnificence, so that the biggest rivalled the imperial palaces in size. They retained nearly all the traditional elements of Chinese architecture: one important exception was the central, multistoreyed shrine, the pagoda. At the centre of Lo-yang's Yung-ning temple, built from A.D. 516 on, was 'a nine-storeyed pagoda framed in wood. This rose 900 feet, and had a mast 100 feet higher still. It was visible from a distance of 100 *li* from the capital.' Some exaggeration entered this account: the pagoda probably rose only between 300 and 400 feet above the temple grounds, but it was certainly high enough to be conspicuous.[43]

Until European buildings were widely introduced into the coastal provinces of China in the late nineteenth century, the pagoda was the most striking alien element in the Chinese landscape. Though inspired by Indian Buddhism, its architectural ancestry is not clear. Apart from the mast and the parasols the Chinese wood pagoda has little in common with the masonry Indian stupa. In its architectural elements the three-storeyed wood pagoda of the fourth

13. Pagoda in An-hui province

century appears to have more points of similarity with the Han watch-towers (*t'ai*), and beyond them in time, the pleasure-towers and hunting-towers of the Chou princes in the feudal period.[44] On the other hand it has been said that Chinese Buddhism adopted the tower form as a focus of worship because it came under the influence of the Kushan Buddhist and architectural tradition, a tradition that passed into China by way of the oasis cities of the Tarim basin.[45] Wood is the traditional building material of the Chinese. But as early as the sixth century A.D. some of the pagodas were nearly solid pillars of brick. In profile, in the use of masonry but particularly in decorative detail, they reflected strongly Indian influence.

Sui dynasty: population change and engineered landscapes

After more than three-and-a-half centuries of disunion China was brought under one rule again in A.D. 589 by Yang Chien (541–604). The Sui dynasty which Yang Chien founded was shortlived (590–618), but in that short period the autocratic rulers of Sui compelled the Chinese to exert great effort and aim at great achievement. Internally the achievement consisted in large-scale engineering works, particularly in the field of canal-building and irrigation, but also in building roads and cities. Externally Sui China enlarged its sphere of influence northwestwards into Chinese Turkestan and southwards to Champa and Formosa. The Sui dynasty bears certain resemblances with the Ch'in dynasty of Shih-huang-ti. Neither was able to benefit from its own strenuous labours. Historians have traditionally condemned them for their excesses. Both were succeeded by long dynasties of hallowed memory.

According to the census of A.D. 609 the population of Sui China was 46 million. A modern scholar has revised this figure upward to 54 million.[46] As compared with the population of the Later Han empire in A.D. 140, the population of loessic uplands, centred on the Wei-Fen valleys, had shown an increase, to about 11 million people. Most of them must have been of non-Chinese descent although by the seventh century they were well assimilated. The number of people living in Ch'ang-an and vicinity may have been as large as 1,800,000. South China, in spite of the heavy influx of settlers from the north and occupation by a number of Chinese dynasties during the Period of Disunion, appears to have been sparsely populated. The entire region south of the Yangtze River was treated as one vast province, out of a total of nine, in the geographical sections of the *Sui Shu*.[47] It seems likely that the figures given for South China in A.D. 609 are defective. In any case, compared with the census of A.D. 140 that of A.D. 609 does show a gain in certain parts of South China, notably over the lake swamps of Hu-pei. By the fifth century the isolation of the southeast coast was broken. On the other hand, Kuang-hsi and Yun-nan fell outside the sovereignty of the Chinese state.

In the short period of Sui rule, monumental feats of construction were initiated or accomplished. The Great Wall was fortified with the labour of some 1 million people and at a great loss of life. Near old Ch'ang-an, the founder of Sui caused to be built a new capital on an unprecedented scale. Its walls enclosed an area of 31 square miles. This was the Western capital. The Eastern capital of Lo-yang required 2 million workers for its construction. Large timber was brought in from regions south of the Yangtze River.[48] A huge imperial park with a circumference of several hundred *li* spread beyond the city limits. All the prefectures of the empire were obliged to contribute plants, strange birds and exotic beasts towards its furnishing. Not content with two capitals near the Huang Ho the Sui emperors required the construction of a third capital at Chiang-tu (Yang-chou) north of the Yangtze estuary. The three metropolises were linked together by canals. The linkage was also between the heavily populated old North, with worn soils that could no longer fully support the populace of the great cities, and the rich South which had rice surpluses.

Canal-building during the Sui dynasty began in A.D. 587 with the clearing of a waterway of the mid-fourth century which connected the Yangtze and the Huai Rivers. By the end of the dynasty canals linked the Hai River (on which modern T'ientsin is located) in the north with Hang-chou in the south, and Yang-chou in the southeast with Ch'ang-an in the northwest. Altogether more than 800 miles of canals were constructed during this period.[49] The scale of the project and the landscaping associated with it may be glimpsed from the following description of a segment of the canals as given by a Sung historian:

> From Shan-yang (near Huai-an) to the Yangtze River, the water surface of the canal was forty paces [*c.* 200 feet] wide. Roads were constructed along both banks of the canal and planted with elms and willows. For over 2,000 *li* from the Eastern capital [Lo-yang] to Chiang-tu [Yang-chou], shadows of trees overlapped each other. An imperial rest-house was built between every two official post stations, and there were more than forty such rest-houses.[50]

T'ang dynasty: changing frontier scenes

The population of T'ang China, according to the census of A.D. 742, was 51·5 million. It has been suggested, however, that the figure was higher, probably about 74 million, and that the increase from the Sui census of A.D. 609 was achieved during the prosperous years of the T'ang dynasty from 640 to 755.[51] The T'ang empire, in its expansive phase, made significant impact on the tribes and nations to the west and northwest. By the middle of the seventh century T'ang China extended its power once more to the Tarim basin and beyond by defeating the western Turks. However, in A.D. 751 the Chinese suffered decisive defeat in a battle in which the Arabs took part. An indirect result of the defeat was a permanent change of the cultural scene in the oases of the Tarim basin: from Buddhist houses, shrines and stupas to the cultural artifacts of the western religions, and of triumphant Islam in particular Muslim shrines, mosques, schools, and bazaars remain to the present the characteristic features of the oasis landscape in Turkestan.

T'ang China was indirectly responsible for the withdrawal of Buddhism from the Tarim basin. On the other hand, it helped to establish Buddhism in Tibet. In A.D. 641 the Chinese princess Wên-cheng was married to the first unifier of Tibet, Sren-tsen-gampo, and brought with her to Tibet a great image of Buddha, several volumes of Buddhist scripture as well as a few treatises on medicine and astrology.[52] Characteristically, Tibet received its cultural influences from both China and India, with India the more important of the two; and this dual source was symbolized by the marriage of Tibet's unifier not only to a Chinese princess but also to a Nepalese princess. It is believed that at least three well-known temples in Tibet date back to this earliest historic period: the Trhan-tr'uk in the Yar-lung Valley, cultural heart of Tibet, and Trhul-nang and Ra-mo-che, both in the Lhasa basin. The two Lhasa temples are supposed to have been built originally to enshrine the Buddha-images brought by the two spouses of Sren-tsen-gampo. The image of Buddha the Prince, reputedly brought by the Chinese queen, is now the centre of pilgrimage in Lhasa.[53]

Tibetan legends are anxious to attach their native traditions, however unconvincingly, to those of India. Skill in the making of barley beer, butter and cheese, it is believed, was acquired in Tibet at this time; such foods belonged to the Indian or southwest Asian tradition rather than to the Chinese. As a people the Chinese have shown habitual distaste for milk products. On the other hand, Sren-tsen-gampo's grandson is credited with the introduction of tea from China.[54] Tea has become the national beverage of the Tibetans, who can drink thirty to seventy cups a day. But it is a special kind of tea – a rancid-butter tea – a mixture of Indian and Chinese influences.

Within China proper the main movements of people during the T'ang dynasty were to the subtropical and tropical regions. By the middle of the eighth century nearly half the total population lived in the Yangtze Valley and places to the south. The causes of migration were wars, harassments from Turks and Tibetans, famine, floods, and social iniquity evident in heavy taxation, forced labour, and the extension of tenancy: in other words, the same types of cause as had operated in the past. Only once, under Ch'in Shih-huang-ti, was the equatorward thrust of colonists the result of government policy. South of the Yangtze River the largest increases occurred in southern Chiang-su and Chê-chiang. The southeast coast became fully a part of the Chinese empire during the T'ang dynasty. The isolation of Chiang-hsi, centred on the Kan tributary of the Yangtze River, was broken; by the middle of the eighth century it had more people than Hu-nan for the first time.

The gain in population and the increasing prosperity of the south and southast coast were attributable to the stimulation of commerce. Arab traders expanded their activities in the eighth century. They established factories first on the Canton delta and later in Fu-chien and Chiang-su. Persian and Japanese merchants also plied trade with the southeast coast. The chief emporium for Arab and Persian traders by the mid-eighth century was Yang-chou north of the Yangtze delta. The size of some of these foreign trading communities may be judged by the fact that a local disturbance in Yang-chou in A.D. 760 resulted in the death of several thousand Arab and Persian traders.

While the colonization of South China was not the result of deliberate state policy, that of the marginal lands along the northern frontier was. During the T'ang dynasty the government held very large areas of land, which were set aside to yield incomes for officials, for the upkeep of official buildings and to provide pasture for horses. Extensive areas of northern China were designated as pastures and used by the state for horse breeding. Horses were vital to the maintenance of empire; they required a lot of grassland to feed on. In the middle of the seventh century T'ang China had a stock of 706,000 horses, which were distributed over eight great pasturelands north of the Wei Ho Valley.[55] With the exception of the pastures, government-owned lands were rented to tenants. Income to the government derived from the collection of rents.

In addition to these lands the state owned others over the exploitation of which it had more direct concern. One such category was known as *t'un-t'ien* or land exploited by military-agricultural colonies. The system originated during the Former Han dynasty. It was then devised as a means to settle and protect the newly pacified northwest frontier. During the T'ang dynasty the *'un-t'ien* system of colonies served a similar function of frontier protection and settlement: only there were far more of them. By A.D. 736 more than 900 military-agricultural colonies were established in the northern border provinces. They could be found south of the Great Wall from Yu-kuan on the coast westwards to where the wall ran into the great loop of the Huang Ho; they were established on the outer side of the Huang Ho loop, along the oasis of the Kan-su corridor westwards to the Turfan depression; and in the mountain valleys on the border of Tibet, east of the Kokonor lake. The size of the colony varied from 20 *ch'ing* (370 English acres) to 50 *ch'ing* (928 acres), depending on the fertility of the soil and on whether the land was suited to dry-farming or irrigation agriculture. A largish colony might be garrisoned by several hundred farmer-soldiers. Some of the more fertile and more distant lands appear to have lacked labour for their full development. The Kan-chou oasis of Kan-su corridor, for example, could profit from more settlers. As a memorial to the throne put it in 684:

The military colonies of Kan-chou are all irrigated, and being watered by heavily sedimented rivers their fertility does not depend on the weather.

These forty and more colonies together form a rich region, and hence every harvest is never less than 200,000 *tan*. But because labour is not available there is still some idle land. If additional troops were now stationed here and made responsible for exploiting the resources of the land to the utmos limit, it will not be difficult to obtain an annual harvest of 300,000 *tan*.[56]

The economy and landscape of prosperity

The early decades of the T'ang dynasty were far from peaceful. From abou A.D. 640 onward, however, the years were good until the civil wars of the period 755–65 terminated the first phase of peace and prosperity. The culmination of this first phase occurred during the reign of Hsuan-tsung (715–56) It was a time of wealth and safety. Prices were low. Within the empire a large number of shops and emporia supplied the merchant travellers, who could undertake their long journeys without fear of robbery. Besides the fine and safe highways, an intricate net of canals served to bring the necessities and luxuries from South China to the imperial capitals in the north.

The chief necessity was grain. As the *Hsin T'ang Shu* put it: 'although Kuan-chung (Shen-hsi) was known as a fertile country, the territory was too crowded and its products could not support the capital and accumulate reserves to prepare against flood and famine. Hence grain tribute from the southeast was transported.'[57] Whereas during the Former Han dynasty the chief problem was the efficient conveyance of grains from the North China plain to the Wei Ho basin, during the T'ang dynasty the problem was to bring food into the old Northwest from the far more distant source of southeast China. The amount sent was enormous. It has been said that in a three-year period centred around 735, some 7 million tons of grain were delivered.[58] What did the grains consist of? During the Han dynasty they were undoubtedly wheat and millet. But during the T'ang period the chief crop of southeast China was probably rice. Wheat and barley were introduced to the rice area as early as A.D. 318, when North China had fallen to the barbarians and a Chin prince had declared himself emperor at Nan-ching. The estimated 1 million Chinese who migrated to the South during the fourth century must also have contributed towards the spread of wheat cultivation.[59]

The transportation of necessities to the northern capitals had to compete with the increasing flow of luxury goods – anything from pearls and kingfisher feathers to live rhinoceros – from Canton. Two routes led from Canton northwards, one following the Kan tributary, and the other the Hsiang tributary, of the Yangtze River into the lake plains of the middle Yangtze Valley; thence one could easily sail down the river to Yang-chou, and then up the Grand Canal and the Pien Canal to Ch'ang-an. In fact it was possible to go all the way by boat from Canton, across the southern uplands, down the

Yangtze Valley, up the North China plain and into the loessic uplands of Shen-hsi. The imperial capital, Ch'ang-an, lay at the edge of the great Asiatic steppe; it was nevertheless equipped to handle this flow of goods by boat. In A.D. 743 an artificial lake, a transhipment pool, was built east of Ch'ang-an. As Schafer graphically put it:

> In that year, the fascinated northerner . . . could see the boats of every part of the empire gathered on this pool, loaded with the tax goods and local tribute destined for the palace: scarlet felt saddle cover from the north, vermilion bitter tangerines from the south, pink silk-fringed druggets from the east, crimson alum from the west. These goods were transferred to lighters, whose crews were specially garbed in bamboo rim hats, sleeved smocks, and straw shoes, in the fashion of the boatmen of the Yangtze.[60]

The population of Ch'ang-an, the western capital, was nearly 2 million, 1 million within the city walls and another in the suburbs. The eastern capital of Lo-yang had about a million inhabitants. In the T'ang China of the eighth century, as many as twenty-five cities had populations that exceeded half a million. Even the newer cities of the south and southeast coast like Hang-chou, Fu-chou and Canton had populations that numbered in hundreds of thousands. Probably 450,000 people lived in Yang-chou.

The population of China might have reached 75 million by the middle of the eighth century. This increase in population, both urban and rural, implied a corresponding gain in agricultural output. How was it achieved? It was achieved by extending the arable land in central and South China and by a more intense use of the land in the North. But a change in the type of land-holding might also have contributed towards the greater production. During the Period of Disunion peasant farmers owned small plots of land and received, in addition, land from the government which they could work on and benefit from, at least during their lifetime. In A.D. 624 the T'ang government promulgated a law which reaffirmed the principle of this system of 'equal land allotments'.[61] But very quickly the wealthy began to buy out the poor – despite government prohibitions. This happened because, in the first instance, the T'ang ruler did not abide by his own rules. Aside from giving large allotments to influential persons, the ruler also arbitrarily presented them with grants of land. Thus the Emperor Tai-tsu granted one favourite 1,000 *ch'ing* of land, a mansion, and an estate of 300 households. Numerous other persons received grants of five, ten, or several dozen *ch'ing* of land as well as mansions and manorial estates.[62] Moreover, after the period of civil strife and rebellion (755–65), the government itself competed with the wealthy landowners in acquiring estates to develop. The government was tempted to do this because, as a result of the devastations caused by fighting, there was a great deal of derelict land even in central China.[63] In any case, in the course of the T'ang dynasty small fields and free farmers gave way to great estates and wealthy landowners.

Although deplorable from a social point of view, agricultural production probably increased as a result of the consolidation of holdings. The owners of big estates had the means to engage in ambitious works of reclamation which lay beyond the capability of the small farmer. They were able to make better use of the heavier machinery, such as the three-shared plough, the *lou-l* (plough-and-sow machine), and the harrow; and they could, with their numerous draught animals and field hands, carry out the 'three-fields-in-two-years' rotation system that appeared in China during the sixth century.

Sensitivity to nature and conservation

It is clear that by the end of the T'ang dynasty man had succeeded in transforming large parts of China. The ascendancy of culture over nature finds its most poignant expression in the effect of the literary industry on vegetation. As we have noted earlier, the demand for pine soot in the making of ink for China's vast bureaucracy made appreciable inroads on the pine forests of North China. The self-confidence that man derived from the splendour of his cities and the safety of his roads was translated to greater awareness of the beauty and fragility of nature. During the Han dynasty, nature – especially the forested wilderness of the South – was still too much of a threat to human values to be seen as something that could possess charm and evanescent loveliness. During the T'ang dynasty, however, nature appeared to be not so much threatening as threatened. Whereas the Han poet of *Chao Yin Shih* feared the mountains wrapped in mist and the sheer ravines into which a man might wander and not return, the great T'ang poet, Li Po, wrote, with characteristic misanthropic overtones,

> If you were to ask me why I dwell among green mountains,
> I should laugh silently; my soul is serene.
> The peach blossom follows the moving water;
> There is another heaven and earth beyond the world of man.[64]

The sentiment for nature was translated into decrees that re-enforced the ancient respect for temple precincts and for the grounds around the tombs of the sacred emperors as inviolate refuges, where all living things shared the sanctity of the enshrined or the entombed. The government increasingly recognized the value of forests and laws were promulgated against arson, against the unreasonable burning of fields, and against making fires alongside public roads.[65] There was also some attempt at protecting watersheds for both religious and practical reasons. Thus the T'ang code of institutes states:

On all the Five Sacred Mountains and on the Notable Mountains which are capable of gathering numina and of giving birth to extraordinary things, which can raise clouds and bring rain, having advantage for mankind, all gathering of fuel is interdicted, while prayers and sacrifices shall be made in season there.[66]

Forested landscapes of T'ang China

Despite the many signs of a world transformed for good or ill by human busy-ness, it would be incorrect to envisage T'ang China as the eroded and de-forested country that it was to become in later centuries. The great evergreen broadleaved forest of South China was barely touched, notwithstanding the heavy influx of settlers into the alluviated valleys. The primeval character of the South is suggested by the fact that wild elephants were still abundant in the mountainous parts of Kuang-tung province in the ninth century, and that the rhinoceros still found a home over a broad area in South China, particularly in western and southern Hu-nan. North China too was a far better wooded land than it is today. Shan-tung, for example, is now a deforested and eroded country burdened with the support of a very dense population. In the early part of the ninth century it seems to have been well wooded, wet and sparsely peopled. The Japanese monk Ennin, on his way to the Shan-tung coast in 839, encountered Korean mariners who were engaged in transporting the charcoal they made in Shan-tung peninsula to the treeless plains of the lower Yangtze. Ennin also gave us a valuable picture of what the Shan-tung peninsula was like when he crossed its mountainous promontory in 845:

> The road from Hai-chou up to Teng-chou is impassable. There are broad waste lands, the paths are narrow, and the grass and trees close over them. . . . In the mountains, we would cross a hundred mountains and ford a hundred streams in a single day. In the waste lands, the trees were dense and the grass was thick, and if someone went a little ahead it was difficult to see him. . . . The mosquitoes and horseflies were like rain. . . . The prefectural and subprefectural towns along the way were like single mounds in the wilderness.[67]

Ennin's destination was the Wu-t'ai Mountains in northern Shan-hsi where the twelve great monasteries and many lesser ones formed a major centre of pilgrimage in T'ang China. Today, except for the sheltered precincts of temples and a few deep ravines, the mountains are largely treeless; their ex-posed ribs and the dry, cobble-clogged valleys are in sharp contrast to the image that Ennin's diaries give us. The image is one of a cool, well-timbered land. 'The groves of pines on the peaks and the trees in the valleys grow straight and tall.' Alpine flowers covered the higher slopes. Icy cold water

5

bubbled up out of the ground on the flat summits, and in the deeper valley there even lingered some permanent bodies of ice.[68]

The development of cities

An attempt has been made thus far to evoke images of the Chinese landscape through what is known of the physical environment and of the changes in society, economy, and agricultural techniques during China's Imperial Age. One major element of the landscape, however, needs to be given greater articulation, and that is the town or city. In fact, few features of the humanized landscape are as sharply defined or as visually striking as the walled city in China. It is moreover a feature that has shown remarkably little change in basic conception down the ages. A visitor in the twentieth century, approaching a Chinese town, might be confronted by a monolithic expanse of wall rising sharply above the cultivated fields; what he sees would not be very different from what the Japanese visitor, Ennin, could have seen in T'ang China.

I have indicated earlier that the Chan-kuo period of the Chou dynasty was a time when many new towns came into being, apparently in response to the growing call of commerce, and that even the capitals had lost their character as citadels. The Ch'in dynasty brought this trend to an end. It discouraged commerce, and sought to destroy the power of the old and rich families through a policy of centralization which was carried to the extremity of insisting that these families move their household to the imperial capital, Hsien-yang, in the Wei Ho Valley. The result was the inflation of Hsien-yang, in size and in wealth, at the expense of the old feudal centres. New cities were founded during the short Ch'in dynasty; for example, the *hsien* capitals in the Hsiang Valley south of the Yangtze. But these were political and administrative in character; they functioned as fortified centres of Chinese power, a function that was especially evident in newly developed land. The cities, large and small, tended to resume the closely guarded, citadel character that they had in the earlier part of the Chou dynasty; only in the Ch'in period the walls were built as much as a means of controlling the citizens within as to ward off possible marauders from without.

The Former Han dynasty inherited the centralized governmental framework of the Ch'in, including the physical system of routes convergent upon the capital, and the walled cities that made the authoritarian pattern of control operational. The Han capital of Ch'ang-an retained and augmented its unchallengeable position as primate city – a city far superior to its rivals in the number of its palaces, in architectural splendour, and probably in population. Ch'ang-an was looted and burnt after the brief interregnum of Wang Mang, during a time when several claimants to the throne struggled for power. The victorious claimant founded the Later Han dynasty (A.D. 25–220) and moved his capital to Lo-yang. However, following the sacking of Ch'ang-an, the new mperial seat failed to achieve supremacy – at least numerical supremacy. As late as A.D. 111 the population of Lo-yang (1,010,827 inhabitants) was probably less than that of Ch'eng-tu, capital of the fertile Ssu-ch'uan province, which had at least a million people within its walls and some 350,000 in the suburbs.[69]

During the reigns of the first seven emperors of the Former Han dynasty the policy of moving the residences of the wealthy families to the capital was continued. But these measures did not stem the rising power of the great families, nor did they prevent the weakening of the central government. In the Later Han dynasty the system of social control exercised within one pyramidal structure of power had lost much of its effectiveness. An expression of that control – the walled town – had also declined. Nevertheless we can make a few generalizations on Han towns, for during that long span of Chinese history they displayed certain traits which marked them off from city development in both the preceding and succeeding periods.

Han towns, according to Miyazaki, may be grouped into three classes *hsien*, *hsiang*, and *t'ing*, on the basis of size. The smallest unit was the *t'ing*. Its population numbered hundreds. Where there were several *t'ing*, the largest among them might have had a population of a couple of thousand or more, and such a large *t'ing* was known as the *hsiang*. Similarly, the principal *hsiang* became the prefectural town or *hsien*. The density and size of these settlements probably depended on the agricultural productivity of the region, for Han towns were in fact mostly agricultural towns. They may be called towns rather than villages by virtue of their physical separation from the countryside, and in view of the highly regimented nature of the life of the inhabitants, a regimentation imposed from above.

The dominant element of the Han townscape was the wall. It separated a settlement from the outlying fields, and by creating an enclosure facilitated the regimentation of life within. The Han town, whether large or small, had the character of a succession of walled-in rectangles. There was the town wall (*ch'êng* or *kuo*) with gates on the four sides. Within the wall the settlement was partitioned into a number of wards or *li*. The number of wards varied with the size of the town. The expression 'ten *li* one *hsiang*' suggests the size of the *hsiang*. Ch'ang-an itself had as many as 160 wards. Streets separated the wards, which were in turn surrounded by walls (*yuan* or *ch'iang*). Each ward had only one gate opening to the street during Han times, and contained up to one hundred households, each of which was again surrounded by a wall (*ch'iang*). Very narrow lanes led to the gates of the individual households. The inhabitants, to get out of town, would thus have to pass through three sets of gates: that of their house, that of their ward, and that of their town. Moreover, all the gates were guarded and closed at night. City streets after sundown must have been eerily empty. Within the wards, by moonlight one could probably catch sight of young lovers climbing over the *ch'iang*. The scene has indeed become a cliché of Chinese romance. It was reprehensible to climb over the *ch'iang* but to negotiate the town *ch'êng* would have been a crime subject to severe punishment.[70]

During the Former Han dynasty, there were 1,587 *hsien*, 6,622 *hsiang*, and 29,635 *t'ing*; that is a total of 37,844 walled settlements. If we assume an average of some 2,000 people per town, this would mean that the entire population of the Former Han empire (*c.* 60 million) lived in walled enclosures of varying size. This is the opinion of Miyazaki, who believes that few people lived outside of them during the Former Han dynasty, and that indeed the enclosed existence was the norm for the Chinese since antiquity.[71] Other views are certainly possible. Thus Eberhard believes that during the Western Chou period, Shang villages existed side by side with the Chou walled towns, and that in feudal China farmers left the towns to live in temporary shelters in the fields throughout the summer season, only to return after harvest; and that these temporary shelters eventually became villages.[72]

During the Later Han dynasty, the total number of towns appears to have diminished. There are several plausible explanations: the decline of population in general but, in particular, over the North China plain; the increase in size of towns that survived, and the growth of numerous small villages (the *ts'un*) in the neighbourhood of new frontier towns and in newly cleared fields. During the Period of Disunion, a period of barbarian occupation of North China and mass movements of people to the south, the rigid system of control based on supervision at the successive wall gates had broken down. Villages increased at the expense of the smaller *hsiang* and *t'ing*. The *hsien* maintained their numbers; they were almost as numerous during the T'ang dynasty (A.D. 618–907) as during the Han. But they were larger and modified in the direction of greater freedom for their citizens. Thus, whereas the enclosed ward *li* of Han times had only one gate to the street, the ward of T'ang times (more commonly known as the *fang*) had four gates. During the Han period, very few of the noble families possessed the right to establish a gate in the *li* wall so that their house could front the avenue. Under the T'ang, not only high-ranking nobles but also Buddhist temples were authorized to have their private gate in the *fang ch'iang*.[73] However, the *fang* gates were closed at night. Even in the remote frontier town of Canton and in the bustling quarter reserved for foreign merchants, this was the case.

Compared with Han cities, those of the T'ang dynasty were far more active in trade, far more urban and cosmopolitan in character. The coasts of south and southeast China, for example, attracted an increasing number of visitors from overseas. Canton had become the largest port in the South, with a population of 200,000, a majority of whom were foreign traders and 'barbarians'. Ships belonging to Brahmans, Arabs, Persians and Malays sailed into the estuary, loaded with aromatics, drugs, and other rare and precious things.[74] Yang-chou, near the junction of the Yangtze Chiang and the Grand Canal, had most of the characteristics of a bustling, bourgeois city. Its population of 450,000 was dominated by a rich citizenry engaged in trade, in the transhipment of goods from all parts of South China and from overseas to the great cities of the North, and in banking and industry. Yang-chou exploited its focal position in the T'ang waterways by distributing salt, tea, precious stones, aromatics, drugs, and costly damasks and tapestries. It manufactured bronze mirrors, felt hats, silk fabrics, and embroideries, woodwork and boats. It refined sugar.[75]

The two great northern capitals of T'ang China were Ch'ang-an and Loyang. Each had more than a million people within its walls. Both had great markets, a variety of luxury manufactures and many foreigners. The foreigners included Arabs, Persians and Hindus, who could also be found in large numbers in the cities of the South; but in addition the northern capital of Ch'ang-an had visitors from the north and west, Turks, Syrians, Tartars and Tibetans; and from the east, Koreans and Japanese.

We must make the distinction, however, between the old northern cities and the new urban centres of the South. The latter, despite their large population and the wealth of boisterous commerce, were architecturally crude – as one might expect of places at the remote frontier. Canton, for example, was a wealthy but also flimsy town, 'its triple wall surrounded by a crowded mass of thatched-roofed wooden houses, which were periodically swept by disastrous fires, until in 806, an intelligent governor ordered the people to make themselves roofs of tile'.[76] The northern capitals, on the other hand, were paradigms of tradition and imperial splendour.

What are the main elements of this architectural tradition? The oldest element in the design of the Chinese city is the rectangular wall, oriented more or less to the cardinal directions. The earliest sign of this appeared in the prehistoric Lung-shan settlement of Chêng-tzu-yai, but the pattern became much clearer by the late Shang dynasty. In the Eastern Chou period there were numerous examples of the rectangular city and variations on the rectangular shape, such as two walled rectangles built side by side, or one attached to the corner of another, or a box-within-box pattern. Archaeology confirms the antiquity of these designs and their modern progenies can still be seen. Peking is the best-known example. Less old but still ancient elements of the capital city are the central or northern location of the palaces, and the grid pattern of the streets. By Chan-kuo times, the characteristics of a royal city were already enshrined in ritual books. They were: proper orientation, a rectangular shape girdled by walls, twelve gates in the walls to represent the twelve months; an inner enclosure to contain the royal residences and audience halls; a public market to the north of the inner enclosure; a principal street leading from the central south gate of the palace enclosure to the central south gate of the city wall; two sacred places, the royal ancestral temple and the altar of the earth on either side of the principal street.[77]

These elements of the city plan reflected the ancient Chinese conception of the universe, and of the role of the emperor as intermediary between heaven and earth. The city is a microcosm. The arrangement of its parts is the visible expression of cosmological beliefs, which are fundamentally that of an agricultural people. Thus the Four Quadrants in the heavenly vault were translated into the Four Directions or Four Seasons of the terrestrial grid. Each side of the square may be identified with the daily position of the sun or with each of the four seasons. The Polar star and the celestial meridian writ small became the royal palace and the main north–south street through the city. The palace at the centre dominates the city as the Polar star the universe. It separates the centre of profane activity, the market, from the centres of religious observance. The ruler in his audience hall faces south, the world of man.

Such a pattern probably never found architectural expression in all its details. It is nonetheless remarkable how closely the pattern has been followed in certain periods of Chinese history. The Ch'ang-an of Sui and T'ang dynasties, for example, was properly oriented, and had three gates on each of the three walls; its altar of earth and the royal ancestral temple were correctly located with respect to the central north–south axis. However, the palace quarter was backed against the north wall instead of being placed at the centre: this departure pre-empted the space for the official market, which was divided into two sections and set in the eastern and western parts of the capital. The Ch'ang-an city plan is known to have served as a model for the construction of the Japanese cities, Kyoto and Nara; it has doubtless influenced the construction of a large number of cities – those with some political pretension – in China, and, moreover, the canons of urban design, so lucidly illustrated by T'ang Ch'ang-an, may still be discerned in cities that have survived into the middle of the twentieth century, whether this be a small *hsien* town of grid pattern or Peking.

What did Ch'ang-an look like during the T'ang dynasty? The poet Chü-I, who had a pavilion in the southeast corner of the city, described a night scene as follows:

> Hundreds of houses, thousands of houses – like a great chess-board.
> The twelve streets like a huge field planted with rows of cabbage.
> In the distance I see faint and small the torches of riders to court,
> Like a single row of stars lying to the west of the five gates.[78]

Night life in Ch'ang-an was quiet. The main streets were empty except for official riders. The *fang* gates were closed. Daytime, however, would see a great deal of life – especially in the western market. But first let us take note of

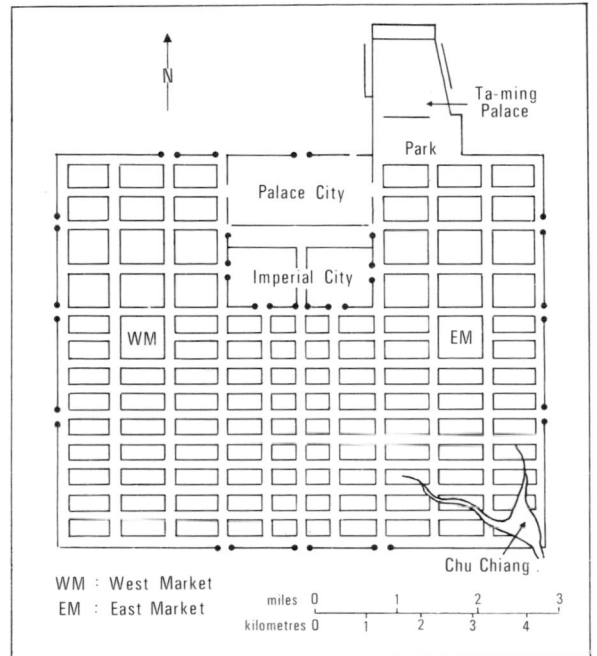

WM : West Market
EM : East Market

miles   0   1   2   3
kilometres 0   1   2   3   4

14. Ch'ang-an under T'ang dynasty

a few statistics that will give us an idea of the size of the metropolis.[79] The basic framework, grandiosely conceived by the founder of the Sui dynasty, was inherited by the T'ang rulers. Its rectangular shape measured 6 miles east-by-west and 5 miles north-by-south (Fig. 14). Streets divided the walled city compound of some 30 square miles into a grid pattern, in which the main elements were the Palace City and the official quarters placed at the centre, next to the northern wall; the western and eastern markets, the Ch'u Chiang park in the southeast corner, and the 110 *fang* which were walled off from the streets. Twenty-five broad carriageways bordered by drainage ditches, footpaths and fruit trees divided up the city: eleven ran from north to south and fourteen from east to west. The north–south streets were remarkably broad, more than 450 feet across, and the east–west ones were not much narrower. They must be thought of as straight, clean and open spaces – impersonal and forbidding – serving, one would think, more to isolate *fang* residential quarters than to connect them. The upper classes lived mostly in the eastern part of the city, the lower classes in the western part, which therefore probably had the higher concentration of people. Of the two markets, the eastern one – visited by the well-to-do – was less populous and had, by the beginning of the ninth century, become largely residential. The western market, on the other hand, was 'a busy, raucous, and multilingual cluster of bazaars and warehouses, whose visitors were also entertained by prestidigitators and illusionists of every nationality, not to mention story-tellers, actors and acrobats'.[80]

Although about a million people lived within the walled city of Ch'ang-an, there were nevertheless areas of sparse population in the huge compound of some 30 square miles. A broad strip in the southernmost part of the city was thinly peopled; it had mostly cultivated fields, gardens and a few scattered shrines. At the southeast corner was the water park of Ch'u Chiang, a place richly decorated with beautiful plants and pavilions and frequented by the gentry. The poet Po Chü-i 'liked to go there on horseback, dismount, and stroll among the willows along its banks. Richly planted with trees and flowers, including willows, poplars, pink lotuses, marsh-grasses and reeds, and attracting wildfowl of every sort, the gardens brought visitors from among the élite every season.'[81]

The existence not only of gardens but also of cultivated fields and wastelands within the walled compound is a well-known characteristic of northern Chinese cities. Visitors to China in the nineteenth and early part of the twentieth century have often commented on this intimate mixing of the rural and the urban. It is an ancient trait and probably derives from the fact that in the founding of a new city the wall was frequently the first structure to be built. The wall defined a world first, separating it – so to speak – from the unconsecrated land beyond; the enclosure was then filled, to varying degrees, by people. It is improbable that the great walled compounds of the Eastern Chou dynasty were packed with people. Neither archaeological nor literary evidence, nor what we know of cities in modern times, suggests that this was the case. Some of the Chan-kuo cities appear to have had very crowded quarters, but such crowding could well exist side by side with open fields: it is one of the paradoxes of the Chinese city. In Han times the cities were partitioned into *li* or wards. Han Ch'ang-an had as many as 160 wards. But many of them were rural or agricultural units. In fact, the word *li* now means a unit of distance, a village or hamlet, and carries no urban association.

Chapter 6
Architecture and landscape

The 'ahistorical' landscape

In Europe one can readily detect vestiges of the past in the present landscape. There are, for example, the ruins: megalithic monuments, Greek temples and theatres, Roman aqueducts and coliseums, hollow and vegetated shells of ancient monasteries, churches and castles. The ruins may be insignificant numerically and yet play a lively role in our present conception of European scenery. They may dominate the countryside through sheer bulk or strategic location, but even more so through the potency of accreted romance. Then there is the fact of architectural revival: past forms are occasionally resurrected and given a new lease of life in the midst of their modern descendants.

The European landscape is historical in the sense that it invites one to see time as progressive change. By contrast the Chinese landscape is 'ahistorical'. One may feel that it is old: the walled city, the hump-backed stone bridge, the rock-and-water garden, the pagoda and the pavilion give the impression of age and permanence. But in so far as the works of man seem changeless as the works of nature, they have no evident 'story'; relics that recall stages in the past are not apparent. The impression of age is justified by the conservatism of certain basic forms of Chinese city-planning and architecture. But the impression that the forms have shown no discernible change or that the buildings themselves are of great antiquity is mistaken.

Antiquity of form and transiency of matter are characteristic of most man-made features on the earth's surface: in China even the more grandiosely conceived architecture is not exempt. Attention has been drawn to the city wall. Some of the less monumental architectural elements in the Chinese landscape may now be described.

The bridge

The bridge is often a conspicuous landmark in the flat, water-riddled plains of the lower Yangtze Valley and in South China. The visual prominence of the bridge in both the countryside and in the cities encourages statistical exaggeration. The most famous error is attributed perhaps unjustly, to Marco Polo in his highly enthusiastic description of Quinsai (Hang-chou), capital of the

Southern Sung dynasty. He is supposed to have said: 'There is a story that it has 12,000 bridges between great and small, for the greater part of stone, though some are of wood.' A. C. Moule believes that an early copyist had missed a line, and that Polo probably said there were 100 great bridges in Hang-chou – enough, anyway, to impress a Venetian.[1] No accurate survey exists on the number and style of bridges in China. According to Fugl-Meyer, in a book published in 1937, there are some $2\frac{1}{2}$ million of them. The density is twelve bridges per square mile in the intensively cultivated parts of the country; the highest, more than twenty per square mile, occurs – as we may expect – in the watery land of Chiang-su province. The hilly but densely settled Ssu-ch'uan basin has a remarkably high average density of ten bridges per square mile. An-hui, Shan-tung, and Hu-pei provinces are also richly peppered with these structures.[2]

The style of bridges shows geographical variation. In North and central China arch bridges are conspicuous. Most bridges of military or commercial importance that were built in the late Ming and Ch'ing dynasties were supported by arches. Masonry structures using huge stone slabs as beams (stone truss bridges) also exist but they appear to be relic forms of earlier times. The stone-truss style is widely used in numerous minor structures, such as decorative bridges in gardens and bridges that bestride the plethora of side canals in the Yangtze Valley, where the water is too shallow to allow the junks to enter, and hence high arches are not necessary. In subhumid China north of the Yangtze Valley, where horses or ox-drawn carts are frequently used for transportation, the approach to the arch bridges is usually level. In the lower Yangtze Valley, however, most bridges are built for pedestrians, donkeys and mules. They are commonly hump-backed. A steep flight of steps leads up to them on both sides, making them impassable for wheeled traffic. These humped structures with horseshoe or circular arches allow the passage of boats and at the same time form a highly visible and picturesque element of the flat landscape.

One of the most famous bridges in China is the flat-arched An-chi bridge of Chao-hsien in Ho-pei. It is a thing of beauty as well as a superb achievement in engineering. It has a long span of 122 feet 10 inches but a rise of only 23 feet from the abutments to the crown of the arch. In Europe such very flat arches of large span had to wait until about 1567, when Ammanati's bridge in Florence (span of 96 feet) was built. The An-chi bridge of Chao-hsien, however, was built between A.D. 605 and 616. It is one of the oldest structures in China and has been in continuous use from the time of its construction to 1954, when a new bridge was built nearby to save it from further wear.[3]

Bridges in South China, south of the Yangtze Valley, are characteristically of the stone-truss type. The situation is roughly the reverse of that in North China. In the South, it was the stone-truss bridge that served commercial traffic and the arch style that was most frequently used for decorative purposes.

15. *Two bridges:* Above: *Suspension bridge across the Mekong River on the Burma Road:* below: *A 'moon' bridge in the Summer Palace, west of Peking*

near temples and in gardens. The stone-truss bridges of southeastern China appear to date back to the Southern Sung dynasty (1127–1279). They were remarkably long. Some had a total length of more than 4,000 feet; and huge stone slabs, as much as 70 feet long and weighing some 200 tons, stretched from pillar to pillar.

Western China, which includes Ssu-ch'uan, Kuei-chou, and Yun-nan, has two distinctive types of bridge in the more remote and rugged regions; the cantilever and the suspension. These were used for all bigger spans. The arch structure was used for smaller spans of less than 100 feet, whereas truss frames are seldom seen except in primitive plank bridges. Over the sparsely populated, mountain country of Yun-nan and Ssu-ch'uan the cantilever bridge, with its grey-tiled roof and prominent rest-house at either end, is often the most conspicuous manmade feature in the landscape. It is one of the few places where people pass through with any regularity, and thus serves as the gathering and marketing centre for the neighbourhood. Wood is the main structural material and there is no lack of it in the mountains. The other common type of bridge in western China is the single-span suspension bridge, made of cables of twisted bamboo. On each side of the gorge a substantial house rises above a stone foundation. These houses shelter the gears used for tightening cables, but in addition they are places where travellers can rest and where toll may be collected. In time of origin iron-chain suspension bridges appeared later and imitated the principle of the bamboo structures. They do not require tightening gear; they do, however, have a house at either end. The iron-chain suspension bridge is itself an old invention. According to Needham, it was constructed in China at least as long ago as the sixth century A.D.,[4] and from China it had spread into Tibet and the Himalayan countries. The Sui and T'ang dynasties extended roads and iron suspension bridges into the southwest. But those that we see today, suspended over the great rivers of Mekong and Salween, probably date from Ming times. The Ming emperors sought to tie the sparsely settled regions of the southwest to the Chinese *oecumene* by extending a net of paved trails and bridges deeply into the mountainous country. The roads were built primarily to facilitate the movement of troops. The engineering achievement was remarkable, though not always wise. Iron suspension bridges vaulted the great rivers whereas stone bridges crossed the smaller streams. The latter were usually hump-backed and this caused great difficulty to the pack animals of caravans.

Historically, the oldest type of bridge in China was made of wood. Bridges in the Chou dynasty were wooden structures built on the principle of the pontoon or planks supported by pillars. The Chinese character for bridge, *ch'iao*, has the 'wood' radical, and it is a character of great antiquity. By the Former Han dynasty, long stone slabs were being substituted for timber and the wooden plank bridge was transformed into the stone-truss bridge. The reason for the substitution is not known. There was no shortage of timber then, and of course houses continued to depend on wood for their framework and this dependence has persisted through history. Another, and more recent, example of substitution took place in Fu-chien province during the Sung dynasty. In this case, the construction of great stone-truss bridges was clearly an imitation of the wooden, cantilevered structures in the mountainous interior. Again there is no evident reason why the substitution of material occurred. If high-quality timber was difficult to get, so were the great stone slabs, 50 to 70 feet long, that served as planks. The stone arch bridge appeared in China during the Later Han dynasty. H. Fugl-Meyer suggests that the inspiration, as distinct from the technique, of using the arch in bridge construction might have come from Parthia and Rome; and that the inspiration for the pointed arch – a form common in western China and very old – might have come from Buddhist India. The technique of construction, however, was distinctly Chinese. The Roman arch was of massive masonry and rather gross in appearance compared with the Chinese arch, which was a thin stone shell loaded with loose filling.[5]

No actual example of the Han arch bridge now exists. The earliest structure extant in China is the An-chi bridge of A.D. 605–16, but it displays such perfection that we may assume it has had a long history of development. The thin-shell arch, using a minimum of stone, is also a necessity of alluvial plains, particularly on the uncompacted base of the Yangtze delta. The stone bridge has shown little further development since it reached a peak of elegance and efficiency by the Sui dynasty. The numerous bridges that we see in the lower Yangtze Valley may not themselves be of great age but the form and the technique of construction have ancient roots. The stone bridge is an old and little-changing element of the Chinese landscape. Its converse is the stone quarry; it too has become a noticeable feature of the landscape. 'Almost everywhere in the Yangtze delta where a rocky hill of suitable material lifts its rounded profile above the muddy front, a cut into the hill can be seen from afar.'[6]

The house

Little is known about the historical geography of the Chinese bridge. Relatively more is known about the Chinese house – although lamentable gaps of knowledge exist with regard to even this fundamental feature of the Chinese landscape. Since eastern China can easily be divided into two parts, a sub-humid North and a humid South, we may think that domestic architecture will respond to the differences in environment and yield distinctive styles. To a degree this is true. Thus the flat-roof house is more common in northwestern China than in the South, where roofs are steeply pitched to shed rain. Or, it has been noticed that the walls of peasant houses in North China are made of pounded earth and sun-dried bricks. In South China the same materials are used, though they are evidently less adapted to the climate. A partial remedy is to cover the outer surface with a thick layer of mud, and to this is sometimes added a final coating of whitewash. Furthermore, in central and South China bamboo wattle and plaster frequently enter wall construction, and bamboo often replaces wooden timbers in the structural frame.[7] Such differences may be multiplied in detail; yet the fact remains that the fundamental characteristics of the Chinese house are remarkably uniform throughout the sinicized parts of the country. These are: the curtain wall principle of construction, with skeleton made of wood; the gabled roof of tile or straw thatch; the arrangement of house units around a courtyard.

The prehistoric houses of North China were semi-pit dwellings of roughly square or circular shape. The frame was made of wood, and the roof too might have consisted of radiating poles plastered over with wattle and mud. The roof sloped down from the ridge-pole in the case of the larger, rectangular houses. The circular houses had conical roofs whereas the roofs of the squarish houses were pyramidal. In some cases, it would seem that the pyramid came down to the ground, and the house looked like a tent. It is clear that the flat roof was not a part of the early Chinese tradition even in the driest parts of the country. Its common occurrence in the mountainous regions of western China suggests Tibet and central Asia as sources of origin. The semi-pit dwellings of Neolithic times continued to be built during the Shang and Western Chou periods. In Shan-tung province they have been reported even in the early decades of the twentieth century.

A basic architectural change took place in the later part of the Shang period. This was the introduction of the gabled, rectangular house built on the principles of an earth foundation, a timbered framework that supports the roof, and curtain walls as distinct from weight-bearing walls. In the Shang capitals at Cheng-chou and An-yang this type of building had prestige: they were official and ceremonial structures or they housed people of importance such as the aristocrats and the esteemed craftsmen in bronze. Common people continued to live in Neolithic semi-subterranean dwellings.[8] In the course of time, however, the above-ground rectangular house also came to be widely used by the common people. There was then no fundamental distinction between the unit house of the poor and that of the wealthy. The distinctions, and these were important cumulatively, lay in the size of the unit, the kinds of material used in roofing and in making the walls, the degree of sophistication in roof construction, and the number of such units.

For the peasant farmer the house in its simplest form may well be just a single unit divided into several rooms. The characteristics of such a unit in the materials used and in the manner of construction departed little from those of the Shang ceremonial house. The difference is that in Shang times the house was held in such high esteem that its consecration required human and animal sacrifices. The process of adoption of the Shang house by common people went on contemporaneously with the elaboration of the Shang house for ceremonial and aristocratic usage. There were changes in the materials of construction. Tiles came into use as early as the Western Chou period and bricks during the latter part of the Chou dynasty.[9] By the Han period both materials were in common employ for the larger buildings although the poor continued to depend on thatch for roofing. The most striking changes of the fundamental building unit took place in the shape of the roof. The low-pitch, gabled roof was the earliest, and it continued to be the widely adopted shape for domestic architecture. For ceremonial halls and the houses of the rich a variety of other shapes evolved, such as the fully-hipped, the half-hipped and the pyramidal. The fully-hipped roof appeared in pre-Han times. This has always been given pride of place and was used for the most grandiose structures. A modified form, which gained popularity during the T'ang dynasty, was the half-hipped roof.[10] Pyramidal coverings were characteristic of the smaller temples and pavilions.

The development of the curve in the roof line has imparted a special distinction to Chinese building and so to the Chinese landscape. However, through unimaginative imitation in the last few centuries the curved roof has become an architectural cliché; so much so that to declare a building Chinese nowadays one need only add a curved roof on it – even if it were a skyscraper. The novelty of curvature in the roof appeared at least as early as the Later Han dynasty. It reached a peak of rakishness in important buildings during the T'ang-Sung period. The roof was massive and high-pitched; it was by far the most prominent feature of the building. Yet, because of the jaunty upward sweep of its eaves and the lustre from the enamelled tiles the roofs had elegance, even airiness.

What further development could logically ensue from the curved elegance of the Sung ceremonial hall? Not more curvature – which would have led to grotesquerie – but rather, it would appear, a return to greater simplicity and horizontality in overall shape; a search for the formal, the clean, and the monumental. In these respects the Ming hall differed from the Sung.[11] The Ming hall, however, seems to be the end of the line in the long evolution of the basic Chinese building from its début as a ceremonial house of the late Shang dynasty. The 350-odd years of the Ch'ing dynasty (1644–1911) had much to add to Ming architecture in the way of detail but little that was fundamental.

The courtyard

Even more conservative than the evolution of the basic structural unit of the Chinese house is the evolution in the spatial arrangement of these units. As soon as the first raised, rectangular and gabled houses appeared in Shang times, a right-angled alignment of the separate units may be discerned.[12] At the An-yang site we can already see a rudimentary courtyard pattern in which the open spaces were defined by buildings oriented in an east–west or a north–south direction.

The courtyard pattern was at first confined to the ceremonial centre of the city; it became identified with the royal complex of palaces. The pattern then extended to clusters of official buildings, to the residences of the aristocrats and large landowners, to their country farmsteads, and finally to the household of the middle-class farmer, to anyone, in short, who can afford more than just the single unit. The permeation of the courtyard pattern to the social and economic level of a well-to-do farmer was already achieved by the Han period. The pattern, therefore, has been a characteristic element of the Chinese scene for different classes of people, and in different parts of China, for a very long time, perhaps over 1,500 years. The pattern is ancient but the exemplars that we can see today, such as the palace complexes of Peking, are all relatively recent in construction.

The fundamental form of the courtyard pattern is of course the rectangle. The rectangle is the traditional way in which the Chinese have symbolized the cosmos. The city, as a cosmic paradigm, has displayed a characteristic rectangularity – oriented to the cardinal directions – since the early Chou period. Since the middle Chou period the city has shown a basic division into two parts: an official and ceremonial quarter, and the quarters in which the populace lived. The official quarter or palace city was normally placed near the centre of the walled compound or at the northern edge: from that position it dominated the world of man. Within the palace city, the arrangement of the halls duplicated certain features of the greater city. The throne or audience hall lay in the middle of the succession of courtyards. The imperial residences were clustered around the 'inner' (i.e. northern) courts, whereas less important official buildings distributed themselves around the 'outer' (or southern) courts.

The pattern was again duplicated at a still more modest level in the home of the wealthy. There may be two courts, separated by a central building which was the guest hall, or the place where visitors were ceremonially received. To the north, arranged around the inner court, were the residences of the parents and the older children of the household. The parents' suite lay on the north side whereas the children's rooms lay to the west and to the east. South of the guest hall were other rooms for guests and children, located on the west and east sides of the outer court. Along the south side, next to the street, were the kitchen and the servants' quarters.[13]

At the most humble level is the home of a well-to-do farmer. It may consist of three units arranged like a horseshoe around a small courtyard, with the open side enclosed by a wall. The unit on the north side contained a living room or work room at the centre, and two bedrooms. Of the two side units, one was a kitchen, the other a barn and a place for implements. In all these patterns there existed a hierarchy of locations, with the central or northern (south-facing) locations the most important.

Wherever a homestead has more than one courtyard the rule for some kind of functional and social distinction between the 'inner' and the 'outer' courts held fairly consistently. But orientation to the cardinal points was far less consistent. As we may expect, the cardinal points exerted their maximum influence on the alignments of city walls and streets. The city, standing alone on a flat plain, had the least need to compromise with the canonical traditions. The royal city could also freely follow the accepted paradigm. The houses within the city would have to consider the exigencies of their neighbours and the alignments of the streets. Southward orientation was frequently compromised. Farmsteads, too, not uncommonly departed from the cardinal points even when they had the courtyard pattern and stood in isolation. The dictates of tradition exerted less force in the countryside, and the homes found greater need to adjust themselves to physical features.

According to Boyd, houses of the Ming dynasty (1368–1644) which were preserved at the southeastern extremity of An-hui province in central China faced mostly to the south-west, and occasionally to the southeast; this was for various local reasons, such as to avoid a prevailing wind from the due south, and to gain winter sunlight, which in the moderate latitude of southeastern An-hui is rather high.[14] But even where traditions were forgotten the need for letting winter sunlight into the rooms demanded that the main units of the building face a southerly direction. The need was made all the more compelling by the fact that the outer walls seldom had windows. The blank outer wall of Chinese homesteads, be they sumptuous or humble, is probably the most commonly shared feature of the Chinese house.

The theme just pursued takes on a rather theoretical air because too little is known of the numerical importance and the geographical extent of the courtyard pattern at different times in Chinese history. The patterns I have enumerated, from the rectangular city to the rectangular farmstead, were common enough through the Ch'ing dynasty (1644–1911), and can still be seen today, but how far backwards in time can they be traced? That they existed in antiquity is well established – archaeologically, for cities, and in clay models for modest homesteads of the Han period. This is one more illustration of the remarkable conservatism of form, but of form in its principal characteristics, not in the details which have shown important changes, as the details of the unit house have changed. In the Ch'ing dynasty the courtyards of the wealthy home were spacious and surrounded by single-storey houses. On the ratio of the area of courtyard to area of covered buildings, the home of the wealthy falls between the palaces at one extreme and the modest farmstead at the other. Most rural buildings in modern times are one storey, although one-and-a-half and two-storey buildings occur: their courtyards are usually small compared with the rooms around them. In earlier periods of Chinese history, it would seem that the two-storey or even multistorey house was far more common, and that the enclosed courtyard was small compared with the bulk of the multistorey structures around them.

Pottery models of houses, buried in tombs as evidence of the dead man's worldly possessions, give us a striking impression of country houses in the Han period. These belonged to the well-to-do: they showed a walled courtyard, with houses on one, two (L-shape), or three sides (U-shape). Even some of the apparently small and simple houses had two storeys. The courtyard and the ground floor were used for livestock and probably the storage of food, as in modern times. The wealthy and the great, as distinct from the merely well-to-do, had sumptuous mansions the general layout of which was similar

16. Pottery model of five-storey house with courtyard (Han dynasty)

to that of later periods: courtyards succeeded each other along the main axis, with a corresponding increase in privacy; buildings were assembled around the courtyards, with the left balanced against the right and the main hall on centre at the rear. The height of these buildings is not known except that the main hall might be two-storeyed.[15]

In the virtual absence of funerary models and in the extreme scarcity of other forms of evidence (such as painting), we know little about the domestic architecture of the great T'ang period. The murals of Tun-huang grottoes suggest the prevalence of the courtyard pattern for religious institutions, and probably also for the mansions of the wealthy. The centre hall commonly had two storeys but, in some cases, the side buildings too appear to have had more than one floor. Very little is known about the structure of buildings in the poorer and more crowded quarters of the city. A funerary model of the Han period showed a very shallow court backed by a towerlike structure of five storeys which might have been a town house.[16]

In the crowded Sung (1127–1279) capital of Quinsai (Hang-chou) the houses were packed close together. A Chinese account described them simply as 'lofty' (kao), but the accounts of Marco Polo, and of Arab and European travellers of the fourteenth century, give the impression that the houses were multistoreyed. Friar Odoric reported structures of eight to ten floors.[17] The houses of the rich were rectangular units arranged in spacious grounds to form more or less closed courtyards. These houses, according to Gernet, had a ground floor only, or one storey at the most.[18] In the Sung dynasty, then, there was a clear distinction between the spacious courtyard layout of the wealthy and the compact multistoreyed structures of the poor; at least this kind of distinction held in the city.

In the Ming dynasty, country houses that have been preserved to the present in An-hui province are two-storeyed, compact structures with very narrow courtyards, rather like some of the Han dynasty farmsteads. These houses have a fortress appearance that the mansions of the wealthy in the cities do not have. It seems probable, therefore, that the high, compact nature of farmsteads owes something to the needs of defence. That the lofty and compact building may be a response to hostility is suggested by the imposing communal houses of the Hakka. The Hakka ('Guest People') were natives of the Huang Ho plain who migrated south to Fu-chien, Kuang-tung and Kuang-hsi when North China was invaded by non-Chinese peoples, particularly during the twelfth century. In South China the Hakka found themselves in the midst of un-friendly local populations whose dialect they could not understand. The Hakka's response to this was to become inward-looking, somewhat contemptuous but also defensive; architecturally their complex attitude was expressed by build-ing walled, lofty structures which were either rectangular or (surprisingly) circular in shape, and enclosed small rectangular or circular courts.[19]

17. *Street and entrance courtyard to a town house. From a Sung painting, 'Return of Lady Wen-chi to China'* *(courtesy Museum of Fine Arts, Boston)*

Nature preserves, parks and gardens

The courtyard, whether of a rich man's home or of the emperor's palace, was characteristically paved. Vegetation was conspicuous by its absence; at most it occupied a modest corner in the vast expanse of flagstones and earth. In a country house the courtyard sheltered livestock and must necessarily be cleared of trees, which were planted outside the walls. The imperial courtyards were also without plant life. The Forbidden City of Peking illustrates this lifeless austerity. The courtyard was a part of the ceremonial life of man: it shared the rectilinearity of the house, of the streets, and of the city. It was not a place where one could discard ceremony and social distinctions, and commune with nature.

Where, then, could one do this? Where could the Chinese escape the Confucian rigours and indulge the Taoist side of his make-up? The answer would seem to be: for the farmer, wrestling with nature in fact left little time for contemplative communion; for the scholar-gentry there existed a variety of possibilities – the miniature gardens in his own city home, the public and semi-public artificial landscapes, and the 'grass hut' in the countryside; for the imperial household there were the summer palaces and great hunting parks beyond the confines of the city.

In the remote and long Chou period of Chinese history, the garden was not a separate concept that could be divorced from the great hunting grounds and zoological preserves of the kings and feudal lords. The *Shi Ching* gives us portrayals of vigorous hunting on the one hand, and of busy rural life on the other, but no clear images of the cultivated garden or the contemplative appreciation of wild nature. By the Han dynasty the emperors of a centralized empire were able to command immense pleasure parks which contained a multiplicity of symbolic associations, a multiplicity of uses and purposes that, in later times, became separate and specialized. The pleasure park of the second century B.C. lay beyond the western wall of the capital Ch'ang-an. This is a fact we may note: the emperors of China have often preferred to obtain their pleasures outside the walled confines of the city, outside the domain of propriety and order. Thus, during the T'ang dynasty, only a few decades after the city of Ch'ang-an was completed, the emperor began a pleasure garden north of the great walled rectangle of his capital. This was the famous Ta-ming Kung. And, 'of the six important Ch'ing dynasty emperors with whom we associate the palaces and gardens of Peking, only one, Ch'ien-lung, died in the city as he wintered there. The other five died in their gardens or detached palaces.'[20]

What was the nature of the imperial park? From the description of the poet and historian, Pan Ku (A.D. 32–92), we gather that the park west of Ch'ang-an was immense, surrounded by a circular wall of more than 400 *li*. Within it were mountains, thickets, forests and marshes. This suggests a natural land-scape. On the other hand, there were thirty-six palaces and buildings, magic streams, marvellous pools, lakes with islands crowned by fairy rocks. The park was stocked with exotic plants and animals from distant countries, including 'unicorns' from Katigara, horses from Ferghana, rhinoceros from Huang-chih and birds from T'iao-chih. It was, in short, a juxtaposition of nature and art The artificial landscapes were designed to reflect Taoist magical beliefs. From the centre of man-made lakes rose pyramidal islands in imitation of the three legendary Isles of the Blest in the Eastern Sea. The entire park may be seen as cosmos, idealized and in reduced scale. In it the emperor indulged in a curious mêlée of secular and religious activities. He hunted lustily. After the slaughter, he and his entourage feasted and were entertained by dancers, clowns and jugglers. At the end of the festivities he might climb up one of the great towers which commanded the landscape, and there commune with nature in solitude.[21]

In the centuries that followed the fall of the Han dynasty the outdoor spaces became more specialized: there existed hunting parks, wild-life preserves, landscaped gardens of varying degrees of splendour in the country, and miniature gardens in city residences. Hunting was essentially a royal and aristocratic sport. The great T'ang royal park still provided hunts for rabbits, adjutant-storks, and white geese. Non-Chinese emperors, such as Kublai Khan, engaged in great hunting expeditions. But, under the tender influence of Buddhism and moralizing Confucian officials, killing for sport declined in popularity. Hunting parks developed into nature parks or wild-life preserves, and these were separate from the elaborately landscaped gardens. The two great Manchu emperors, K'ang Hsi (1662–1722) and Ch'ien-lung (1735–96), for example, established gardens and parks in the Western Hills beyond Peking. Two of them were nature preserves with only scattered buildings. They had roots in the Chin (Jurchen) and Ming dynasties. Three were very large palace complexes set in the midst of magnificent gardens.[22]

During the later part of the Period of Disunion (*c.* A.D. 200–600) there developed in China a new sensitivity to nature that was not in evidence before. This new sensitivity was characteristically associated with the poet-recluse. It has had an extraordinary impact on Chinese painting and gardening, and has affected the Chinese landscape far beyond the confines of royal parks and aristocratic estates. There were two intertwined elements in this appreciation of nature: one was the desire for the solitude and simplicity of the farmer's life. The other, tinted by Taoist mysticism, was the yearning to escape wholly from the life of strife to a secluded valley far away in which people lived as immortals, in peace and contentment. The rich and powerful could create whole landscapes to simulate the idyllic world, though on a scale far less pretentious than that of the Han emperors. In such a garden there might be a grotto for dragons, an artificial mountain for the immortals, fish ponds and rtificial waterways. The basic elements of the Chinese garden (as of Chinese landscape painting) then, as now, were *shan* and *shui*, mountain and water. The humble scholar could not afford anything so grand. He could afford, however, a small secluded garden in his courtyard, which contained no more than a few trees, a pool, and some potted shrubs and flowers. Or he could retire to a country cottage, perhaps his native home, and there live a life of simplicity, surrounded by a rustic garden and the fields. As the archetype of the poet-recluse, T'ao Yuan-ming (A.D. 365–427), expressed it:

> I empty the cup and lean on the window
> And joyfully contemplate my favourite branches,
> And joyfully savour the peace of my cottage.
> Sometimes I wander in my garden
> Where there is a door that is rarely open.
> I lean on my staff at my leisure
> And sometimes lift my head and look around.
> Idly, the clouds climb the valleys;
> The birds, weary of flying, seek for their nests.
> Light thickens, but still I remain in the fields,
> Caressing with my hands a solitary pine.[23]

The awakening interest in gardens during the Period of Disunion may have been inspired, according to Michael Sullivan, by the new environment in which the artist-scholars found themselves after the great migrations to the South.[24] A change of environment could stimulate new interest in it; especially since, with the migration and consequent disorder, ties with official life were loosened. In the South, moreover, nature could be enjoyed in relative comfort. The scholar need not traverse wind-swept plains to enter forest-clad hills, in which he could hear the chatter of monkeys and the roar of waterfalls. If landscape paintings yielded any evidence, we could say (with Oswald Siren) that the gardens which best corresponded to the Chinese feeling for nature were those attached to the huts or study pavilions of the scholar-officials.[25] The characteristic elements of such a scene would include a nest of pavilions, bamboo groves, scattered pines on craggy mountains that faded into the distant mist, and flowing water on whose banks grew flowering shrubs and broadleaved trees. Abundant illustrations of this genre of landscape – the polar opposite of the formalism of courtyards and cities – may be seen in the painting of the Sung, the Ming, and the early Ch'ing periods.

We have treated of private domains, whether royal parks or gardens of the gentry. There also existed parks and gardens of a public or semi-public nature. Great estates attached to Buddhist monasteries belonged to this category. The ground of Chinese sensitivity to nature may rest on Taoism and on certain Shamanistic beliefs that had been incorporated in Taoism, but the expression of this sensitivity in the shape of gardens owed much to the concrete examples set forth in the Buddhist estates. Thus, Yang Hsuan-chih's book *Lo-yang Chia-lan Chi* probably exerted considerable influence on the Chinese conception of the garden. In this book, Yang (who lived during the second half of the sixth century) described the beautiful Buddhist edifices and grounds, in and near Lo-yang, that had suffered decay with the fall of the Northern Wei dynasty.[26] But one had no need to rely on literary means for propagating the idea of the garden. Buddhist temples were abundant in China from at least the fourth century onwards. They were located not only in the cities and on highways, where they provided hospitality to travelling officials and merchants, but also in the mountains, surrounded by vast and beautifully cared-for estates, where they received pilgrims from near and afar.

Another type of the semi-public park was that which surrounded the 'gardened tumulus (*yuan ling*)'. It had long been a custom in China to treat the grounds around the tombs of the sacred emperors as natural parks, in which all living things partook of the holy character of the spirit of the deceased. Such places served the separate human needs of religion and recreation. Entry into these places seemed rather strict, to judge by the T'ang criminal code. On the other hand, in the eighth century the code was so relaxed that the great mausoleum-parks had become pleasure grounds for the diversion of the gentry. The normal atmosphere, however, was one of quiet dignity and beauty.[27]

The third type of park was more truly public, and had recreation as its primary purpose. These were the large artificial landscapes created in one corner of the walled city or just outside it. The gorgeous water-park of T'ang Ch'ang-an has already been described. It was the haunt of the gentry and upper classes, and although the 'common people' who lived in the other side of the city were not known to be specifically excluded, they probably were not welcome. Besides the serpentine lake on which one could go boating, there were beautiful pavilions, and walks bordered by willows, poplars, and assorted flowers.

The most famous of all the public parks in China is the West Lake of Hangchou. Its beauty has been celebrated by poets and artists for more than a thousand years. As is characteristic of Chinese beauty spots, the landscapes surrounding the lake, and the lake itself, are largely artificial. The natural scene of the Hang-chou area was a deltaic flat, sluggishly drained by a few streams. Out of the flat alluvium, islands of bedrock obtrude. When the streams were dammed, perhaps as early as the first century A.D., a lake collected behind the dyke so that the basic elements of the Chinese landscape – mountains juxtaposed against alluvial banks and water – were formed. By the beginning of the ninth century, when the poet Po Chü-I was the prefect of Hang-chou, the lake had already a long reputation for beauty, a beauty that was to be enhanced by the secluded estates of Buddhist monasteries and of the great families in the mountains. The lake had been artificially enlarged during the course of centuries, and since it was shallow it was always in danger of being choked with mud and aquatic plants. Between 1086 and 1093, another famous poet and prefect of Hang-chou, Su Tung-p'o, memorialized the Emperor for funds which were needed to embellish and maintain the lake. By 1275 the lake was over 9 miles in circumference and 9 feet deep. Military patrols looked after its maintenance; it was forbidden to throw rubbish into it or to plant water-chestnuts in it. For centuries, through T'ang and Sung times, the Chinese bestowed zealous care on the lake and its surroundings. New buildings, for example, had to harmonize with the landscape. The Buddhist pavilions and towers amply fulfilled this requirement. However, notwithstanding the care and the regulations, the lake and its parks were open to the people. The lake, according to a description of 1275, always had hundreds of boats of all shapes and sizes. On feast days the parks and gardens on the lakeside

> were invaded by a holiday crowd who came to admire the rare flowers and exotic trees. Some of them taking with them something to eat, and carrying musical instruments, made a day's excursion on the shores of the lake or on the hills surrounding it. Others hired boats for several cash coins and enjoyed the pleasure of seeing some of the most beautiful and celebrated scenery in China pass before their eyes.[28]

Chapter 7
From the Sung to the Ch'ing dynasty

Periodization of Chinese history is at least as controversial as that of Europe
I have followed what seems to be a widely shared opinion that the end of the
Chou dynasty (c. 250 B.C.) marked the end of 'antiquity' or the 'feudal period'
The next period began with the unification of China under the Ch'in and continued until the decline of the Manchu or Ch'ing dynasty (1644–1911). This
is a very long span of some 2,000 years. Clearly it can be subdivided in several
meaningful ways, depending on the criteria one chooses. If one had to make
one division, there seems to be tentative agreement among scholars that it
should fall in the tenth century A.D. Or, to put it more flexibly, an important
series of interlocked social and economic transformations began in tenth-
century China and continued through the Sung period (960–1279). These
transformations occurred within the Chinese tradition: no major foreign
patterns of thought were incorporated during this time. Some of the changes
within tradition remained as characteristic features of the Chinese scene until
the first part of the twentieth century.

Sociological innovations during this period included the appearance of a
middle class ('small gentry' families) under the patronage of a relatively small
group of established great families; the appearance of greater social mobility
the spread of education to the class of merchants and artisans; a general tendency towards popularization, particularly in literature, literary styles, and
plays.[1] Economic changes may be subsumed under the terms 'commercialization' and 'regional specialization'. As we have observed earlier, progress in
these directions had already begun during the T'ang dynasty, but by the later
part of the Sung period it had brought China to a type of economy akin to that
of modern times. The key economic area of China had shifted to the South
so had the preponderance of population. The North and northwest were increasingly dependent on rice produced in the Yangtze delta and in the smaller
fertile areas of Ssu-ch'uan, Hu-nan, and Chiang-hsi. Regional interdependence
replaced regional self-sufficiency. Fertile areas exported rice and might in
return receive from the less fertile areas commodities such as salt, metals, sea
fish, and tea; or locally produced specialities. The less fertile areas might also
exploit their geographical location to provide such services as banking and
transportation, or function as a depot for foreign and interregional trade.
Urban population increased rapidly in South China. Market fairs grew into

mall towns and small towns into cities. Some cities grew to enormous size and
wed their prosperity, not primarily to political importance as had been charac-
eristic of northern cities in the past, but to commerce.

The Sung period: agricultural economy and landscape

n the Sung period new lands were opened to agriculture, new crops were
dded to the rice fields of the South, and new agricultural techniques were
ntroduced. Two kinds of population change correlated with these innovations:
n increase in the total population and a mass shift of the population to the
outh. At the peak of T'ang prosperity the total number of people living in the
mpire may have been as large as 75 million. Thereafter, rebellions and inva-
ions probably reduced it so that by about A.D. 980, when the Northern Sung
ynasty consolidated its empire, the number was 60 or 70 million people.
'opulation then climbed to an estimated total of more than 100 million around
100.[3] Admittedly these figures are educated guesses, for the period's census
ata are unreliable. More certain is the mass shift of population. According to
Cracke:

> As late as the middle of the eighth century, the Yangtze Valley and the
> areas farther south still held only 40 to 45 per cent of China's people. [But]
> by the end of the thirteenth century this area reported no less than 85 to 90
> per cent of the nation's population, and no less than 20 per cent were estab-
> lished in the valleys of Fu-chien and eastern Chê-chiang along the southeast
> coast.

The increase in total population, the high densities on the small alluvial
lains of southeast China, the existence of possibly five urban areas by the
ear 1100 with populations that exceeded one million, all suggest the existence
f a productive agricultural base. There is indeed evidence of agricultural
xpansion, but before we look into these technological innovations, let us con-
ider first the changes in society that encouraged the acceptance and develop-
nent of new methods. We have noted earlier the rise of great families and
heir great estates during the Later Han dynasty. In the succeeding Period of
Disunion attempts had been made to break up the estates and to redistribute
he land to small farmers – in a system known as *chün-t'ien* or 'equal land
llotments'. By the T'ang period, however, the *chün-t'ien* system was breaking
own although it was still formally in the books. In the course of the Sung
ynasty great estates were once more thoroughly established, especially in the
rowded parts of southeastern China.

Besides the old families, a new middle class had risen and climbed the ladder
f success through the examination system and by attaching themselves to the
owerful old families. The new class of scholar-gentry in turn became large

landowners. They acquired wealth and commanded the labour of a large number of tenant farmers who found themselves in greater legal servitude to their landlords than their predecessors had ever been during the T'ang dynasty.

Servitude of large numbers of people was a social evil that received minor compensation in the form of collective security against the exigencies of unscrupulous officials and against natural disasters. The system had its small virtues when the landlord was enlightened, and it was usually in his interest to be so. Economically, the large estates had reserves of wealth which enabled them to capitalize their operations on a scale far beyond the reach of small farmers. As Twitchett summarizes it:

> The great landlords of the lower Yangtze Valley installed complex water driven machinery for pumping irrigation water, for draining their fields and for threshing and milling their grain. They also invested in the large variety of improved and complicated field implements which are described and illustrated in the rich literature on agricultural techniques published during the late Sung and Yuan.[4]

The reclamation of marsh and lake lands brought hardships to small farmers who depended on them to regulate drainage and irrigation, and who probably also used the resources of the lakes to supplement their food. An official of the Southern Sung dynasty wrote:

> After the reigns of Lung Hsing (1163–64) and Chien Tao (1165–73) not a single year passed without the powerful clans and families following one after another in the occupation of large areas of lake-bottom land. Thus the people were deprived more and more of the benefits of reservoirs and lakes and marshes have all become land during the last thirty years.[5]

Not only the owners of large estates, but small farmers also encroached upon the waters, turning lakes, ponds, and marshes into cultivated fields. The government appears to have given encouragement to the practice. Thus, in order to persuade the refugees from the north to cultivate the marshy grounds near Su-chou in the Yangtze delta area, the government provided them with seeds, exempted rent for the first three years, and required only low rent thereafter.[6] In Chê-chiang province, reclamation had proceeded so far that there arose the danger that reserves of water would not be available to relieve the land in times of drought. A memorial to the throne of 1196 stated:

> Tracts of reclaimed land cover hundreds of thousands of *mu* in Che-hsi [Chê-chiang]. Tanks, ponds, reservoirs, streams, and creeks are all turned into farms. No trace of any storage for surplus water can be found and no

water to relieve drought is available. If not strictly prohibited, the situation will become worse, and years of good harvest can hardly be expected.[7]

Despite the forebodings of some anxious officials the government itself, as we have noted, did nothing to abate the trend: on the contrary, official agencies undertook the more ambitious reclamation works and so set an example to the landlords. On other fronts they instructed farmers in the use of new techniques and in the application of a wide range of manures – including lime, green manure and vast quantities of human waste from the large and growing cities. Most of the fertilizing practices had been discovered much earlier, but it was during the Sung period that they won wide acceptance. Government agencies also helped to spread the knowledge and use of new varieties of wheat and rice. From the twelfth century onwards farmers experimented with early ripening strains of rice so that a second crop could be planted in the warm areas. There were attempts at interseeding, that is, mixing different varieties of rice in one field, or mixing rice with beans.

New irrigation methods evolved with the spread of rice. The practice of periodic draining destroyed malarial mosquitoes. This meant that large areas which were unhealthy before, say, the year 1000 could now be settled and absorb large population. After about 1100, fish were kept in the shallow water of the rice fields. Several advantages accrued: the fish ate mosquito larvae and thus helped to cut down malaria; they produced fertilizer for rice, and were a valuable source of protein as food.[8]

During the reign of Chen-tsung (998–1022) in the Northern Sung dynasty twenty *tan* of drought-resistant rice were imported for seed by the government from southern Annam.[9] The drought-resistant rice was first established in Fu-chien and from there spread northwards to the Yangtze delta where it became especially common. This new introduction probably enabled the farmers to extend their arable lands beyond the bounds set by irrigation.

Rice was the dominant crop in the lower Yangtze Valley and in South China during the first part of the Sung period. This dominance the government attempted to break. A decree of the late tenth century said:

> While people north of the Yangtze grow various cereals, people south of the river rely solely on *keng* rice [non-glutinous and late ripening]. Although there may be climatic and topographical reasons for this, it is in accordance with ancient practice to grow a wider range of crops so as to stave off flood and drought.[10]

To encourage the growing of dry crops, the government ordered that southern tenant farmers should not be required to pay additional rent for the harvest of dry crops. Farmers in Chiang-su and Chê-chiang were particularly able to take advantage of this. They began to grow a double grain crop of autumn-sown wheat of an early ripening variety followed by spring-sown rice. The wheat was grown purel as a cash-crop for sale in the cities of the lower Yangtze area, where a hug market in grain swiftly grew up. The cities also provided an insatiable marke for every variety of vegetable and other food products raised especially fo sale.[11]

Outside the densely settled areas in which large cities provided a read market, government exhortations toward the growing of dry crops had littl effect. Thus Hu-pei in the middle Yangtze basin did not appear to respond Today it is a leading wheat-producing area, but wheat assumed importance i the lowlands only after the 1730s.

The foremost rice-growing region in China during the Southern Sun dynasty was the Yangtze delta. It has been the country's granary since th T'ang period. Other major producing and exporting areas were the Ka Valley of Chiang-hsi, the Hsiang Valley of Hu-nan, the Hsi River plains an delta of Kuang-tung (an area of great landlords), and the Ssu-ch'uan basin Ssu-ch'uan had acquired dense population clusters and sophisticated agricul tural techniques long before the middle Yangtze basins and South China wer developed. It maintained this superiority in agriculture during the Sung period Thus, while double-cropping was unusual in most parts of rice-growing Soutl China, Ssu-ch'uan was said to grow three or four crops a year.[12] It continuee to exercise its ancient skills in irrigation. Sung histories contain many reference to irrigation canals and reservoirs and to the repairing of dykes in the area surrounding Ch'eng-tu, Mei Shan, and Ch'ing Shan. The land under irrigatio in some of these districts ranged between 72,400 and 340,000, and sometime up to 1 million *mou*.

The areas in the Southern Sung empire which needed to import rice wer Hu-pei and the Huai River basin in the north, eastern Chê-chiang, Fu-chien and the coastal districts in the south. The northern borders of the contractee Southern Sung empire were ravaged by battles with the Chin (Jurchen) state The southeastern coast needed to import rice from the Yangtze and Canto deltas because of its large urban population. The economy of crowded place like eastern Chê-chiang and Fu-chien depended on activities other than grow ing rice, such as fishing, mining, salt works, tea, handicrafts, and a flourishin sea trade.[13]

Effect of the Northern Sung industrial revolution

In addition to gains in food production, China during the Sung dynasty mad rapid progress in coal-mining and in the manufacture of iron.[14] Industria growth, particularly in the Northern Sung period (960–1126), was part of th remarkable economic expansion which led China into new social and economi tructures that were more flexible than anything it had known in the past. The extent of China's industrial development in the eleventh century was comparable to that which took place during the earlier phases of England's industrial revolution. It was stimulated by the demand for iron currency, iron and steel weapons, agricultural implements, salt pans, nails, anchors, and armour.

In agriculture, for example, the Chinese farmer of the eleventh century made heavy demands on iron for his implements, probably to a greater extent than his counterpart in the early years of the twentieth century. The importance of the market for iron farm implements was such that by 1083 the state saw fit to monopolize it. To meet the demand the total output of iron from the Northern Sung mines and smelters was probably of the order of 75,000 to 150,000 tons annually, or greater than in any other period in pre-nineteenth-century Chinese history.

The rapid growth of ironworks exerted pressure on the timber resources, which were already heavily pressed to meet the needs of large city populations and of shipbuilding. Many hundreds of thousands of tons of charcoal were swallowed up by the metal industries. In addition, there was the demand for charcoal in the manufacture of salt, alum, bricks, tiles and liquor. The Northern Sung period must be seen as a time of rapid deforestation. North China suffered first, but the forests along the frontier regions came to be protected by the government in the belief that trees hindered the movements of the semi-nomadic herdsmen who plagued China's borders. Firewood and charcoal for the cities and the industries had to be transported from the South. There was an acute shortage of fuel in the North, a shortage which was partially met by the effective substitution of coal for charcoal in the eleventh century.

Enough has been said to suggest the extent of economic development during the Sung period. Metal industries reached an unprecedented scale in the North. New patterns of industrial location sprang up. Cities were the traditional centres of manufacturing, but the heavy industries required locations closer to the sources of demand or to the sources of raw material. Ironworks, for example, were established near the salt-producing areas to supply the iron salt pans, at the shipbuilding yards to provide for anchors, nails, and armour, and at the iron mines to reduce transportation costs. Food production increased. It increased in response to the rapidly growing population in South China. The greater production of food in turn enabled more people to be supported.

An economy of regional specialization and exchange throughout the moderately and densely populated parts of China replaced the older order of a high degree of regional self-sufficiency in food and manufactures. By the eleventh century paper money entered into circulation, and the coinage of iron and copper reached proportions never again approached in Chinese dynastic history.

Commerce and the shaping of Sung cities

The foci of commerce were the great cities that had sprung up in the Sung period. By 1100 at least five cities had populations that exceeded 1 million only one of them, K'ai-feng, lay in the North. There were a number of othe: cities that approached the five giants in size at this time. In 1126 the Sung empire lost North China to the Jurchens, but the southern metropolises con tinued to grow rapidly during the next two centuries. In several instances the prefectural populations appear to have doubled, tripled, or even quadrupled by 1290. Among the most striking increases, three were on the southeast coas (Hang-chou, Su-chou, Fu-chou), and one (Jao-chou) near the inland trade route from the Yangtze to Canton.

In contrast to earlier periods when cities achieved economic importance only after their designation as national capitals, during the period between the tenth and the thirteenth centuries, cities that were chosen as capitals had already achieved importance as trade centres at strategic points. K'ai-feng, for example became the capital of the Northern Sung dynasty. Before its selection it was a regional seat of administration which owed its economic importance, however primarily to its location on the arterial canal from the South.[15] As the capita of Northern Sung, K'ai-feng was far from being just a political centre. I developed industries and manufactured for export as well as for local con sumption. Its products included textiles, printing, ink, metalwork, and porcelain.[16]

An interesting consequence of the growing commercialization of cities wa: that cities – even when they functioned as capitals – had lost the traditiona rigidity of rectangular walls, with the interior space organized more or les according to some ancient canonical principle. The walls of great urban area: in the Sung period were irregular. One reason was that they were frequently built to enclose commercial districts that had grown up in a haphazard way beyond the confines of an older core. We may recall that something like thi: had taken place a very long time ago, during the Chan-kuo period of the Chou dynasty, which was a shortlived phase of commercial expansion. The traditiona shape of the political city was a rectangle, a rectangle imposed rather arbitrarily on the landscape – in response to the emperor's conception of his own grandeui – rather than a shape imposed by the expansion of population. K'ai-feng, ir contrast, had grown in size as it gained commercial importance. Successive new walls were built to enclose the suburbs that spread unplanned beyond the city gates. The result of this history was that, although the city lay on a leve plain, it lacked the symmetry that marked the earlier national capitals, and tha would later distinguish Peking.[17]

Quinsai (Hang-chou), the capital of the Southern Sung dynasty, was, to judge by the rhapsodic descriptions of Marco Polo, the greatest city in the

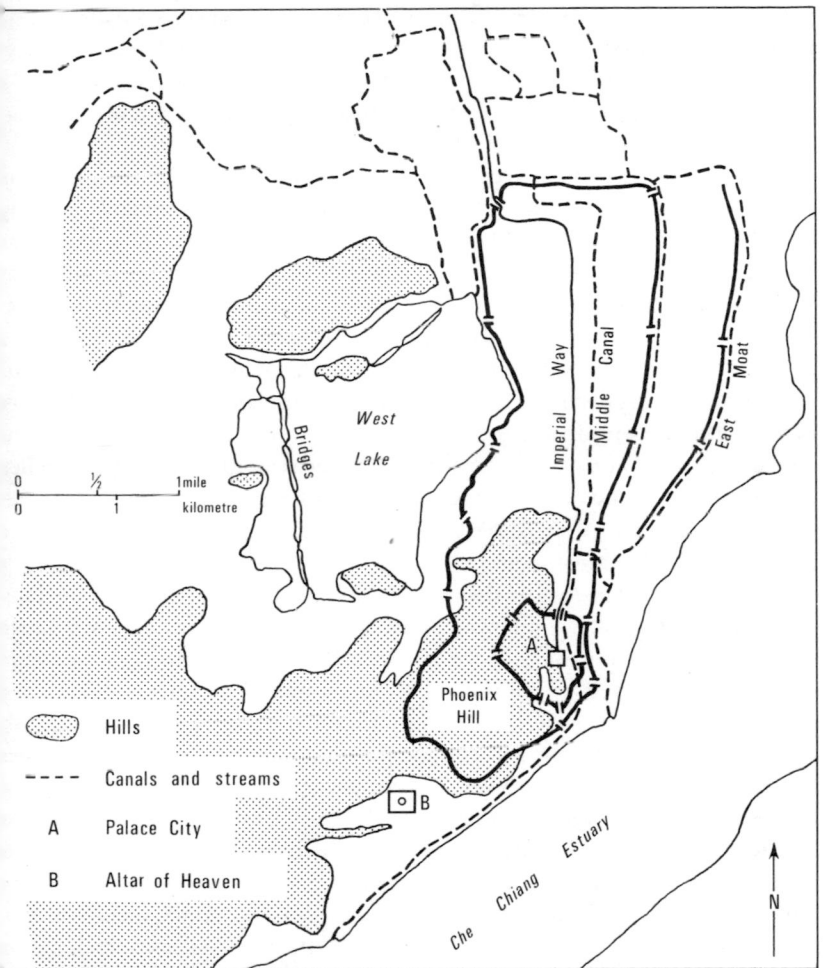

Key labels on map:

West Lake

Bridges

Imperial Way

Middle Canal

East Moat

Phoenix Hill

A

B

Che Chiang Estuary

N

0 ½ 1mile
0 1 kilometre

Hills

Canals and streams

A Palace City

B Altar of Heaven

8. Hang-chou (Quinsai) in the thirteenth century

orld (Fig. 18). But its greatness lay in its population, wealth and urbanity, in
ιe beauty of its famous lake, parks and gardens; it did not lie in physical size,
ι physical spaciousness or grandeur of conception. In all major points Hang-
ʰou failed to follow the canonical rules of city building. The walls enclosed
highly irregular area determined to a large extent by the lake to the west and
Ἷhê-chiang estuary to the east. They were pierced by thirteen irregularly
)aced gates. The Palace City lay at the southern end of the walled compound
ιstead of the more traditional central or northern location. The geometric
entre of the city was occupied by a pig market. The Palace City itself spread

over the wooded eastern edge of Phoenix Hills and its serpentine walls rose an
fell with the undulations of topography. The Imperial Way did follow the city
north–south axis but even this main artery compromised the canonical pre
scription by introducing two right-angle turns half a mile north of the Palac
walls in adaptation to the relief.[18]

Hang-chou substituted irregularity and human charm for the order an
grandeur of the 'cosmicized' cities of the north. In physical dimension Hang
chou was far less imposing than, for example, the Ch'ang-an of the T'an
dynasty. Its rampart enclosed an area of less than 3·5 square miles in contras
with T'ang Ch'ang-an's spacious enclosure of some 30 square miles. I
Imperial Way was magnificently paved, but the street's width of 180 feet wa
scarcely half the width of the grand north–south avenues of Ch'ang-an. Durin
the Southern Sung dynasty Hang-chou had an abundance of landscaped chart
in the southern quarters of Phoenix Hills where the officials and rich merchant
established their homes, and also in the suburbs bordering the lake, wher
great monasteries and elegant houses of the wealthy might be found. But Hang
chou also achieved an intensity of urban life compared with which the life c
a T'ang Ch'ang-an must seem pale.

A part of this intensity was the result of population concentration. In Hang
chou a population of $1\frac{1}{2}$ million was concentrated in an area of some 8 squar
miles both within and without the walls. In Ch'ang-an of the eighth century
a million people lived within the walled compound of 30 square miles. Larg
parts of the T'ang capital were in fact rural. Sung Hang-chou beyond th
Phoenix Hills was, in comparison, packed with houses and people. The highe
densities (more than 200 persons per acre) were distributed along the narro
lanes in the neighbourhood of the Imperial Way.[19] The dearth of building lan
was such that it appears to have encouraged the construction of multistoreye
houses. These houses opened to the streets, in contrast to those of T'ang typ
The lower levels were used as shops for selling noodles, fruits, thread, incens
and candles, oil, soya sauce, fresh and salt fish, pork and rice, and a grea
variety of luxury goods. The upper levels probably served as dwellings
although some tea-houses and taverns of ill-fame had singing girls there.[20]

Perhaps the greatest contrast, reflecting to the full the social and economi
changes that had occurred since the end of the T'ang dynasty, was in the nigh
scene. Cities of the T'ang type were pretty dead at night. The *fang* gates wer
closed. What activities there were after sundown had to be pursued within th
wards. Outside, the broad avenues were eerily empty, except for a few guard
and night riders on some official mission. In Sung Hung-chou, on the othe
hand, animated life continued with little abatement until very late into th
night. Around the Imperial Way the night scene was brightened by multi
coloured lamps which lit the entrances and courtyard of restaurants an
illuminated the shop displays.

Hang-chou, as the capital of the Southern Sung empire, was distinguished
y affluence, cultural eminence, and political power, but not by size nor by its
eterodox physical layout. At least three others, Fu-chou, Jao-chou, and Su-
hou, surpassed it in total population. These sprawling urban areas, as well as
thers that approximated to them in size, showed none of the rigidities of the
lder northern cities. They owed their importance far more to commerce than
o political power. Physically, this commercial orientation was expressed by
he fact that the southern cities lacked spatial ordering: business activities were
o longer confined within the government-supervised walled markets. Com-
nerce and manufacture operated in shops that were scattered throughout the
ity and that spread beyond the city gates into the suburbs.

The northern antithesis: Cambaluc or Ta-tu

n striking contrast to the unplanned growth of the great cities of the Southern
sung empire was the planned capital of its Mongol neighbour to the north,
Cambaluc or Ta-tu, seat of Kublai Khan. Construction of Cambaluc began
n 1267 on a site to the north of the destroyed capital of the Chin (Jurchen)
dynasty (its location corresponds roughly to the northern city of Peking).
When the Sung emperor selected Hang-chou as his temporary capital in 1135
t was already a prosperous prefectural city with a quarter of a million people.
But Kublai Khan's capital was built more or less *de novo*. Its nucleus consisted
f no more than a cluster of summer palaces left behind by the Chin.

Despite the fact that the city was built for a Mongol emperor and the chief
rchitect was a Muslim the plan of Cambaluc displayed nearly all the traditional
haracteristics of a grid-patterned Chinese capital.[21] As described by Marco
Polo, Cambaluc was almost a perfect square, with the prescribed set of three
gates along each side of the walls. The streets were straight and wide and laid
ut like the grid of a chessboard. Within the outer enclosure were two walled
precincts, the innermost of which housed the Khan's Great Palace, the Ta-
ning Tien.

Given the political pre-eminence Cambaluc rapidly attracted a large popula-
ion and flourishing business. When Marco Polo arrived in 1275 the city was
till very new. Yet it already bustled with activity. In Cambaluc 'there is such
multitude of houses and people, both within the walls and without, that no
ne could count their number'.[22]

Ming and Ch'ing urbanization

The Mongol dynasty was overthrown by Chinese rebels from central and
South China. Nan-ching (Nanking) became the first capital of the Ming
dynasty (1368–1644). It was a reasonable choice for Nan-ching lay in the area

of rebel strength and near the centre of population and wealth. Southeastern China continued to prosper. Most of the new walled cities established during the Ming period were established there. The giant urban areas of the Sung dynasty remained although their relative size and importance shifted. Su-chou for example, maintained a registration consistently in excess of 2 million persons. Nan-ching gained new importance after it became the national capital. A huge but highly irregular wall was thrown around it. In 1403 the new Ming emperor moved the court north to Peking. Nan-ching thus lost its political pre-eminence but economically it continued to flourish. The Jesuit missionary Matteo Ricci, compared it favourably with Peking and Nan-ching's population of 1,093,620 probably exceeded that of the northern metropolis.[23]

The Ming emperors gave shape to the Peking of modern times. It was built on the site of Cambaluc but the walled compound became somewhat smaller and was shifted slightly to the south. It retained the square shape and in fact improved upon the geometric regularity of the Mongol (Yuan) capital, for by shifting the frame to the south the inner walled precincts were more centrally placed. However, not long after the completion of the new compound in the 1420s, a large suburb consisting of several hundred thousand families developed beyond the south wall. Traders from all parts of the empire and from foreign countries set up shops and homes there. A new wall was planned which would give the box-within-box pattern of the city another layer, but only a segment could be completed. The result is roughly what we can still discern: two walled compounds adjoining each other.

The succeeding Ch'ing or Manchu dynasty (1644–1911) was a period of large-scale city building. More walled cities were created then than during any previous dynasty, with the possible exception of the Han. The new settlements were located both in frontier regions, such as Manchuria, southwestern China and Taiwan, and in the older settled areas such as the Yangtze delta and the southeastern coastal provinces.[24] However, this great gain in the total number of cities was not matched by the addition of any striking novelty to the urban scene. In overall plan and in the construction of individual buildings the old traditions persisted with little change. Peking exemplified this conservatism. The Manchus occupied Peking for more than 250 years; in that time they merely maintained the Ming framework, remodelled the palaces and temples and added a few new ones.

The new fact in urbanism that eventually emerged towards the end of the Ch'ing dynasty was hardly rooted in native genius. This new fact was the grafting of Europe to China. The most striking manifestation of the process lay in the treaty ports, for in them we could see the incongruous juxtaposition of two cultures. The treaty ports were shortlived as expressions of political injustice, but as expressions of the infiltration of Western commercial-industrial values to the Chinese ethos they indicated a permanent reorientation. The impact of Western techniques and values on the Chinese landscape will be a theme in the next two chapters on modern China. In the meantime we need to return to the older China, a country and a civilization in which remarkable changes had indeed occurred, but they occurred largely within the flexible framework of the Chinese tradition.

Changes in rate of population growth

Population in China, it has been suggested, reached a peak of 70 to 75 million by the middle of the eighth century. Thereafter it levelled off, and – after the Huang Ch'ao rebellion in A.D. 874 – showed a slight decline to possibly 60 or 70 million people at the time of the consolidation of the Northern Sung empire. Although census figures remained persistently below 50 million there is reason for believing, on the basis of economic and technological changes towards greater intensity of resource use, that the population of Sung China around 1100 was at least double that number. Mongol conquest of the Southern Sung empire undoubtedly caused some contraction in population. With the restoration of the Chinese House the total number of people could have been 75 or 85 million, according to modern scholars.[25]

The Ming period (1368–1644) saw a rise of population to perhaps 150 million by 1600. One hundred years later the population probably remained the same or showed a slight decline for there had been a change of dynasty in the interim. But during the Ch'ing or Manchu dynasty (1644–1911) population increased at a rate it had not, in recorded history, attained before. The 150 million people around 1700 was more than doubled one hundred years later. By the middle of the nineteenth century population reached a peak of some 430 million, but towards the end of the dynasty it fell to a figure of around 340 million.

North China under the Mongols

Changes in population are related to changes in economy and find expression in the landscape. From the tenth century onwards, the Yangtze Valley and South China entered a phase of rapid economic expansion compounded of steep increases in population, corresponding gains in food supply, the development of commerce and the growth of great cities. The theme has already been treated. North China, on the other hand, had a more fluctuating history. From the tenth century it was invaded and occupied by the Khitans, the Tanguts, the Jurchens, and the Mongols; the last finally succeeded in occupying the whole of China in 1279.

Population in North China undoubtedly fluctuated with the successive invasions, and with the changing policies of the nomadic and semi-nomadic conquerors who were uncertain in their response to the sophisticated, agricultural civilization they subdued. Drastic alteration in the landscape occurred when the invaders sought to confiscate agricultural land in order to turn it into pastures. The Jurchens had attempted this. In the early years of Ogodei certain Mongols sought to turn large tracts of North China into grazing land. Fortunately this was not rigorously carried out, although some farms – in particular those in the northern part of the North China plain – were turned into pastures, and confiscation for this purpose continued until Kublai Khan specifically prohibited it.[26]

The conversion of agricultural to pasture land was probably a cause in the decline of grain production in North China: after the Yuan empire had extended over the whole country, large quantities of grain were sent to the northern capital from the Yangtze delta. Transportation was effected in two ways: via maritime routes in ships that sailed close to the coast and via the newly constructed Grand Canal (1266–89) in grain barges.

The Grand Canal was the greatest engineering project carried out by the government during the rule of Kublai Khan. The earlier Sui canal no longer served well except for the southern sections, since it was designed to supply the capital at Ch'ang-an, and not the Yuan capital at Peking (Cambaluc or Ta-tu). The Grand Canal functioned as the main artery of communication between North and South China during the Yuan, Ming and even the Ch'ing dynasties. It expressed the persistent economic dependence of the North on the South.

This dependence made the capital area in the North vulnerable. Maritime routes were harassed by pirates and suffered from the navigational uncertainties of open-sea sailing, while the inland canal route was constantly threatened by the little predictable behaviour of the Huang Ho. One evident solution was to make the lands around the capital more productive – at least productive enough to save transportation costs and render the capital self-sufficient in regard to basic food, particularly for the army. So in 1352 the Yuan emperor ordered that all government land and land formerly used for military colonization in the Hai Ho drainage basin be distributed to tenants to be cultivated. At the beginning of this venture the government even provided wages, oxen, farm implements and seeds. The government also brought in farmers proficient in the cultivation of irrigated land and experts in irrigation works from the Yangtze provinces to instruct the peasant tenants of the North. These measures met with some success but not enough to make the North independent in the basic grains: hope, however, persisted through the succeeding Ming and Ch'ing dynasties.[27]

Population growth and agricultural expansion: Ming and Ch'ing dynasties

The Ming period was a time of rapidly expanding agricultural production through the opening up of new land and the gradual diversification of crops.

nd it saw the rise of a more varied economy. Population had grown in a more or less linear fashion, according to Ho Ping-ti. The congested areas remained where they had been since the Sung period, that is, in the lower Yangtze Valley and in the southeast coastal regions. The northern lowlands gained population rapidly. They had suffered most from the devastations that followed the downfall of the Mongols, but from the early fifteenth century onwards they enjoyed the peace of a stable government and the stimulus of having had the national capital of Peking in their midst. The Huai River basin and the lake plains of Hu-pei were sparsely populated. Much arable land there still awaited systematic development. Such southern provinces as Kuang-tung and Hu-nan had low population densities.[28] Into the southwest the Ming government built military roads and bridges and established military-agricultural colonies. The mountainous region had pockets of dense aboriginal population but remained marginally Chinese. Not until 1420 did Yun-nan and Kuei-chou become Chinese provinces. Sinicization proceeded in the remote lake basins of Yun-nan through the agricultural efforts of garrison troops, and of civilians who had been forcibly sent there from the Yangtze delta.

During the Ming period population probably increased at a steady rate until it reached some 150 million by 1600. Food production rose correspondingly. In 1602 the total officially registered land reached 176 million acres, which is 75.8 to 86 per cent of the various estimates of J. L. Buck for China proper in the 1930s.[29] In spite of government efforts since the Northern Sung dynasty to encourage the diversification of crops, rice remained the dominant grain in China and might have contributed as much as 70 per cent of the total national food output in the seventeenth century.[30] But the situation was soon to change. The relative importance of rice was to decline drastically as dry crops, and in particular the New World introductions, spread into new lands and environments that were unsuited to wet-rice cultivation. The consequent gain in food output, combined with a long period of peace, enabled the population of China to rise at an unprecedented rate through the century between 1750 and 1850.

It is difficult to ascertain the causal relationships between food and population increase. Was it the availability of new sources of food that led to growth in population, or should one say that as population increased during the Ming and early Ch'ing dynasties new food crops came to be accepted, and their cultivation led in turn to the possibility of further gains in population? Something like the latter seems to have taken place. The Ming and early Ch'ing period was not only a time when the acreage under farms expanded but also a time of agricultural diversification. The growth of cotton, for example, spread beyond the North China plain and the Wei-Fen valleys to the Hu-pei lowlands, to central Ssu-ch'uan, and even to Yun-nan and Kuei-chou where cotton spinning and weaving became a common rural industry. Sugar-cane and indigo helped to transform the economy of many southern regions.

Tobacco, introduced during the late Ming period, brought wealth to such diverse localities as Lan-chou in Kan-su, Ch'eng-tu plain in Ssu-ch'uan, Shan-hai-kuan at the northern end of the North China plains, and Pu-ch'eng and Lun-yen in Fu-chien.[31]

New World food crops, such as peanuts, maize, and sweet potato, appeared in China in the late Ming period. According to Ho, peanuts arrived in the Canton area as early as 1516.[32] Maize and the sweet potato were recorded in south western China (Yun-nan) and in coastal Fu-chien around the middle of the sixteenth century. They gained local acceptance readily enough, but wide spread popularity was achieved much later, in the second half of the eighteenth century. Before 1700, for example, peanuts were a delicacy. In the eighteenth and early nineteenth century they made inroads into hitherto little developed areas such as western Kuang-tung, the remoter parts of Kuang-hsi and Yunnan, and the sand-bars of Ssu-ch'uan. The peanut is tolerant of light sandy soils, and was therefore able to colonize areas that would be quite unsuited to rice. Maize entered China through both the overland India to Burma route and the maritime routes before the middle of the sixteenth century; but up to 1700 maize was grown mainly in the southwest and a few spots along the south eastern coast. Sweet potato spread more quickly, for the Chinese were already accustomed to the Chinese yam and taro and found the American tuber a desirable substitute because of its rich food value and tolerance to drought. However, for reasons not well understood it was only in the eighteenth century that these New World plants found wide acceptance and spread rapidly into areas that had formerly seen little use; the peanut into localities of sandy loam and the maize and sweet potato into the hitherto forested and sparsely settled highlands of South China.

Landscape changes in three areas

The constructive and destructive aspects of landscape change as population increased in the Ming and Ch'ing dynasties may be reviewed in three areas. These are the northern Shan-hsi province, the Ssu-ch'uan basin, and the highlands of South China. The physiography of northern Shan-hsi and South China was such that the clearance of the forest cover often led to severe erosion. Ssu-ch'uan, on the other hand, was able to absorb the great gain in people: the expansion and intensification of land use appear not to have taxed unduly its rich natural fundament.

North China

Of North China bordering the Mongolian plateau, I have sketched the idea that, during prehistoric and early historic periods, the landscapes were appreciably more humid than they are in modern times. Northern Shan-hsi and

Shen-hsi were well wooded and the woods were gradually displaced by scattered groves and grasslands, with an occasional lake and stream, as one penetrated into the Mongolian plateau. In the last two centuries a visitor would encounter much drier scenes: the treeless and largely waterless steppe of Mongolia then extended southwards into the nearly treeless and dissected plateaux of North China.

Between these extremes and for many centuries the landscapes at China's north border were dichotomized into the steppes of Mongolia and the extensive forests in the higher and more rugged parts of Shan-hsi and Shen-hsi. In the T'ang dynasty, for example, northern Shan-hsi was forested. Various literary sources, including the diaries of Ennin, attest to this. During the Northern Sung period inroads were made into the forests by the great monasteries and by soldiers given permission to farm. At the same time officials sought to protect the forests on the ground that trees provided a barrier against the penetration of nomadic invaders from the steppe. In any case, the extent of clearing during the Northern Sung and Chin periods was modest, for at the beginning of the Ming dynasty the ancient forested condition remained. In 1506 a traveller into the Wu-t'ai mountains of northern Shan-hsi recorded how 'tall pine and ancient fir reached the sky and obstructed the valley; deer played on the cliff; birds sang in the thicket'. He spoke of a myriad torrents, of the music of rushing and running water, and of the remarkable fragrance and coldness of the water from a spring.[33]

The deforestation of Shan-hsi appears to have begun on a massive scale in the middle of the sixteenth century. A Ming scholar reported:

At the beginning of the reign of Chia-ching [1522–66] people vied with each other to build houses, and wood from the southern mountains was cut without a year's rest. The natives took advantage of the barren mountain surface and converted it into farms. . . . If heaven sends down a torrent, there is nothing to obstruct the flow of water. In the morning it falls on the southern mountains; in the evening, when it reaches the plains, its angry waves swell in volume and break embankments causing frequent changes in the course of the river. . . . Hence Ch'i district was deprived of seven-tenths of its wealth.[34]

In a gazetteer dated 1596 it was reported that

When the timber by the streams was gone the wood cutters went into the midst of the valleys in crowds of a thousand or a hundred, covering the mountains and wilderness; axes fell like rain and shouts shook the mountain . . . [Eventually] the beautiful scenery of Ch'ing-liang became almost like a cow and horse pasture.[35]

Deforestation was deplored by the late Ming scholars not only because of its effect on streams' flow and on the quality of the soil in the lowlands, but also because of their belief (an old argument for conservation) that the forests on mountain ridges were effective in slowing down the horse-riding barbarians. The protestation of the scholar-officials led in 1580 to the issue of an imperial edict which prohibited tree-cutting. Forests re-established themselves on the mountain slopes, but as the Ming rule came to an end and the demand for farmland continued to increase with rising population the forests were once more being cut down.

Deforestation proceeded despite the prohibition decreed by the Manchus in 1683, and it led eventually to the barren, gullied or cobble-choked landscapes of much of Shan-hsi in modern times.[36] The protected groves around the temples and monasteries bear melancholic witness to the probable forest wealth of the past (Fig. 8). Closer to the steppe, at Yin-ch'uan (Ning-hsia) where the Great Wall crossed the western arm of the great northern loop of the Huang Ho, there is evidence of drastic deforestation and economic decline. W. W. Rockhill reported how Father Gerbillon, who journeyed with the Emperor K'ang-hsi to Ning-hsia in 1697, was impressed by the size and prosperity of the place. The houses were built so close together that there lacked room even for courtyards. Father Gerbillon noted that 'building timber is here very cheap, because they go to get it in that chain of mountains which is to the northwest [Ho-lan Shan], where it is so abundant that from the neighbouring localities, more than 400 or 500 *li* away, they come to buy it at Ninghsia'. In contrast Rockhill reported in 1892 that not a forest tree was to be seen, only a few poplars recently planted along the irrigation ditches.[37]

Ssu-ch'uan basin

The Ssu-ch'uan basin is a mountain-bound and physically isolated unit of China's chequerboard physiognomy: nonetheless it was absorbed into the mainstream of Chinese civilization at an early date. In the Chan-kuo period it already boasted at least two areas of moderately high population density: one was centred on the irrigated Ch'eng-tu plain, the other in the Chia-ling Valley. In the Later Han period Ch'eng-tu city and suburbs claimed a population which equalled, if not excelled, that of the capital at Lo-yang. The prosperity of the Ch'eng-tu plain rested on its irrigation system. The prosperity of the Wei Ho basin in Shen-hsi also depended in part on its waterworks. We have seen how the Cheng-kuo canal of the third century B.C. had contributed to the basin's productivity. But, in comparison with those of Ssu-ch'uan, the Wei basin waterworks were more sensitive to disruption caused by invasions and rebellions; they also had greater difficulty in coping with the problems of silting and salinization.

Agricultural wealth was maintained in the Ssu-ch'uan basin despite the existence of local population pressure and deforestation. It was able to achieve a relatively stable level of prosperity at least in part because of the favourable characteristics of the Ssu-ch'uan environment. Thus, compared with the North, Ssu-ch'uan has a mild and equable climate with adequate, dependable precipitation. Compared with the southern highlands, the soils of Ssu-ch'uan are far more fertile, notwithstanding the fact that much of the Ssu-ch'uan soil was developed *in situ*, on bedrock, and not on transported alluvium.

The early start that Ssu-ch'uan had in the more intensive forms of land use, compared with practices in other parts of the Yangtze Valley and in South China, persisted into later times. As noted earlier, during the Sung period double-cropping was unusual in the rice areas but in parts of Ssu-ch'uan three or four crops were grown in one year. Despite the early application of intensive agriculture, which supported small pockets of dense population, Ssu-ch'uan basin as a whole was sparsely peopled. In the thirteenth century the more rugged ridges within the basin and the mountain slopes surrounding it were still essentially a wild and forested country. Ssu-ch'uan's oldest Chinese clans seldom date back beyond the early Ming period. Its gains in population through immigration during the Ming period were, however, largely lost during the devastating peasant rebellion in the second quarter of the seventeenth century. Population so declined that between 1650 and 1850 Ssu-ch'uan became the largest recipient of immigrants: yet in 1786 its registered population was less than 8·5 million. In 1850 Ssu-ch'uan had more than 44 million people.[38] The large population of that province was therefore a phenomenon of the Ch'ing dynasty and achieved, it would seem, in less than seventy-five years.

Unlike the canals of the Ch'eng-tu plain the intricate patterns of land use that we see today have no long ancestry. They evolved as the population rose: they reflect the successful sustenance of the enlarged population through the adaptation of traditional and newly introduced crops to a rich and varied environment. An altitudinal crop pattern was established in which the newly introduced peanuts occupied the sandbars of streams and rivers, the traditional rice was grown on the terraced valley flanks and hillslopes, maize and sweet potatoes from the New World took up terrain less accessible to water, and the so-called Irish potato occupied the lofty flanks of the encircling wall of mountains.

Southern (Yangtze) highlands

The hilly surface of the Ssu-ch'uan basin was able to sustain the mounting population pressure of the later Ch'ing period without suffering from serious soil erosion. Quite otherwise was the response of the southern highlands to subjection under the plough.[39] Up to the beginning of the eighteenth century the southern highlands were forestclad areas of limited use to the peasant farmers, who were packed in the small alluvial valleys and coastal plains.

Wet-rice was the dominant crop and it required the kind of careful water control that could be practised with relative ease only in the heavy soils of the valleys and on the lower hillslopes.

By the second half of the sixteenth century maize and sweet potatoes were added to the crops grown in the southeastern coastal provinces. However, they appear to have contributed little to the needs of this heavily peopled region until increasing population pressure forced the southeastern peasants out of the small alluvial plains to tackle the forested hills and mountains of the interior. In this venture into a new environment the pioneering peasants relied heavily on maize and sweet potato. They moved into the mountains in large numbers from the beginning of the eighteenth century and continued to do so until the time of the T'ai-ping rebellion (1851–64). The introduction of the Irish potato into the region by 1800 enabled even high and steep mountain slopes to be used.

The population of China as a whole increased nearly threefold (from less than 150 million to 430 million) between 1700 and 1850. Much of this gain was made possible through the introduction of New World crops, which permitted the extension of farming into the hills and mountains. Unfortunately this move into the interior highlands soon upset the rather precarious balance of nature. The peasant farmers ignored the most elementary measures of soil conservation in their urgent need for food and for getting maximal returns in a minimal period out of land that did not belong to them. Forests were cleared and crops were planted up and down the hillslopes. The heavy yields of the first few years encouraged the practice wherever land was available. But it was not long before the heavy rains removed the topsoil. Gullies ate into the deeply weathered rocks and brought coarse alluvium to the rice lands of the valleys, from which it had to be laboriously removed. By the third quarter of the eighteenth century soil erosion had become a serious problem in the Yangtze highlands. Erosion caused the silting up of rivers and lakes and accounted for the increasing frequency of floods. By the beginning of the nineteenth century mountain cultivation caused so much damage that laws were passed to the effect that no lease should be renewed for tenant maize farmers in the lower Yangtze provinces, and that mountain slopes should be used for tea planting or for the growth of *Cunninghamias*.

The hills and mountains of South China support fewer people in the twentieth century than they did in the first part of the nineteenth. Areas under cultivation as well as the total population had shrunk in provinces such as Chiang-hsi, An-hui and Chê-chiang. The stratified pattern of land use – wet-rice on the narrow valley floors and dry crops on the hillslopes – had largely given way to a pattern in which the hillslopes (after about 1820) reverted increasingly to secondary forests, coarse grasses, and tea and tree plantations.

Part Four
Tradition and Change in Modern China

Chapter 8
Stability and innovation: 1850–1950

Foreign travellers to China in the early part of the twentieth century have popularized the view of the great antiquity – indeed the unchanging character – of the Chinese rural scene. The attitude was not one of condescension. On the contrary it revealed respect for a way of life that showed such stable adaptation to the physical environment. A mystical philosopher like Count Keyserling was impressed by the 'absolute genuineness' of the Chinese peasant, child of the soil who wrung 'from nature her scanty gifts by ever more assiduous labour', and who, after death, returned to it in trust.[1] The notion of permanence was also conveyed by the American agronomist F. H. King in his well-known book, *Farmers of Forty Centuries*. The title itself is suggestive of something almost timeless. He visited China, Japan and Korea, at the turn of the century in order, not to give advice as a Western scientist, but 'to learn how it is possible, after twenty and perhaps thirty or even forty centuries, for their soils to be made to produce sufficiently for the maintenance of such dense populations as are living now in these countries'.[2]

The route followed in this book shows how misleading it is to impute permanence to the Chinese landscape. 'Unchanging China' is an illusion sustained by Western romanticism and a blindness to the movements of history. In a few special contexts it can be said that the Chinese rural scene has been remarkably stable; for example, in the arrangement of houses, in the courtyard pattern of the farmsteads, and in the persistence of certain staple crops and field patterns. It is possible to pick out certain villages in the loess area or on the North China plain at the turn of the century and show that the basic livelihood of these communities has departed little from that of their Late Neolithic predecessors. One can point to certain areas, the Ch'eng-tu plain, for example, and plausibly argue that here not only the pattern of the individual settlements but their spatial relations show little progressive change over long stretches of time. Irrigation works and the dense population they made possible have persisted for something like two millennia despite the periodic disruptions caused by civil strife and rebellion.[3] The present Ch'eng-tu landscape of irrigation canals and small settlements, each shaded by clumps of bamboo, *nan-mu*, and cypress, has some claim to antiquity as a landscape type.

However, the Ssu-ch'uan example is not representative. Few other parts of China can compare with the Ch'eng-tu plain in the intensity and stability of land use. The Wei-Fen valleys and the North China plain are also ancient centres of Chinese settlement, but they were more vulnerable to the periodic onslaughts of man and nature, more sensitive to national political upheavals and foreign influences than was the relatively isolated Ssu-ch'uan basin.

The middle Yangtze Valley and South China were areas of progressive colonization from the North since the end of the Later Han dynasty. Their landscapes therefore show progressive alteration – alteration that follows from having more people and hence more villages, from adopting the more intensive forms of land use and from the introduction of new crops that enable the farmers to move into new settings. The individual villages may retain traditional forms, but the appearance of the countryside must alter as population increases and more villages emerge on the scene.

Finally, a very important new force entered the Chinese economy at the beginning of the period (1850–1950) we are considering: this was the introduction of Western commerce and industry to China. At first westernization affected mainly the coastal treaty ports; from there its influence gradually made its way to the inland port cities and, in time, to the neighbouring countryside. These remarks point to the illusiveness of the idea of permanence when applied to China. Certainly the beginning of the twentieth century was not an apposite time to emphasize the static character of the Chinese scene, whether we mean by this the political scene, the economic scene, or the visible landscape. However, before I describe some of the kaleidoscopic changes in the period 1850–1950, it is helpful to pause and look at representative tableaux of China in the 1930s.

Types of landscape: *c.* 1930

Earlier in the book attention was drawn to the possibility of dividing China into three climatic provinces along two lines. It serves a useful purpose to recall the division at this point. One line begins near the crest of the Great Hsing-an Mountains in the north, swings southwestwards across northern Shen-hsi to the city of Lan-chou, and then continues southwestwards nearly as a straight line to the edge of the high Tibetan plateau north of Lhasa. This line generalizes the fluctuating boundary between the dry northwestern half of China and the subhumid/humid southeastern half. It was a major vegetation boundary separating the treeless northwest from the wooded southeast.

The vegetation history of China is the documentation of the withdrawal of trees from the wooded southeast and their replacement by the cultivated grasses, so that the climatic curve came to demarcate, as it did in the 1930s, the boundary between the agricultural and non-agricultural halves of China. Northwest of the boundary agricultural landscapes appear as small scattered oases at the edge of, or surrounded by, overwhelming nature. The high plateaux and gorges of Tibet, the barren sand-dunes of the Tarim basin, and the expansive steppes of Mongolia dwarf the works of man. Southeast of the boundary the total area of uncultivated land (corresponding with the mountains, lakes, marshes, and areas of salt-impregnated soil) still exceeds that of cultivated. Nevertheless over broad territories agricultural landscapes are pervasive and the works of man – the shrines, temples, and monasteries – are discernible even in the least frequented fastnesses of nature.

This then is the primary geographical division of China: natural landscapes dominant on the one side, man-modified landscapes dominant on the other. A second division occurs within the southeastern half, and separates the sub-humid 'continental' North from the humid subtropical South along roughly the latitude of the Ch'in-ling Mountains. The following differences in landscape have been noted by G. B. Cressey: In the North, one encounters large areas of level land, with hills; bare fields and brown, dust-laden scenes in winter; dry crops of wheat, millet, and sorghum; dirt roads for two-wheeled carts and draught animals; mud-walled houses; cities with wide streets, open spaces for agriculture and rectangular walls. In the South, one sees a far more rugged topography; landscapes that are green at all seasons and watery scenes; evidences of intensive land use, the most prominent of which are the sculptural forms of the wet-rice terraces; flagstone trails for coolie carriers and sedan-chair transportation; houses of brick and woven bamboo walls; crowded cities with narrow streets.[4]

19. Terraces and stepped pyramids in northern Shen-hsi

Loessic uplands

North and South China are each in turn divisible into smaller and smaller regions, into smaller and smaller units of landscape. In North China the uplands of the middle Huang Ho basin offer a striking variety of scenery, natural and manmade, in the thick blanket of loess. J. G. Andersson, the Swedish geologist, describes an excursion in the loess region as

> a wonderful experience, in which the wanderer often stops short with surprise and even trembling before perpendicular drops of 30 metres or more. Or he may meet thin, fantastic pillars of the yellow earth, or he will glimpse bits of landscape through natural tunnels or arches which remain standing for some time while the washing away of the loess proceeds.[5]

To these physical wonders are added the expressive responses of the Chinese farmer. In the more humid areas the loess-draped hills have been elaborately terraced to look like stepped pyramids (Fig. 19). Benches, which are loess platforms fringed by stone walls, are built even into the small patches of 'yellow earth' that still hang precariously on the rocky slopes. The cave dwelling is another distinctive response of the Chinese farmer.[6] It attains the greatest popularity in Shen-hsi, western Shan-hsi and southeastern Kan-su provinces

20. Loess country, near Cheng-hsien, Ho-nan Province, with some cave dwellings

for there the loess is thick and timber is scarce. The cave dwelling requires little timber, and has the further advantage over surface structures in that it is cooler in summer and warmer in winter. Wherever a steep expanse of thick loess is exposed, as along the side of a gully, it is a fairly simple matter to make a vertical face of it and then dig into the loess with a shovel. Loess dwellings are usually about 30 feet long and 8 to 15 feet wide, the width depending on the strength of the material. Some villages in Shen-hsi are unique in China in that they occur at several levels: the above-ground houses stand at the edge of an artificially steepened ravine, and into the loess face of the ravine may be dug not one but two horizons of cave dwellings. Cave dwellings must of necessity be built farther apart from each other than the surface houses, and it would be interesting to know whether the greater physical distances have any effect on the social organization of these distinctive settlements.

North China plain

East of the uplands the plains of the lower Huang Ho basin are a mosaic of tiny, rectangular strips the directions of which change normally at right angles (though sometimes at a low angle) from field-block to field-block. In summer a bird's-eye view emphasizes the intricacy and the extreme fragmentation of the landscape for the crops are then in varying stages of growth, each farmer having planted at a slightly different time, and the fields are a glorious palette of yellows, browns, and different shades of green; but unlike the artist's palette the colours are sharply discrete. From the air too the viewer is struck by the generally tree-less character of the plain, so that it is hard to imagine, as some authorities have suggested, that it was once wooded. Yet trees can obviously survive. One sees them strung out along the roads and clustered in the villages, where the willows and poplars provide the essential fuel and construction material.

The large nucleated settlements of the North China plain are only about a mile apart. From the ground one can readily see a number of them on the flat horizon marked off by clumps of trees. Settlements are connected with each other by footpaths and cart tracks. They are fairly evenly distributed. There is, however, a tendency for them to be concentrated on the higher ground, and to avoid the rivers which are of little use for transportation and may be dangerous in times of flood (Fig. 21).

In North China a village of average size has 500 to 700 people. It is one of eighteen to two dozen villages served by a market town in an area of about 20 square miles. The farmland controlled by a village varies greatly in size. In Ting county of Ho-pei province it ranges from a minimum of 40 acres to a maximum of 5,000 acres, with the average at 525 acres.[7] Population density on the village croplands depends partly on the fertility of the soil. It may be as low as 450 persons per square mile in areas of poor sandy soil; in areas of rich soil it reaches 1,450 persons per square mile.[8]

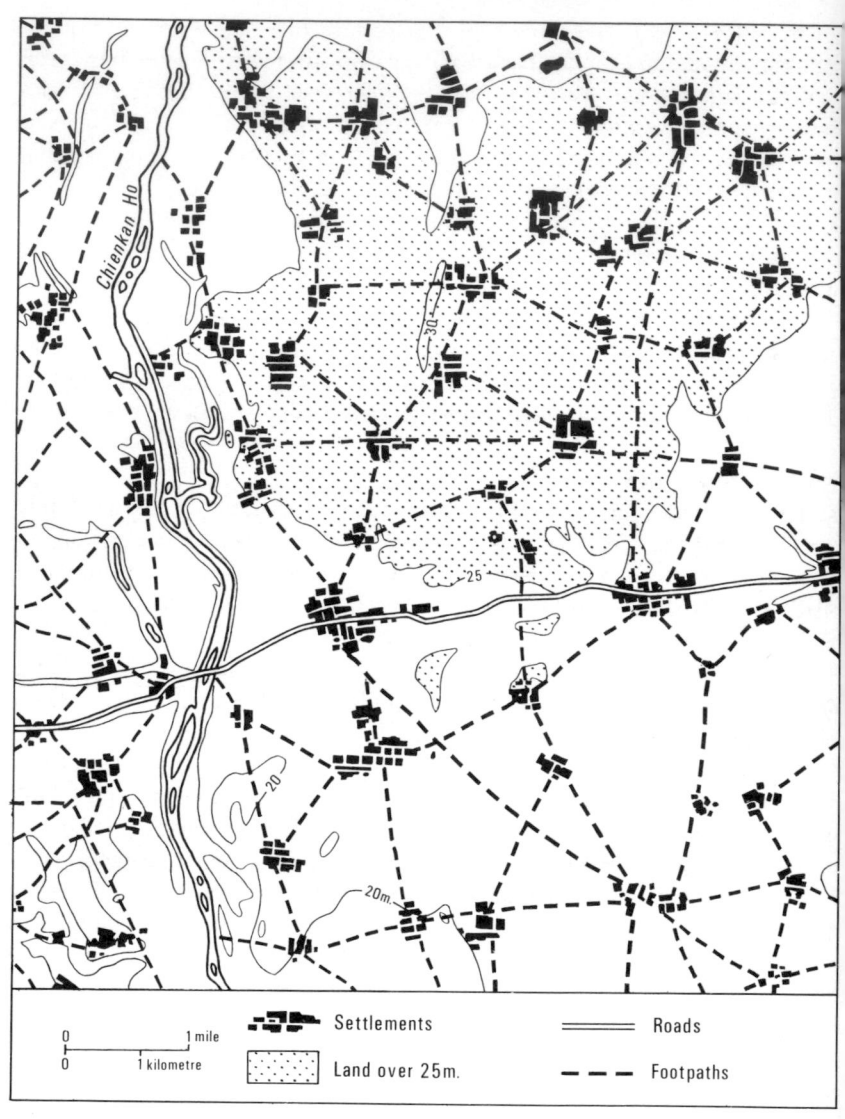

A villager's farm ranges in size from small holdings of a quarter of an acre to 2 acres, to large holdings of 6 to 10 acres. The farms are fragmented into tiny plots scattered in several localities. It is wasteful of time to go from plot to plot, and wasteful of land to build numerous paths to enable the farmer to reach his fields. The usual rationale given for the extreme fragmentation is that even on the alluvial plain, within the environs of a village, the characteristics of soil vary significantly, so that the possession of land in soils of different quality is an insurance against the possibility of complete crop failure for any one family. Other causes of progressive fragmentation are the practice of dividing the paternal inheritance equally among the sons, each of whom will want his share to be distributed over different kinds of soil, and the habit of acquiring small bits of land – instead of whole fields – from neighbours. The very small plots may be only 10 feet by 100 feet whereas the large ones exceed an acre. The fields are therefore a crazy-quilt pattern, but a very colourful one in the growing season.

Villages in North China are compact. Many are surrounded by walls with gates that can be closed at night, but even without the walls they may look closed-in and fortified when viewed from the outside. Houses are built close together, presenting blank faces to the outside world. The number and length of the streets in a village depend on the nature of the terrain and on the number of families. Some of the streets are very narrow lanes which terminate before they reach the countryside.[9] Most of them are bordered by walls in which the only openings are the gateways that lead into courtyards. The wealthier families have their own courtyards. The main living-room and bedrooms are built on the north side of the courtyard and open to the south. Walls may be made of burnt brick. (In villages close to the mountains the foundation and lower walls of a rich farmer's house are made of stone.) The roofs are tiled. Besides the main house on the north side of the courtyard, subsidiary structures accommodate farm animals, implements, and hired labourers. The poorer families live two, three, four, or even five or more families in one courtyard.[10] Their houses are made of sun-dried brick or pounded earth. The roof is thatched or made of sorghum stalks plastered with mud. Beyond the village are the vegetable gardens, and beyond the vegetable gardens are the graveyards of the different village clans. Of Taitou village in Shan-tung province Martin C. Yang says:

> There is no general cemetery; each clan buries its dead on land which is believed to be favourable to the future generations of the clan. When the clan becomes large and several branches split off, each branch chooses its own ground for burial. After a number of generations small graveyards or isolated mounds are scattered everywhere around the village.[11]

The oldest graveyards are often the farthest away from the village centre. As the generations of dead and living both multiply they tend to move in on each other so that the newest grave mounds appear right at the fringe of the village.

22. Terraced rice-fields in the Ssu-ch'uan basin

Ssu-ch'uan basin

Rural landscapes of central and South China are dominated by rice fields, whether these are the small square plots on the Yangtze plain or the elaborate tiers of Ssu-ch'uan which achieve an almost architectural splendour (Fig. 22). The physical environments are richly varied, as also the rural landscapes that have evolved in them. The Ssu-ch'uan basin is supreme in these respects. It has an extraordinarily high average population density of some 650 persons per square mile although perhaps no more than 5 per cent of the basin is level. Elevation in the basin ranges from less than 2,000 feet along the floors of the Yangtze River and its tributaries to about 4,500 feet at the crest of the numerous sandstone ridges that traverse the basin. The highest summer temperatures, outside the deserts, have been recorded in Ssu-ch'uan. At an elevation of less than 2,000 feet the climate is tropical. Cultivated crops, besides rice, include the very important sugar-cane, cotton, maize, sweet potato, tobacco, and peanuts. In addition, one finds citrus fruits and such tropical plants as *litchi* (*Litchi chinensis*), *lung-yen* (*Euphoria longana*), the Chinese olive (*Canarium album*), and the *Clausena punctata*. Above 2,000 feet farmers may continue to plant rice in flights of terraces wherever irrigation is practicable. But maize begins to displace rice as the staple food, and winter crops become less and less common as one approaches the upper limit of rice cultivation, which is about 4,000 feet. The basic settlement types of isolated farmsteads, hamlets, and villages are all represented in the Ssu-ch'uan basin. The very rich Ch'eng-tu plain has a large part of its population in isolated farms and small hamlets surrounded by groups of trees and bamboo. Small settlements also appear to be characteristic of the zone where rice fields give way to dry crops.[12] Farmsteads frequently display the courtyard pattern, and those in the wet-rice zone give an air of substance and wellbeing that one rarely sees on the North China plain.

Yangtze plains

In contrast with the ridge-and-valley topography of Ssu-ch'uan basin the alluvial plains of the middle and lower Yangtze Valley are almost perfectly flat. Water, as Cressey says, is the key to the landscape (Fig. 23). It occurs in many shapes and sizes. There are first the large and shallow lakes bordered by marshlands. We have noted earlier how these great bodies of inland water occupy a part of the geosyncline that has undergone slow but persistent downwarping. The process tends to prolong the life of these lakes while the alluvium brought into them by the Yangtze and its tributaries tends to shorten it. At flood stage the total area of the main lakes, Tung-t'ing Hu, Po-yang Hu, Tai Hu, Hun-tze and Kao-yu Hu, is of the order of 7,000 square miles.

The middle Yangtze River, even when it is not in flood, is an impressive body of water a mile or two across. Bordering it are abandoned meanders (ox-bow lakes), intricate nets of bifurcating and confluent channels, standing bodies of water temporarily ponded by sand bars or dykes, and small streams that flow away from the higher land surrounding the main channel of the Yangtze. In addition there are the manmade waterways, the canals, the irrigation ditches and linear ponds. Cressey reports that in the southern delta around Shanghai the canal mileage is 150,000, and that 'one square mile surveyed near Shanghai shows a total of 27·8 miles of canals and linear ponds, with an average spacing of 380 feet. Half of these waterways are navigable for small boats, for the canals are usually 10 to 20 feet wide. An average width of only 10 feet would represent 5 per cent of the area.'[13]

In the watery environment of the Yangtze plains average population density reaches 1,200 persons per square mile. Over many rural areas it exceeds 2,500 persons per square mile. High yield in the rice fields and double-cropping have made the compaction possible. Densities on the North China plain seldom approach it. Farm holdings on the Yangtze plains are much smaller than those in the North. In areas of wet-rice cultivation farms of half an acre to $1\frac{1}{2}$ acres are the rule. The shape of the fields also differs from that of the North. The irrigated plots in the Yangtze delta are of squarish shape in contrast to the

23. *Watery landscape of streams, canals, and ponds in the middle Yangtze plains*

narrow strips of North China. The square plot is bounded by irrigation ditches and linear ponds; its shape appears to follow from the evident practicality of adopting the grid pattern for the watering and drainage of the mud flats. The rectangular strips of North China, on the other hand, seem to result from the use of the ox-drawn plough, whose low manoeuvrability encourages the farmer to cut the long furrow. On the Yangtze delta the hoe rather than the plough is used on the tiny square plots. Rice fields do, however, also appear in long strips in response to the topographic situation. Thus fields that fringe the larger rivers are narrow rectangles oriented in the direction of the slopes of the levees and at right angles to the direction of stream flow.

Excessive fragmentation, as elsewhere in China, plagues the already minute farms. Plots in an irrigated rice field differ significantly in value, not only because of the variations in soil quality, but also because the plots receive irrigation water at different times and are drained of water for winter planting at different times. Since the plots that lie close to the canal or stream receive water first farmers who own them make an early start in transplanting the rice seedlings from the nurseries; and since the fields are frequently the shape of a very shallow saucer, plots at the centre of the field may be so difficult to drain after the removal of the rice crop that they cannot be used for winter wheat or rapeseed. For these reasons a farmer would wish to avoid certain portions of the field, and an equitable distribution requires that his holdings include both the favoured and the handicapped plots. A field, defined as a mud flat bounded by canals or streams, may be only a few acres or tens of acres in size. The plots are subdivisions of the field and are separated from each other by dykes or irrigation ditches. Very small ones have dimensions of only 100 feet by 70 feet. Partition of the land among male heirs sometimes requires that the larger plots be further subdivided. One way of demarcating these tiny units is to plant a tree on the dyke at either end of the plot. The rural landscape is thus one of extreme parcellation.[14]

Compact villages are the rule on the North China plain. In contrast, the Yangtze delta has almost every type of rural settlement, from the single farmstead to the small town, with hamlets and villages of varying size in between (Fig. 24). Villages of the lower Yangtze Valley are larger than those of North China and may have a few shops that serve not only the villagers but also the dispersed population in the countryside. The region south of Lake Tai is dominated by villages with populations in the neighbourhood of 1,500, located 1 or 2 miles apart. In the centre of every several tens of villages is a market town, which collects basic produce from the surrounding villages and distributes the manufactured goods from the outside cities.[15] Communication among the settlements is by boat on the dense net of waterways. The largest villages tend to grow at the confluence or at the point of bifurcation of the streams. This description, however, has to be modified for the deltaic area closer to the sea.

Eighty miles east of Lake Tai dispersed farmsteads rather than villages are the rule. The landscape of dispersed farmsteads is as flat and watery as that of nucleated settlements south of Lake Tai but it has fewer natural watercourses; it is dominated by manmade canals and ponds. Almost without exception houses are located on waterways but the waterways are so closely spaced that the houses appear to be evenly dispersed. Every farmhouse has its courtyard

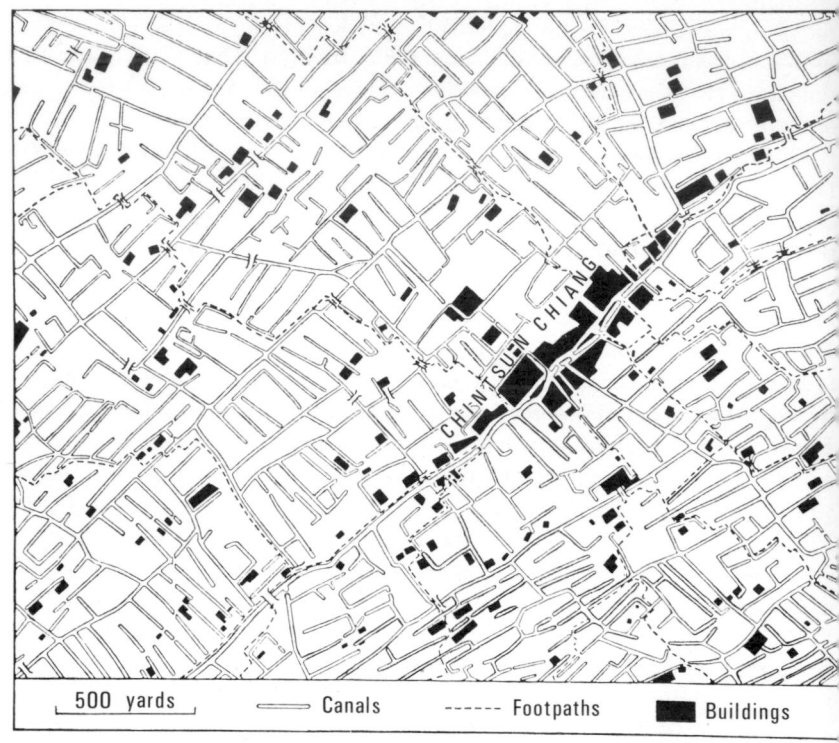

| 500 yards | ⟹ Canals | ------ Footpaths | ▮ Buildings |

24. Settlements, canals, and linear ponds in the Fenghsien district of the Yangtze delta (Cressey)

for threshing grain and other domestic uses. Unlike those in North China courtyards in the delta region are unwalled except for a possible hedge.[16] In small towns houses are built in close proximity or as a connected structure along the watercourses. The front room, used for manufacturing silk, dining, and sitting, opens out to the road, and beyond the road, to the stream. Behind the front room is a small kitchen, and behind the kitchen a bedroom or bedrooms. Either in front or behind the house is an open space which may be used for threshing grain or for growing vegetables; but it also functions as a public road. The courtyard pattern is rarely seen.[17]

Few of the landscape features thus described are evident from the level of the ground. The surface of the Yangtze delta is so flat that vistas are narrowly circumscribed: canals are hidden by reeds and farmsteads by stumps of broadleaf trees and bamboo. Among the more prominent features in the landscape are the numerous grave mounds and stone bridges. Grave mounds, some 8 to 10 feet high, are built in clusters along the dykes. Some of them are shaped like small houses, with walls of burnt brick and pitched, tile roofs. Cressey estimates hat grave mounds in the Fenghsien district of the delta occupy from 5 to 10 per cent of the arable land. The most elegant, and probably also the oldest, structures in the rural scene are the numerous bridges that span the streams and canals. Most of them are made of stone slabs resting on stone pillars but arched stone bridges also exist.

Southwest China: Yun-nan

In sharp contrast to the flat central and lower Yangtze plains are the sculptural landforms and wooded landscapes of south and southwest China. Yet, notwithstanding the differences in physical environment the human response may show remarkable uniformity. Consider, for example, Yun-nan province. It is an elevated plateau with an average height above sea-level of some 6,000 feet. It is a step below High Tibet but rises well above the surrounding regions of Ssu-ch'uan, Kuei-chou and Indo-China. Its equable climate and long growing season result from the combination of high elevation and low latitude. Its surface is compounded of mountains and canyons, hills and lake plains, most of which show a distinct north–south alignment. Population is concentrated on the small lake plains, but the surprising fact is that in these remote, isolated pockets population densities reach 1,500 to 2,000 persons per square mile of cultivated land, densities matching those of the Yangtze delta.

The Tali region illustrates some of the peculiarities of Yun-nanese geography. Topographic units of the region are strung out in narrow north–south strips. Tsang Shan at the western border is a forested, asymmetrical block mountain that rises to 18,000 feet. Streams run down the relatively gentle eastern flank of the block and build at its base an alluvial plain some 2 to 3 miles wide. East of the plain is the narrow Tali lake, and rising steeply out of the eastern border of the lake are the bare slopes of a limestone range. The strip of alluvium is probably not much more than 100 square miles in area; yet it contains some 100 villages as well as the city of Tali, which has a population of 20,000. The average size of a farm per family of five persons is 1·5 acres. It is as small as most farms on the Yangtze delta. Like the Yangtze delta by far the most important crop on the Tali plain is rice. Other similarities in environmental adaptation, despite the differences in environmental context, include the growing of wheat in the drained rice fields in winter, the importance of fishing to villagers crowded along the edge of the lake, the technique of cormorant fishing, and the use of the lake for transportation.

The chief reason for the similarities of land use between the Yun-nanese lake basins and the lower Yangtze valley is that many of the Chinese settlers in southwest China are descendants of farmers who were compelled to migrate from the lower Yangtze valley westward during the Ming dynasty. In the mountain fastnesses of the interior the immigrants sought out those aspects of the environment which allowed them to persist in their habitual ways of life.

They ignored those aspects of the environment – the mountains and the forests – which were alien to their experience. In this attitude the Chinese immigrants might have been encouraged by the Min-chia, who preceded them as settlers of the Yun-nanese lake plains. Like the Chinese the Min-chia were rice farmers and lowland dwellers who entertained an aversion towards mountains. But they differed from the Chinese in one important respect: they kept cattle on the rather poor pastures at the foot of the Tsang Shan and milked the cattle to make cheese.[18]

South China

From High Tibet the land drops to the level of the Yun-nan plateau and from the Yun-nan plateau it descends to the intricately dissected mountains and hills of South China, and from the mountainous interior of South China to the small pockets of alluvium along the coast. The essential character of the South Chinese landscape lies in the juxtaposition of mountains and narrow ribbons of alluvium that reach up the winding streams into the interior (Fig. 25). The character of the mountain landscape varies from place to place. In the south-eastern provinces of Chê-chiang and Fu-chien and in the southwestern province of Kuei-chou, tropical weathering of igneous rocks in the one area and of limestone in the other has produced jagged peaks and precipitous, even overhanging, slopes. This is the scenery of the landscape artist.

Elsewhere, mountains are less precipitous: some retain their natural vegetation, which is a luxuriant, mixed evergreen broadleaved forest. Large areas in Yun-nan, Kuang-hsi and Hai-nan island are thus wooded. Larger areas, however, have been modified in varying degrees by man. In Kuang-tung province, for example, deforestation has been extremely severe (Fig. 25). Mountains once wooded now support coarse grass and shrubs. In Hu-nan, Chê-chiang, and Chiang-hsi, the cleared mountain slopes may be covered with tea bushes or with plantings of the *Cunninghamia*. Crudely made terraces for maize and sweet potato can frequently be seen in the southern highlands. Since 1958, however, commune labour has transformed some of the barren hills of South China into elaborately terraced fields (Fig. 26).

Population is concentrated on the alluvial ribbons and pockets. Terraced rice fields follow the dendritic pattern of the streams. In the narrower alluvial belts rice fields stretch across the width of the valley floor, so that from the ground they look like a long flight of low steps, and from the air a glittering chain of beads. Land use reaches maximum intensity on the deltaic plains along the coast. By far the most important crop on the Canton delta is rice, and two harvests in the year are common. Occasionally it is possible to grow vegetables between the November harvest and the spring planting. The fields are mostly fallow in the winter, although some areas raise winter wheat. Sugar-cane competes with rice on the lowlands. Sweet potatoes are grown by the

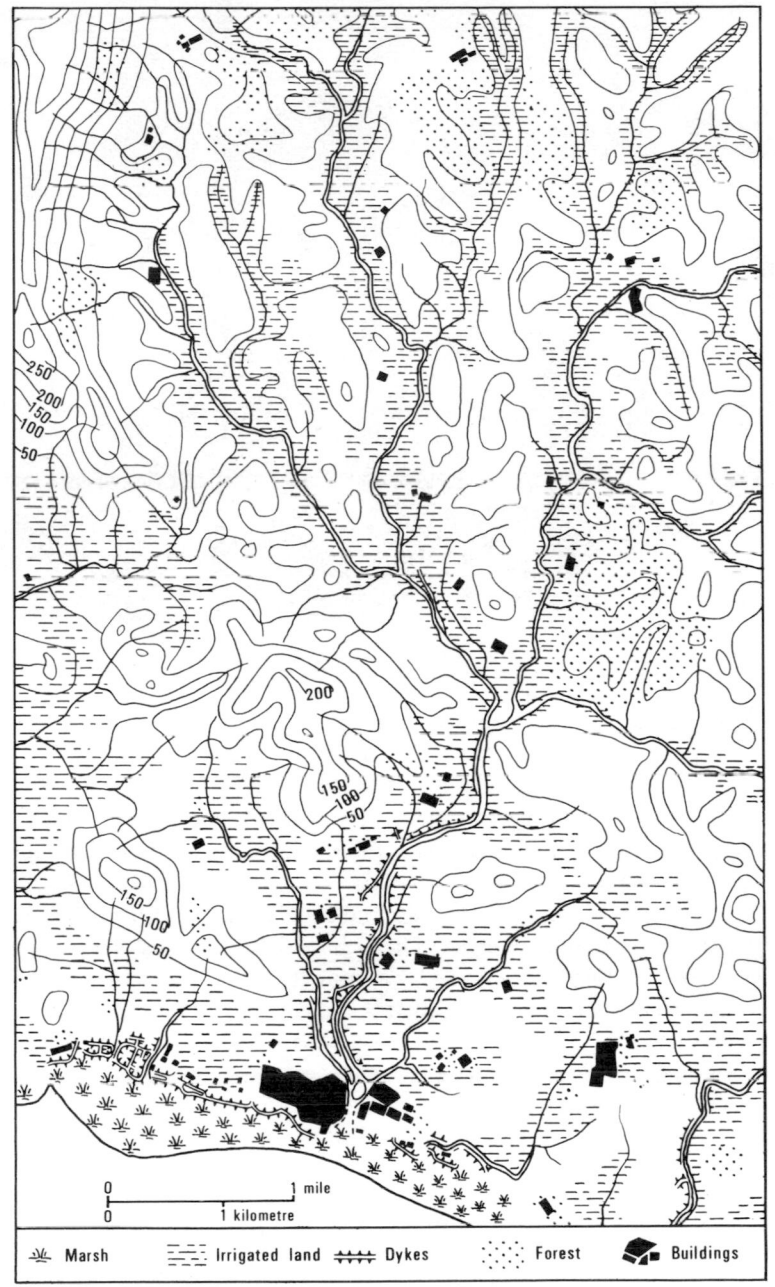

Marsh	Irrigated land
Dykes	Forest
Buildings	

25 Topography, land use and settlements in the New Territories, Hong Kong.
The pattern is characteristic of much of the southern part of Kuang-tung
province. Note the limited tree cover

161

26. Terraced fields built with collective efforts, Kuang-hsi

poor on hillslopes. The higher patches of alluvium support a profusion of
fruit crops, including the pineapple, citrus fruits, litchi, lung-yen, papaya,
guava, banana and persimmon.[19]

Population density per square mile of cultivated land on the Canton delta
is as high as that on the Yangtze delta. The two areas have much in common.
They share such traits as rice fields, numerous watercourses (the bulk of which
in both areas are manmade), the importance of fishing and the silk industry.
There are also evident differences. The Canton delta is broken up by numerous
islands of protruding bedrock; the Yangtze delta is not. The Yangtze delta also
lacks the profusion of tropical fruits that lends distinction to the landscape of
the tropical region. Villages are the characteristic form of rural settlement on
the Canton delta, but unlike those in the lower Yangtze, they tend to avoid the
rivers (which not infrequently break their dykes and flood the rice fields) and
seek the higher alluvium among the orchards or locations at the foot of the hills.

Types of population and landscape change

The humanized landscapes thus far described are representative of what could
be seen if one were to travel in China in the 1930s. These are sketches captured
in a moment of time. Let us now take the broader time span between 1850 and
1950 and consider how, within it, the Chinese scene has altered. The more

significant transformations may be said to be due to: (1) natural population increase, (2) natural and manmade disasters, (3) extension of frontiers, and (4) impact of Western commercial and industrial civilization.

Natural population increase and landscape change

For the country as a whole population appears to have reached a peak in 1850. China then may have had 430 million people. By 1910–11, the end of the Manchu (Ch'ing) dynasty, the figure dropped to 340 million. Some forty years later population rose to 583 million. As the next section will show, population and land use fluctuated sharply within the century under consideration as a result of both natural and manmade disasters. Here we shall attend to those areas that showed an upswing in population as a result primarily of natural increase. Even in the oldest and most densely settled parts of China, new villages arose in areas that were already cluttered with villages.

Consider, for example, Ting *hsien* (county). It is one of the 120 *hsien* of Ho-pei province, located on the western side of the North China plain, some thirty-seven miles south of Pao-ting. Seventy-six per cent of Ting *hsien* was farmland. Average population density per square mile of cultivated land in 1930 was 1,100. The *hsien* history of 1849 reported a total of 423 villages. In eighty years thirty new settlements had been added. Most villages were surrounded by their own fields. Definite boundaries were fixed between the fields of the different villages. Provincial regulations required that they be marked by boundary stones. In 1929–30, nineteen settlements in Ting *hsien* were not yet recognized as villages. They did not control the farmlands and had evidently been set up because of overcrowding in the older settlements.[20]

Another *hsien* in Ho-pei province showed an increase in the number of rural markets from 23 in 1868 to 37 in 1916. Some parts of South China showed far more rapid rise as the result of local immigration. For example, in the 1890s Chieh-yang *hsien* of Kuang-tung province had 163 villages; forty years later the number had increased to 885.[21]

There is thus evidence of a growing intensity of land use and the accretion of more and more settlements in the countryside, even in the chaotic period between the decline of the Manchu dynasty and the founding of the Republic. It is clear that the process must have occurred repeatedly in the long peaceful periods of Chinese history, and that it was punctuated by retrogression in times of disaster.

G. William Skinner has recently sketched a model for the intensification of settlement and land use in the Chinese rural landscape. Its stages are approximately as follows. The first stage sees a simple distribution of dispersed village clusters, each of which surrounds a small rural market. The marketing areas of the village clusters do not overlap for they are small. At the next stage new villages are established beyond the existing ones. Marketing areas expand until the intervening spaces are filled. The rural landscape is then in stable equilibrium. Empirical data suggest that in such a landscape the average number of villages served by a rural market is eighteen. Further intensification occurs through the segmentation of the older villages. On rich alluvial land a new settlement is established, not on one of the main paths connecting an old village to the market, but on a site equidistant from the market and two old villages. This belief follows from the prior assumption that a village on rich soils will grow quite large before economic pressures encourage pioneer families to move out and establish a new village. By that time, however, a site on the path between two old villages may be ruled out by the inadequacy of arable land which is not already cultivated from the two older settlements.

In mountain land or other less fertile environments the point of village segmentation occurs at a lower level of population – at a time when the old villages are still small so that there may be sufficient agricultural land for the establishment of a new village at the mid-point along the path between the two original settlements. In any case, empirical data suggest that as new villages are founded, the ratio of villages to market town increases from 18 (the landscape of equilibrium) to the 30–36 range. At this stage, new markets emerge to serve the needs of the new villages. The emergence of new markets results in the decline – sometimes precipitous – of the village-to-market ratio to the neighbourhood of 18 or below 18. If the ratio drops below 18, then new villages will appear to restore the average number of the equilibrium model.[22]

The intensification of the rural landscape is thus seen not only naïvely as the multiplication of new villages, but of new and smaller marketing areas, each of which will eventually have an average complement of eighteen villages. Very large marketing areas of 55 square miles or more occur only in mountainous regions or on the subhumid margins of agricultural China. The population of such marketing communities may be as low as 3,000. At the other extreme, very small marketing areas of 6 square miles or less occur only on plains of exceptional fertility near major urban centres. The majority of marketing areas, however, are in the neighbourhood of 20 square miles, a size which puts the most disadvantaged villager within easy walking distance of the town. The average population of the standard marketing community is just above 17,000. It is important to lay some stress on the word community here, for the marketing area is also the largest social unit of the Chinese villager. His experienced world extends beyond his native village and its people to, in the course of a lifetime of marketing and visiting, all the villages and nearly all the people (farmers, artisans, merchants, petty officials) in the marketing area.[23]

Natural and manmade disasters

Disasters can change land use over broad areas. The effect may be temporary, as for example when a river in flood deposits a thick layer of silt over the farm-

and and changes it into a desert. But since the silt is fertile, in two or three years it will again support crops. The landscape shows no evident change except that its surface will be somewhat higher and relations with ground-water level may alter slightly. This type of temporary fluctuation due to flood has occurred with depressing frequency over the North China plain. An example of temporary change caused by man would be when a predatory army has swept over farming country. However severe the disaster, the effect is temporary if the farmers were left on the land.

But disasters can also effect much more permanent alterations in the landscape. For example, floods may deposit thick and extensive layers of sandy material that is too coarse for the successful cultivation of grain crops; so the farmer adapts to the change by planting peanuts and sweet potatoes. He may do the same on the sandy beds of abandoned stream channels. Rebellions and wars can bring about prolonged alterations in land use by changing the regional pattern of population distribution.

The major natural disasters in China are drought, flood, and earthquake. It is appropriate to regard the two great floods of the Huang Ho, one in 1855 and the other in 1938, as manmade in the sense that they were induced by man. The agent, however, is water, and the effect of flood water on the land is quite different from that produced by raging armies. The worst of natural disasters, causing the most widespread famine, is without doubt the lack of rainfall. Droughts and floods have occurred with such frequency and have been so widely recorded that one historian made use of the data to infer the history of population movement.[24] In the modern period perhaps the greatest natural calamity (measured in terms of the number of lives lost) that the world has known took place in North China. This was the famine caused by near rainlessness between the years 1876 and 1879. Four provinces, Shen-hsi, Shan-hsi, Ho-nan, and Ho-pei, were hit. Some 9 to 13 million people perished from hunger, disease, or violence during the famine of 1877–78 or shortly thereafter. The population of the region was drastically reduced. Shan-hsi, for example, had more people in 1850 than in 1953, and Shen-hsi became one of the leading recipients of immigrants during the last decades of the Ch'ing dynasty.[25] Famines caused by drought had recurred at short intervals in North China. That of 1920–21 made some 20 million people destitute and brought about the death of half a million people. The starving people in the worst-afflicted districts consumed not only the entire reserve of food but also all other vegetation, including ground leaves, flower seed, poplar buds, thistles, poisonous tree bean, cotton seed, roots, and elm bark. In some localities whole villages were emptied of people.[26]

Among natural agents, next to drought, floods bring the greatest calamity. The effect of floods on the land is more evident and tends to be more permanent than that of drought. This is especially true of the North China plain where the

Huang Ho, within the century now under consideration, changed its cours
over hundreds of miles three times. The first time was in 1855. The mouth
the Huang Ho swung north from the mouth of the Huai River to a positio
north of the Shan-tung peninsula. The main reason for the breakage of the dyl
and the swing northward of the lower Huang Ho was that the dykes borderir
the lower Huang Ho received very little attention in the early part of tl
nineteenth century. At the same time a great deal of effort was expended t
keep the Grand Canal open where it crossed the Huang Ho at Huai-yi
Since the government was using all its resources to protect the junctio
preventing the water there from overflowing, the Huang Ho was forced to fin
outlets higher upstream. It did so by a series of floods in 1835, 1841, an
1843, and finally in 1855 the entire lower course of the river swung north. It
new course cut through the Canal at Chang-ch'iu and put it completely out c
commission.[27]

After the change the river channel became very unstable. Even moderat
water levels could produce dangerous flooding. Between 1887 and 1889
break occurred in the southern dyke in Ho-nan province although the wate
level was not especially high. More than 2 million people perished throug
drowning or from starvation. Nearly the whole of Ho-nan south of the rive
was inundated.

In 1938 the bank of the Huang Ho was deliberately breached at a point a fe
miles east of the crossing of the river by the Peking-Hankou railway. Th
breach was made so that the flood-water could block the advance of the invad
ing Japanese Army. The river swung south and meandered over a broad stri
of good farmland to the Huai River. It remained in this position until 194
when it was redirected to its northern course. Thus for nearly nine years som
2 million acres of land were partly or wholly out of production.[28] Perhaps mor
than 800,000 people perished either directly or indirectly through this man
induced flooding.

With the draining of the flooded area after the return of the river to the ol
course, it was found that the local character of the soil had changed. Som
parts were covered by fine sand and clay and became less productive tha
before the flood. These were planted with peanuts. Other parts received a ric
layer of silt and became more productive. They soon yielded good crops c
wheat, cotton, maize, millet, and a variety of vegetables. It is probable tha
there were important changes in field patterns, in the distribution of lan
holdings and in settlement forms as the farmers proceeded to re-establis
themselves on the new land, but detailed information is lacking.

Earthquakes are another type of natural disaster that leave an impact on th
landscape. They are far more localized and cause less damage than drought
and floods. In the faulted loessic uplands, however, earthquakes are frequen
and severe enough to be significant as agents of landscape change. As to fre

ucncy, historical records indicate that fifty destructive earthquakes occurred
in eastern Kan-su during the interval between A.D. 996 and 1920, or one great
jolt in every 18·5 years.[29] Loess covers extensive areas in eastern Kan-su and
Shen-hsi provinces. The effect of the earthquake is to loosen the loess, causing
it to slide into the river valleys and block streams. The east Kan-su earthquake
of 1920 initiated numerous slides. The total area affected by them was as large
as 15 million square metres.[30] Since many houses in the loessic uplands were
cave dwellings dug into the friable material, earthquakes can bring death to
amazingly large numbers of people. Landslides buried grain stores as well as
whole villages. Almost a quarter of a million people were killed during the
Kan-su disaster of 1920 or died of starvation shortly after.

These calamities of nature, awesome as they were, met more than their
match in the incredible destruction of lives and property by man. In the period
between 1850 and 1950, there took place in China the T'ai-ping and Nien rebellions, the Muslim rebellions, the incessant civil wars in various parts of the
country from 1917 to the establishment of the Nationalist government in 1927,
the battles between Nationalists and Communists from 1928 to the time of
the Sino-Japanese war (July 1937 to August 1945), and their resumption after
the defeat of Japan, until in 1950 the Communist armies gained control over
the whole of mainland China. In the sheer number of people killed this period
in China must be counted as one of the bloodiest in world history.

The T'ai-ping rebellion of 1851–64 was perhaps the most brutal civil war
known to man. Conservative estimates put the number of people who died as
a result of the rebellion at 20 to 30 million. The worst affected areas were the
densely populated valleys of South China and the lower Yangtze basin. In
1850 the valleys were packed with villages, farmsteads and elaborately irrigated rice fields. Population pressure was such that the poorer people, as we
have seen, encroached on the forested hillslopes and planted there crops of
maize and sweet potato. Following the incessant destruction and slaughter,
'The valleys, notwithstanding the fertility of their soil, are a complete wilderness. . . . Here and there a house is barely fitted up, and serves as a lodging to
some wretched people, the poverty of whom is in striking contrast with the rich
land on which they live.' This desolate landscape was described by the German
geologist Richthofen thirteen years after the end of the rebellion.[31] It serves to
emphasize the slowness of recovery if destruction has been intense and widespread.

For some 200 years following the mid-seventeenth-century peasant rebellion
of Ssu-ch'uan, the Ssu-ch'uan basin was the largest recipient of immigrants;
in the later part of the nineteenth century, however, the ravaged lower Yangtze
basin took over this role. Tenant farmers in the mountains suffered less than
the valley dwellers. They left the eroded hillsides to possess the rich soils of the
valleys. As Ho Ping-ti puts it, 'The greatest recipient of "surplus" population

after 1864 was the very region where the pre-1850 density of population wa highest.'[32]

Overlapping in time with the T'ai-ping revolution was the prolonged warfar waged by the Nien rebels in the Huai River basin. Again destruction of lif and property was pursued with the impartiality of a typhoon. Over an area o some 6,000 square miles at the An-hui and Ho-nan borderland, the rebels ha completely stripped the countryside so that it contained no trace of huma habitation. The Muslim rebellions in the 1860s and 1870s devastated th northwestern provinces of Shen-hsi and Kan-su. The total loss of human lives both Muslim and non-Muslim Chinese, numbered several millions. Recover of population was slow: in 1850 the population of Kan-su exceeded tha recorded in 1953 by 2·5 million people. The wholesale destruction of village in the loess upland had a permanent effect on the landscape; those that wer rebuilt after the rebellion tended to be the less visible clusters of cave dwelling

Expansion and adaptation at the frontiers

The expansion of Chinese settlements and agriculture beyond the grea river basins that drain to the east is met by three types of environment: th high mountains and deep valleys at the edge of Tibet; the broad steppe an deserts of Inner Mongolia, and the grasslands and forests of Manchuria. Th extent of penetration of the Chinese into these unfamiliar settings and thei adaptation to them have differed in each case.

TIBET. The eastern edge of the Tibetan plateau stands sharply above th Ssu-ch'uan basin. Most of the basin lies below 3,000 feet, but the jagge peaks to the west rise to more than 15,000 feet. The contrast is especially vivi if one follows the old official road into Tibet from the Ch'eng-tu plain. Afte travelling for four days on horseback across the intensely humanized landscap of the Ch'eng-tu region one arrives at Ya-an (Ya-chou) at the foot of the tower ing wall of mountains. The continuous expanse of irrigated rice fields comes t a sharp end. Beyond Ya-an the road enters the high plateau and continue westwards to the trade town of Kan-ting (Tachienlu) and beyond to Lhasa Along this road, at one time or another, passed conquering armies, gift-bearin embassies, and a great variety of goods: tea, cloth, tobacco, spices, buildin materials, oil, needles and other merchandise from the Chinese lowland wood, fox skins and other hides, yak tails, musk and deer horn from Tibet Along this road scattered signs of Chinese penetration may be seen. Thes amount to no more than a few settlements, varying in size from half a dozen t forty or fifty families, that cater to the traffic along the road. Another type o Chinese penetration into the Tibetan plateau is the isolated Chinese agricul tural community. A few have managed to establish themselves on the scattere alluvial fans that are large enough to make irrigated cultivation worthwhile

27. Prayer flags at the summit of the Jetrun La Pass on the caravan route from Ch'eng-tu to Lhasa

The government in the 1930s tried to encourage more colonists to move into the mountain frontier but with little success.[33]

It is perhaps the social isolation of the scattered communities, as much as the physical handicaps of the environment, that has discouraged Chinese

immigrants from coming in any number. The social isolation is a consequenc
of the highly compartmentalized topography. High mountains and deep can
yons cut off the irrigated alluvial cones from one another. The Chinese ric
farmers are surrounded by non-Chinese peoples such as the sedentary an
nomadic Tibetans, the Chiarongs and the Chiangs with their ancient Bon reli
gion, an assortment of tribal groups known collectively to the Chinese as th
Western Barbarians (*Hsi-fan*), the White Lolos of Chinese-Tibetan-Lolo des
cent, and the proud inbred Black Lolos, superb masters of the horse, who hav
successfully rebelled against Ch'ing authority, and later the authority of th
Republican government, and who have demonstrated their hatred of th
Chinese by destroying their towns and villages from time to time.[34]

The northeastern corner of the Tibetan plateau rears above the T'ao Valle
of southeastern Kan-su. The sharp physical boundary between high mountain
and canyons on the one side and the open, much lower valley of the T'ao H
on the other corresponds to a remarkably stable cultural boundary. Even in th
Late Neolithic period agricultural villages occupied the loess-covered terrace
of the T'ao Ho, while the hunters of antelope and herders of cattle, sheep an
goats lived in the mountains. This prehistoric difference in economy persist
to the present.[35]

In detail the cultural boundary is a wavy line; and several agricultural out
liers appear within an area dominated by pastoral nomadism. Moreover, th
lines that separate migratory herders from sedentary farmers do not coincid
with the pattern of ethnic groups. In the agricultural T'ao Ho Valley Chinese
villages and Chinese-speaking Muslim villages occur in random mixtures
they exhibit distinctive styles of life which find visual symbols in the archi
tecture of religious buildings and in their different ways of disposing of th
dead. In occupation there is little to choose between the Chinese and th
Tibetan peasant farmer: both grow barley, some wheat, soy beans and peas
both keep some livestock, and supply wood to the towns. Even architecturall
the villages look much alike. The reason is that the Chinese farmer has adopte
the Tibetan house, which is a two-storey, fortlike timber structure much
superior to the Chinese house. On the other hand the superiority of the heate
Chinese bed, the *k'ang*, is recognized by the Tibetans and adopted by them.

Near the upper limit of agriculture (10,000 feet), where the superiority o
the Tibetan villager's adaptation to environment becomes evident, the Chinese
is willing to modify his own customs to the extent of changing his style o
housing and dress. But the flexible attitude does not apply to religious practices. The Tibetans are Buddhists who owe allegiance to Lhasa, although a
this distance from the centre of Lamaism they also defer to the local mountain
gods and build shrines on mountain tops to the fearsome beings of the aboriginal Bon religion. The Chinese are fundamentally ancestor-worshippers. The
grave mound is sacrosanct to the Chinese but viewed with dread by the Tibe-

ans who throw their dead into the mountain streams or expose them to the vultures.

Above the mountain valleys, on the grass-covered shoulders of the Tibetan plateau, is the domain of the nomadic herders. Some of the nomadic tribes have constructed permanent winter quarters that are made up of sod houses or huts with sod walls and tent roofs. The herders move with their livestock of yak (which carry the heavy black tents used for encampment), cattle, horses, and sheep from six to nine times in the course of a year. It would seem a rather bleak and strenuous life compared with that of the Tibetan villager who lives in his substantial two-storeyed house in the valley. Yet the villager regards it as a more satisfying way of life and not infrequently he abandons farming to become a nomad.

To this sketch of the remarkable cultural diversity of the Tibet–Kan-su borderland we must add the institution of lamaseries. About a dozen lamaseries occur in the mountain valleys alone, and approximately one-third of the males in the northeastern part of Tibet live in them.

MONGOLIA. The Mongolian frontier of China is an open plain or rolling country. For lack of a physical boundary, an artificial one – the Great Wall – was built. It serves for definition as much as for defence. It sets the Chinese domain and the sedentary agricultural way of life apart from the domain of the barbarians, who depend on their livestock and are migratory. The two contrasting economies fall on the two sides of a fluctuating climatic boundary: to the north precipitation is insufficient for the more intensive forms of agriculture, to the south it is adequate, in good years. The northern limit of extensive agriculture normally lies well to the north of the Great Wall. From the later part of the nineteenth century, Chinese farmers have encroached upon the steppeland of the nomads. Where the Chinese colonists have settled, the land 'retains almost nothing of its Mongolian character except the vigour of its air and the immense sweep of its distances'.[36]

It was the trader and the artisan, rather than the farmer, who pioneered this transformation. Their services and goods tended to lead to the breakdown of the self-sufficiency of the nomadic economy. Mongols found themselves in debt. Chinese traders, encouraged by Chinese officials, then negotiated for the purchase of the Mongol land; and this land was thrown open at once for settlement. Thus, according to Lattimore, it was not just the pressure of population that induced the Chinese farmers to advance into the steppe. The advance took place because it received the active support of provincial governments which preferred to collect taxes from the settled Chinese rather than from the evasive Mongols.[37]

The farmers transformed the landscape. At the outer fringe of agriculture cultivation took the form of scattered plots, but within a short distance to the south there appeared extensive and well-tilled fields of grain, oats, wheat barley, millet as well as rapeseed and small fields of potatoes, peas and beans The size of the average pioneering farm was large (about 30 acres) compared with farms on the North China plain, but the yield was low and became even lower after six to eight years of cultivation. A new feature was added to the wide-open Mongolian plains: the Chinese adobe village surrounded by a high wall which protected it against bandits, wild beasts and inclement weather.

A different type of colonization occurred along the great northern loop o the Huang Ho. The loop was regarded as the frontier at various stages in Chinese history. The Great Wall, as it existed from the late Chan-kuo period to the Han dynasties, lay to the north of the loop. On the loop itself military-agricultural colonies were established during the Ch'in, Han, and T'ang dynasties. Sharp geographical contrasts appear in the zone where the Huang Ho turns east at the foot of the Yin Shan. Here one can see in close juxta-position the denuded slopes of the low mountain range, the shallow lagoons the swamps and cultivated fields of the Huang Ho plain (known as the Hou-t'ao district), and the high sand dunes. A similar mixture of sand dunes, water and cultivated fields lies beyond the northeastern corner of the loop, in an area known as the Kuei-hua plain.

Until the later part of the nineteenth century Inner Mongolia, as also Man-churia, was closed by the Ch'ing (Manchu) government to Chinese settlers The policy of exclusion, however, had been relaxed during the 1860s. Chinese colonists filtered into the Huang Ho bend from northern Shan-hsi and Ho-pei The first of these were merchants who imported manufactured goods in ex-change for furs and hides. Then came the artisans, the small traders and poor farmers. Immigrants settled first on the Kuei-hua plain. From there, at the turn of the century, they moved westwards to the Hou-t'ao plain where they encountered colonists from the south; the latter were drawn into the area by the irrigation projects of the Roman Catholic mission of San-sheng-kung. Chinese population remained scanty and scattered, especially in the western area, until 1914, when Inner Mongolia was incorporated into China proper. But it was after 1923, by which time the railroad from Peking had extended as far west on the Huang Ho loop as Pao-t'ou, that families as well as single males entered the region, and Hou-t'ao became predominantly Chinese.[38]

Irrigated farming distinguishes agriculture along the Huang Ho loop from the type of extensive farming on the steppe. The chief grains along the loop are wheat and millet. In addition there are fields of water melons, soy beans, cabbages and other vegetables. Contrasting with the climatic aridity is the pervasive greenness of the irrigated landscape in the growing season: the green of crops and of willow groves hiding the villages and farm houses. A typical house of the poor, whether it stands alone or clustered together, is a flat-roofed mud hut with two rooms: one room is a combination of storehouse,

oolshed and kitchen; the other is the bedroom for the entire family. Prominent in the landscape are the large 'castles' of the wealthy landlords – features
that one does not find on the unirrigable steppe. The 'castle', as Schuyler
Cammann describes it, is 'a large farm, with the farmhouse and all its out-
buildings enclosed by a strong mud wall. The wall was crenellated and pierced
with loopholes for rifles. A high watchtower inside provided a vantage point
for sighting bandits, and the main gate lacked only a drawbridge to look
medieval European.'[39]

The Chinese moved into the Huang Ho loop of the Ordos desert at the
expense of the Mongol herders, who were pushed into pastures of lower and
lower quality. The traditional source of wealth, the sheep, gave way to the
hardier goat. The Mongolian yurt or *ger* is seldom seen. Schuyler Cammann,
who explored the area in 1945, had to make a special effort to find them. They
hide in the canyons and valleys of Yin Shan. In contrast to the modesty of the
gers are the large lamaseries and temples: these form by far the most striking
architectural monuments in Mongolia. The splendour of some of the temples
looks oddly dramatic in the bare landscape. The Beilighe temple, for example,
is a complex of large, square, pink and white buildings that stand above a high
natural terrace. Behind the terrace, and forming a backdrop to the temple, are
the deeply gashed red cliffs of Yin Shan. The vast Bayan Shanda-in Sume
monastery stretches out against the yellow sand of a hillside. Religious architecture is Tibetan, although occasionally the smaller temples have roofs in the
Chinese style. The large buildings, however, are flat-roofed structures of one
to three storeys, elegantly plain individually, but together they make an imposing complex. Another feature that distinguishes the Mongolian lamaseries
from the Chinese Buddhist temples is that the land around them is unusually
bare. Not only do the Mongolian lamaseries lack trees but even the grass in
their neighbourhood looks poor, perhaps the result of overgrazing by the herds
of sheep and goats belonging to the temples.[40]

MANCHURIA. From the end of the nineteenth to the early decades of the
twentieth century the Tibetan frontier of Chinese settlements has seen change
only in the form of local advances and local retreats in a region of rugged,
compartmentalized topography. The Mongolian frontier, in the same period,
saw more decisive advances of Chinese settlement into the steppe and along
the Huang Ho loop. But these probes beyond the Great Wall had taken place
repeatedly in the past. We do not seem to be witnessing here anything radically
new. By contrast the 'floodtide' of immigration into the Central Manchurian
plain in the early part of the twentieth century was a singularly impressive
event. It is the last sizeable piece of 'virgin' land to be opened up to agriculture
in eastern Asia, and it was settled by some 20 million people in a couple of
decades.

Central Manchuria is a gently undulating lowland of some 138,000 squar
miles, surrounded by a forested upland rim. Although the lowland is on
physiographic unit, its drainage is in opposite directions: rivers in the norther
segment flow into the Sungari, which flows northeastwards into the Amu
River: the southern segment drains into the Liao Ho, which flows south int
Po Hai. Various peoples have occupied the several physiographic units o
Manchuria. The western portion belonged to the Mongols. (It is now a par
of the Inner Mongolian Autonomous Region.) Out of it came the Khitan wh
founded the Liao dynasty in China in the tenth century. The northern an
eastern portions of Manchuria, largely forested country, were the home of th
Tungus. Out of this region came the Jurchen, who established the Chi
dynasty (1115–1234), and the Manchu, who established the Ch'ing dynasty
the last imperial house in China. The southern portion of Manchuria, includin
the lower Liao Ho basin and Liao-tung peninsula, were occupied by th
Chinese since at least the third century B.C. It is what Owen Lattimore call
'the Chinese Pale'.[41] Culturally the lower Liao Ho basin is an integral par
of the North China plain: in landscape, in crops and settlement pattern littl
change can be seen as one moves north into the Chinese Pale through th
narrow land corridor at Shan-hai-kuan or across Po Hai from Shan-tung.

It may seem strange that for so long the Chinese settlers stayed essentiall
within the Pale and made little effort to colonize the fertile soils of Centra
Manchuria; and that, in the early decades of the twentieth century, the slow
permeation around the edges of the nucleus and the odd splashes into remote
corners turned suddenly into a strong flow of immigrants. Several facts are
helpful in putting this phenomenon in perspective. One is the physical fact tha
north of the lower Liao Ho basin winter temperatures are increasingly sever
and the length of the growing season shortens. The northward course of river
in the northern segment of the Central Manchurian plain may also have dis-
pirited the Chinese immigrant whose sentimental ties, even after long sojour
in a new country, remain with his old home in Shan-tung or Ho-pei to th
south. Unlike the Western pioneer the Chinese frontiersman (as Lattimor
puts it) has his back to the frontier.[42]

The Chinese moves from his homeland with the greatest reluctance. Colonization of the tropical South took place largely under constraint: the constraint of governmental policy, and the constraint of nomadic invasions, civil
unrest, rebellions and natural disasters that periodically afflicted the North
Yet the South is attractive from the viewpoint of potential agricultural productivity. The northern border is not only less attractive agriculturally but i
is identified in the Chinese mind with the unruly barbarians – with a bare land
of cold wind, loneliness, and bleached bones. There is also the fact that North
China did not seriously feel the 'pressure of population' until population began
to increase rapidly, which was sometime near the opening of the eighteenth

entury. But the Manchurian grasslands were then reserved as the hunting ground of the Manchus; they were closed to the Chinese farmer. In the past Chinese governments have from time to time compelled the people to settle the marginal lands of the northern frontier. The Manchu government, by contrast, forbade the Chinese from making any such move.

Chinese migration into the untilled lands of Manchuria may be seen as a consequence of outside pressure – pressure from the two newly modernized nations of Russia and Japan. Russian designs on the Amur and Ussuri river basins were evident in the middle of the nineteenth century. The Manchus responded to the threat by opening the rich plain north of Harbin to Chinese settlement. The pressure continued. Russia obtained a concession to build the so-called Chinese Eastern Railway across Manchuria to her Pacific port of Vladivostok in 1898, and then the branch line south from Harbin to the tip of the Liao-tung peninsula. The Russian-controlled railway company had political and economic powers over a strip of land several miles wide along the lines. It built the city of Harbin, developed a railway town at Mukden (Shen-yang), and also Port Arthur and Dairen as Russian ports. Japan's interest in Manchuria was whetted by her victory over Russia in the war of 1904–5. The southern branch of the Chinese Eastern Railway came under Japanese control and was renamed the South Manchurian Railway. Japan then invested heavily in the development of resources – coal, iron ore, and agricultural land – to her immense profit. Great progress was made under Japanese direction in extending the railway mileage, in opening up new land for settlement, in mining, and in building up a great iron-and-steel industrial complex.

Against this background of Russo-Japanese designs on Manchuria and what they were able to do for the country economically the Manchu government recognized the urgent need to fill this rich and sparsely settled land with Chinese farmers. All legal bans to Chinese immigration were lifted by 1907 when Manchuria became the three northeastern provinces, and an integral part of China. Railways enabled the immigrants to disperse northwards from the lower Liao Ho basin. Modern exploitation of the immense resources of Manchuria demanded men. At the same time cumulative disasters within China made emigration seem less unattractive. Population in Manchuria rose with remarkable rapidity, from an estimated 15 million in 1910 to more than 30 million in 1931, the year of the Japanese invasion. The maximum rate of immigration was in the years 1927, 1928 and 1929, in each of which more than a million people entered Manchuria.[43] Population continued to rise under Japanese rule to about 44 million in 1940. Acreage in cultivated land rose at a matching rate: from 16·5 million acres in 1915, and 31·3 million acres in 1932, to 40·4 million acres in 1950.[44] By 1950 the best lands were already in use and large areas of virgin soil could be found only in the cold north and the dry west.

The Manchurian landscape evolved very rapidly. Settlements and farms were established along the main railways and their numerous branches Of the rivers the Nonni and the Sungari were followed by immigrants as they pushed northwards into the forests and into uninhabited country. Unlike China proper, agricultural Manchuria lived by the export of its produce Farms close to the service of railways and river steamers had therefore an immense advantage over those that were only slightly farther away. One crop, however, fetched such a high price that it could withstand the cost of distant transportation; this was opium. It played an important part in opening the remote corners of the northern frontier. The settlement of the lower Sungari River, from San-hsing to the Amur, was due chiefly to the success of opium cultivation. Opium first made it profitable to increase steamer services, and then the better transport made it profitable to produce more wheat and soy beans.

Other remote spots along the Amur River were settled because of the exceptionally favourable terms that the government offered. In the uninhabited country, villages were marked out at 20 to 30 miles apart. Building timber was transported to these sites under government supervision. When the settlers arrived they could immediately proceed to build their own houses.[45] Expansion along the western frontier encroached upon the grazing land of the Mongols The stages of penetration were similar to that which had taken place in Inner Mongolia. Traders and officers took the initiative of buying up or expropriating land from the Mongols; it was then open to settlement. New villages were constructed and old ones abandoned in the westward move. This sometimes meant changing good soils for less good ones in a drier climate. However, the farms in the new land were several times bigger and the migrating farmer could sell his developed land at a profit.

The crops that were grown and their distribution reflected the operation of market demand and of climate. The profitability of opium has already been mentioned. Other export crops were sugar-beet, introduced by the Russians, and the immensely successful soy bean, fostered by the Japanese. The soy bean crop reached its greatest relative and absolute importance in the northern part of the Manchurian plain. It was more tolerant of the cooler and shorter growing season than *kaoliang* (sorghum) which required at least 150 frostless days for optimum growth and which reached its greatest importance in southern Manchuria. The drought-tolerant Italian millet pioneered the semi-arid western lands, whereas spring-sown wheat opened up the north. The climatic extremes of northern Manchuria were met by planting experimentally many varieties of wheat in order to find the most resistant strains. They were also met by special methods of cultivation. Thus, to minimize soil erosion in spring from the strong prevailing southwest winds, narrow furrows were tilled in the open land parallel to the wind direction.[46]

Impact of the West

The Chinese landscape is a material expression of Chinese culture. And in so far as the Chinese culture has been enriched by foreign influences, so has the Chinese landscape. But these additions have not been (in most cases) sufficiently important in any period to distort the shape of Chinese culture and alter its course of development. Buddhism was an exception. It added another dimension to Chinese thinking and enriched Chinese institutional life by giving rise to, for example, hostels for travellers and hospitals for the poor. It added to the landscape by introducing such new architectural elements as temples and pagodas. However, Buddhism eventually became a part – even an essential ingredient – of the Chinese cultural tradition. The artfully placed pagoda is very much at home in the Chinese scene.

In the nineteenth century, another alien thought and style of life impinged on China. Unlike Buddhism in the past this new culture was backed by vast economic and military power. It threatened not to add to but to displace the traditional Chinese culture. It introduced unassimilable elements to the Chinese landscape.

In Manchuria we have already taken note of some of the effects of the impact: the railways, the Russian-styled city of Harbin, mechanized farms, coal-mines and heavy, motorized industries were some of the new elements of the landscape. But it was not from the continental border that the new technologies and ethos first penetrated into China. The Russians were encouraged to be rapacious because China's feebleness had already been demonstrated in her futile attempts to resist pressure from Britain and France along the coast. It was along China's coastal borders that the first pockets of aggressive Western culture found root. Unlike the past these new infusions appeared under the panoply of force and they claimed not only military but cultural superiority over their decaying host. China's humiliating defeat in the Anglo-Chinese war of 1840–42 led to the signing of the Treaty of Nan-ching (Nanking) which opened Shanghai, Ning-po, Fu-chou and Hsia-men (Amoy) to foreign trade. These, the earliest footholds of Western commercialism, spread first along the coast and later inland by way of the Yangtze River so that at the end of the nineteenth century more than forty treaty ports were established in China.

Early industrialization

The response of the Ch'ing government to the West's show of force was equivocal. On the one hand, it reasserted the superiority of the Confucian tradition; on the other, it acknowledged the challenge of the West by making a few feeble efforts at developing modern arsenals and the essential industries to support them. As early as 1855 small arsenals were built in Chiang-hsi province. The industrial project at Shanghai, established in 1865, eventually produced small naval vessels, as well as rifles, cannons, gunpowder and cartridges. It was seen that defence required modern transport, communication and supporting industries.

A steamship company and telegraph lines to furnish modern transport and communications facilities were undertaken. In what seems a logical sequence a coal-mine was opened in Chihli (present-day Hopei) in 1877 to furnish fuel for the newly erected arsenals and the steamship line. Transportation of the coal from the pithead to a suitable port led to the construction of China's first railroad. A gold-mine was opened in Manchuria in the Amur River region in 1887 which was intended to help pay for Li Hung-chang's Westernization projects. Both Li and the governor-general at Wuchang Chang Chih-tung (1837–1909), undertook to sponsor textile mills which would furnish cloth for their troops and revenue for their other projects. Chang erected an iron and steel works at Hanyang in Central China to provide raw material for his arsenals and to manufacture rails for a trunk line connecting Peking and Hankow. And gradually flour milling, cotton spinning and weaving, silk reeling, and other consumer-goods industries were inaugurated in the principal cities of the coastal province.[47]

South Manchuria's 'industrial landscape'

Industrialization in China was a haphazard and half-hearted affair compared with what Japan was prepared to do and had achieved in the same period. Coal-mines, ironworks, textile and food-processing factories broke out in clean-edged spots rather than in rashes. Moreover the national pattern was lop-sided. Mechanized industries were overwhelmingly concentrated along the coast, and around the prosperous treaty ports in particular.

Before the Second World War only one part of China could claim to have an 'industrial landscape' of any size and that was southern Manchuria. It had been developed by the Japanese. Although southern Manchuria was far from being the richest mineral region in China, it provided at one time 'about half the coal, a third of the copper, nine-tenths of the steel, and the bulk of the lead, zinc, aluminium and magnesium. Here, too, was most of the heavy industry in the entire country.'[48] The lower Liao Ho basin contained the following elements of an industrial landscape: it had a railway net centred on Mukden (Shen-yang), which was in fact the only 'net' in China. A number of small but highly productive coal basins formed the resource base of several industries. Fu-shun, east of Mukden, was the largest coal-mine in China. Open-pit operations had produced a monumental hollow, some 4 miles long, 1 mile wide, and reaching to a depth of 500 feet. Pockets of medium-grade iron ore also occur and were exploited at Tung-pien-tao, near the Ya-lu River, at Miao-erh-kou on the Shen-yang–Antung railway, and at An-shan. The industry used local iron ore, and coal from Fu-shun and Peng-hsi-hu. Under Japanese direction An-shan ranked among the dozen or so largest iron-and-steel centres in the world. Pig-iron production rose from 370,000 metric tons in 1932 to 1,725,000 metric tons in 1943. An-shan's contribution to Manchuria's total output was 78 per cent. Besides An-shan, two other centres operated in the east Manchurian uplands, Peng-hsi-hu and Tung-pien-tao, and both drew upon local resources of coal and iron ore.[49]

Urban manufacturing

Outside of southern Manchuria iron and steel works are all quite modest operations. One of the more important has already been mentioned. This was Han-yang, established by Chang Chih-tung (1837–1909), beside the Yangtze River in central China. Despite accessibility and the presence of rich local ore the Han-yang steel centre never prospered. Far more successful than the heavy industries, which required large capital investment, were the food-processing, textile and other consumer goods industries. These could be housed in small factories, only lightly mechanized; they could take advantage of the vast pool of cheap labour in the cities and of an inexhaustible market. Excluding Manchuria, industrialization in China prior to the Second World War was largely a phenomenon of the coastal cities. The beginning of urban manufacturing may be traced to the conclusion of the Sino-Japanese war and the signing of the Treaty of Shimonoseki in 1898. The treaty allowed all foreigners to establish manufacturing industries in China. Numerous factories were founded by the Japanese, the Germans, the British and the Americans in treaty ports. Shanghai experienced its first industrial boom. A second one occurred during and after the First World War when the flow of manufactured goods from Europe slackened.[50] By the end of the First World War most of the factories in Shanghai were under Chinese management. Shanghai itself became by far the most important manufacturing centre in China. Half of the country's mechanized factories were small-scale operations which could be housed in private houses or dwellings that needed only slight modification to accommodate the machinery driven by electric power. Workers slept on the premises. Crowding was extreme. Some enterprises were so small that they occupied only one room.[51]

Treaty ports

The impact of the West on the landscape of China was most evident in the treaty ports where foreigners naturally congregated. By their efforts little enclaves of the Occident were grafted on the coast of China, next to her own crowded cities. Foreigners established themselves in the international Concessions. There they built residences that sentimentally duplicated the styles of ideal homes in their respective countries, and large business structures that looked aggressively un-Chinese. At the time when China was opened to foreign trade many of her coastal cities were smaller than they were in the twelfth and thirteenth centuries, and some were in advanced stages of decay. They had lost the vigour and glamour that so impressed early European travellers like Marco Polo and Friar Odoric. They retained their battered walls, their narrow, crowded, smelly streets in the south, and broad, dusty avenues surrounded by mud houses and blank peeling walls in the north. By contrast the European quarters were clean and attractive. Certainly the Europeans thought so.

At the end of the nineteenth century, the Belgian consul in Tientsin compared the European town in the Concessions with an old Chinese city. In the European town, 'The streets are lit by gas, well swept, macadamised, bordered by trees and European-styled houses of grey brick. . . . Together it gives one the impression of a small provincial town.' When one left the European quarter for the Chinese city one was struck by the contrast. 'On the one side, order, cleanliness and little traffic; on the other, filth, disorder, crowd and noise . . .'[52]

The single most impressive monument to Western commercial enterprise in China is the Bund in Shanghai. The Bund consists of a curtain of tall, monolithic buildings that housed the great banks, insurance companies and heavily capitalized firms. It rises as a magnificent front above the broad tree-lined street which fringes the Whangpoo River. In 1893 the curtain of sky-scrapers was yet to be raised, although there already existed some impressive buildings belonging to wealthy firms. A British missionary, in that year of jubilee marking the fiftieth anniversary of the founding of foreign settlements, was moved to say:

Shanghai is the centre of our higher civilization and Christian influence for all of China. We are here in the midst of a people proud and prejudiced in favour of their ancient line of things, and what have we introduced amongst them, for their benefit as well as our own? We might well point to the homes we have formed here. . . . How different is this from what we know to be characteristic of Chinese homes! In front also we have these beautiful *hongs* (trading firms) for the transaction of business, and we may especially remark the Supreme Court, distinguished by the just and equitable conduct of legal matters, in striking contrast to what is represented to us as existing in other places.[53]

Treaty ports, on the whole, expanded at a faster rate than other cities. They were selected in the first place on account of their accessibility and superior transportation facilities. The commerce introduced by foreign traders, combined with the security and, at the same time, certain laxness in the execution of legal matters in the Concessions, encouraged Chinese businessmen to move in. But the increase in population was slow and fluctuating before industries

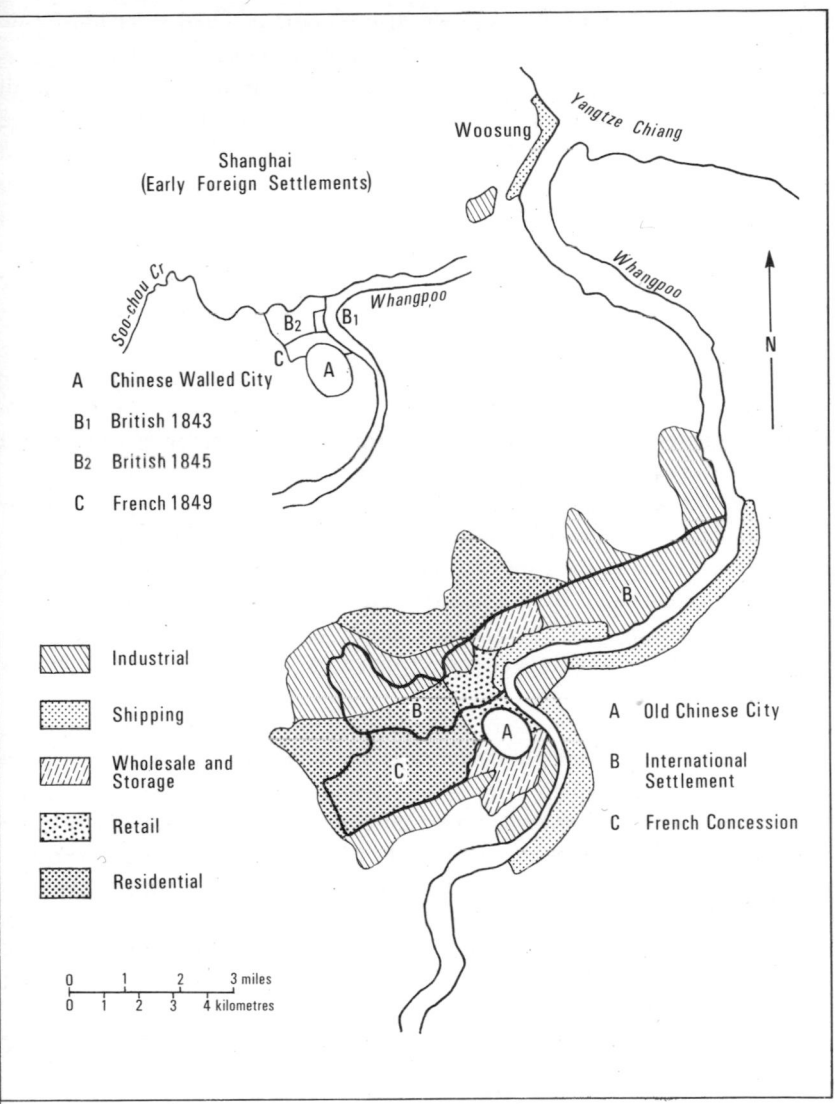

28. *Shanghai in 1936. (After Rhoads Murphey)*

were established. For example, until 1895 Shanghai was an exclusively trading city; its population never exceeded half a million. Rapid and accelerated gain in numbers followed the development of manufacturing after 1895; by 1936 Shanghai claimed some 3·5 million people (Fig. 28). Foreigners had always constituted only a minute portion of the total population. Shanghai's

International Settlement, for example, had more than 1,120,000 Chinese inhabitants in 1935, or more than 99·5 per cent of the Settlement's total population.[54] Foreign impact, direct and indirect, on the urban landscape was out of all proportion to the number of foreigners who actually resided in the city. I have already mentioned the skyscrapers along the 'un-Chinese' Bund, and could have pointed also to the large modern shipyards bordering the Whangpoo River, and to the tree-lined streets bordered by stolid Western-style homes in the French Concession. The International Settlement, by contrast, was extremely crowded (with densities of 300 to 500 persons per acre) and largely industrial. Instead of spacious factories there were rows and rows of small workshops separated by alleyways. Hygiene was minimal. In a relatively peaceful year for China, when the influx of poverty-stricken refugees to the safety of the city was small, the Shanghai Municipal Council collected 5,590 exposed corpses from the streets of the International Settlement alone. But if hygiene was minimal within the Settlement it was non-existent in the appalling slums that spilled to the north of its borders. Here a million people dwelt in squalid huts of bamboo and mud, with no piped water, no light, no drainage, no sewerage. Even in the French Concession it should be said that the air of respectability purveyed by fine homes and clean streets was misleading for, besides the wealthy foreigners and Chinese of good legal standing, there gathered also many wealthy Chinese criminals who profited from the laxness of the French authorities.

It is not possible to capture in a few words the atmosphere of Shanghai in the 1930s. Extreme cosmopolitanism was one ingredient: the staff of a good hotel must be prepared to cater to its clientele in half a dozen languages. Extremes of poverty and wealth was another: on a cold night one may be obliged to step over the inconveniently placed body of a beggar into the warm lushness of a first-rate restaurant. The worship of money and complete amorality seemed not just words in Shanghai but something that one could inhale, smell or touch as one walked down its crowded, colourful streets. Shanghai makes it clear that 'tension', 'richness of texture', 'excitement in sound and colour' are complimentary terms in the appraisal of a great work of art; but that a city, if it is to be liveable and humane, must strive for something less exotic.

Impact of modernized cities on countryside
Rhoads Murphey, in his book on Shanghai, regards the boundary between that city and its countryside as one of the sharpest and most dramatic in the world (Fig. 29).

Even in 1941 it was still possible to walk from the centre of the Bund to the unchanged agricultural countryside in three or four hours. It was less than ten miles, and the rice paddies and peasant villages could be seen clearly from any of the city's tall buildings. . . . Traditional China continued unbroken almost to the limits of the foreign settlements.[55]

The sharpness of the boundary gave one the initial impression that Shanghai, like other treaty ports, exerted little influence on the surrounding country. This impression is of course a mistaken one. Westernized coastal cities in China did not send tentacles of roads, railways and suburban sprawls into the countryside: communication with their hinterlands was achieved mostly by small boats moving back and forth over complicated networks of canals and streams. The cities themselves may have nets of paved roads suitable for motor vehicles but these terminated abruptly at the city boundaries. Shanghai, with 3·5 million people in 1936, had only two rail lines and very few serviceable roads. On the other hand it had an immense mileage of small waterways as well as the Yangtze River itself. The impact of the city on the immediate hinterland was to intensify land use. The first ring of farms was devoted to market-gardening, and the next ring to rice cultivation. The continued high level of

29. *New housing project in Shanghai in the post-1949 era. Note the sharp boundary between the new apartment houses and the fields, narrow paths and villages beyond*

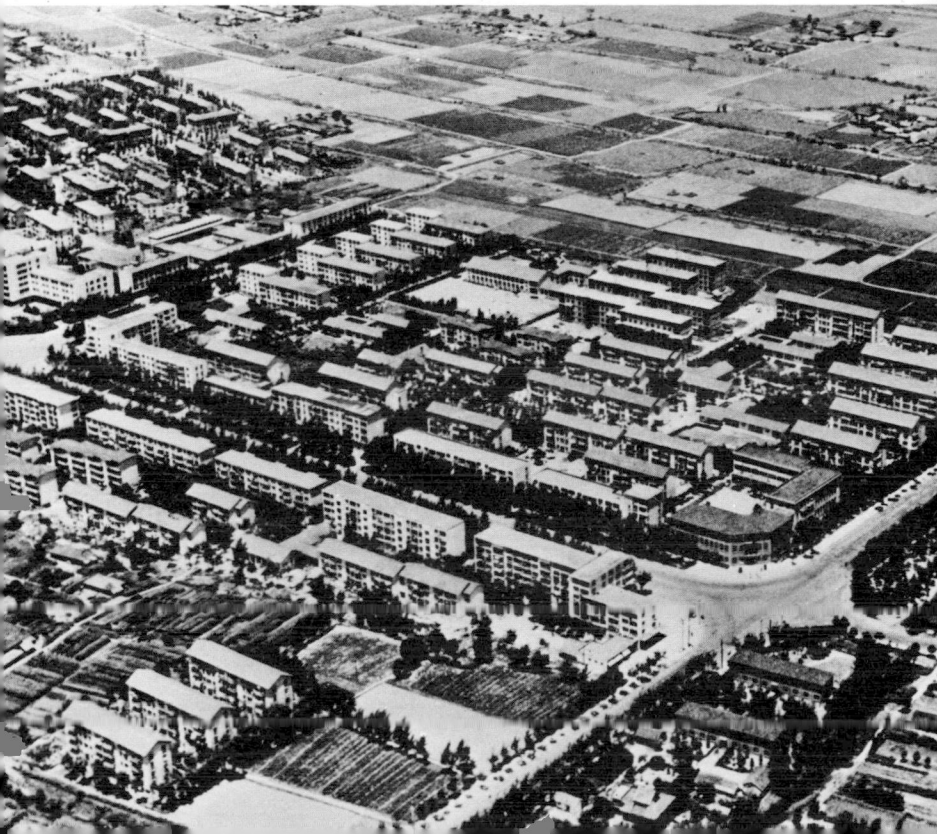

productivity in these intensively worked fields was made possible by the abundant supply of city manure. Industries in the cities created demand for raw materials. Cotton and silk factories in Shanghai stimulated cotton-growing in Chiang-su province and silk production in the numerous small villages of the delta.

However, beyond the immediate fringe the impact of the city on the countryside clearly depends on the ease of transportation. Shanghai's superiority over other cities rested on the relative ease with which it could communicate with its vast market. But it was a relative superiority. Waterways were subject to seasonal fluctuations. Conveyance of goods on the Yangtze River above I-chang, and on the Yangtze's tributaries, contained a large element of risk. Beyond the main waterways, therefore, the countryside remained little affected. Where water arteries were limited or non-existent the size of the area under the influence of a city must depend on the quality and extent of its roads and railways. Now, China's railway pattern was extremely sparse: only 2 miles per 100,000 people as compared with 11 for India and 261 for the United States.[56] Clearly railway transportation has had negligible influence on the countryside. As to roads, total mileage in the 1920s had been variously estimated to be from 9,000 to nearly 35,000! The criterion as to what might pass for a motor road, as distinct from a deeply rutted cart-track, was evidently very lax. Before 1920 perhaps no more than a hundred miles of improved road suitable for motor traffic had been constructed, and these were principally in the vicinity of Peking, Ch'ing-tao, and some other treaty ports. After 1920 the pace of road-building greatly increased. The roads were used mainly for public transportation in rickety buses. Nonetheless the buses proved to be very popular, especially for travelling between rural towns, for they were not only much faster but much cheaper and safer (from the lesser bandits) than going about by the old springless carts.

What would be the effect of modern transportation on the economy and appearance of the countryside? The countryside, as we have seen, may be described as consisting of mosaics of marketing areas each of which had a market centre surrounded by a cluster of villages. All the villages were within easy walking distance of the central market. One immediate effect of modern transportation and modern industries on the countryside appears to be this: it strengthened the old marketing system.[57] Markets grew in size, more marketing-days were established, and new market centres were founded. This could happen long before roads from the city reached even the larger market towns. The existence of a modernized city appears to have the effect of sending successive waves of commercialization within its trading area. These waves travelled well ahead of the extending network of roads. Villages and their small markets responded by intensifying their activity; and if new markets had to be established to accommodate this, then the size of the marketing areas near a city might actually contract. However, as the road net expanded to include some of the larger market towns, these would acquire distinct advantages over the small markets not so served; villagers would find it as quick to go to the larger market by way of the road as to the smaller market by way of a winding path. The smaller markets declined and eventually disappeared; while the large market towns became modern trading centres with expanding trading areas. This process, according to G. William Skinner,[58] was how modernization in the cities (for example, the treaty port of Ning-po) steadily transformed the economic landscapes of the surrounding countryside.

Chapter 9
Communist ideology and landscape

Communist China provides a notable illustration of how the espousal of new social values can quickly alter the face of a nation. Even in the non-Western world change is in itself a banal fact. The appearance of skyscrapers side by side with traditional buildings, the invasion of coastal cities by the paraphernalia of international commerce, the spread of modern transport networks into the interior and the gradual diffusion of their impact on the subsistence economy of the tradition-bound hinterlands are aspects of the progressive infiltration of the world by Western technological and commercial values. The process takes place from selected spots, usually coastal, and along the veins of modern communication. Cities yield first, and as centres of new ventures they become sharply differentiated from the traditional ways of the countryside.

Such a dichotomized economy and landscape has evolved in China in the last hundred years. Its basic features are far from unique for they are shared by other underdeveloped countries in various stages of industrialization. What has taken place in China in the last twenty years is more out of the common in that the countryside has been transformed as radically as the cities. The process of change was not a slow diffusion from a few nodes and routes in obedience to the operation of economic laws, but revolutionary and doctrinaire; a force, fundamentally ideological in nature, has been let loose and its effects permeated rapidly the entire social fabric of the nation. The Chinese case is unique less in the speed of the transformation from one type of society to another than in the fact that it occurred in a vast and densely populated backward country. It is reasonable to believe that an experience of this order must leave a permanent mark on the course of China's future development, but whether the more doctrinaire forms of change can be maintained is very much open to question.

Stages in agrarian reform

Before we take note of the new features in the landscape, let us first review the stages in the transformation of Chinese agrarian society; the stages between the China of 1949, when a Communist government was established in Peking, and the China of the mid-1960s, by which time the vaulting ambitions of the year of the Great Leap Forward have subsided – at least for the time being. Pre-Communist China was largely a country of tiny fragmented farms, the average size of which was only 3·5 acres. Tenancy varied from region to region. In North China 76 per cent of the farmers fully owned their land whereas in South China the proportion was only 38 per cent. The basic source of livelihood and the ultimate source of security for the peasant farmer was his land. The deep attachment to the tiny plot expressed need as much as sentiment. By the end of 1958 China was metamorphosed into a country of communes; their average size exceeded 75 square miles. The farmer lost his land and found himself a worker in an economic unit that may include several thousand households. His security no longer lay in the personal possession of land but rested in his membership in an enlarged social group.

The change in the first decade was thus revolutionary. It proceeded, however, by psychologically reassuring steps. The first step quickly won the sympathy of China's 300 million land-starved peasants, for it consisted in redistributing the 113·6 million acres of agricultural land. If China had many large estates operated by overseers in control of labour teams, the effect of wholesale land redistribution on the countryside would have been dramatic. But this was not the case; no huge, little-used estates existed to be broken up. In South China, where farms were exceptionally small, even landlords may own no more than 20 or 30 acres of land, most of which would be divided into minute holdings among tenant farmers. Land reform meant in most cases the transference of title deeds to the small farmer, and minor adjustments in property lines. Landlords disappeared as a class. Tenant farmers and landless peasants had at last the immense satisfaction of working on their own property. A great social reform had occurred but it left little visible impact on the landscape; China remained a country of tiny fragmented farms.

Land reform proper was quickly followed by the organization of groups of five to eight farm households into mutual-aid teams. Farmers were persuaded to pool their labour during peak seasons and, in general, to co-ordinate their agricultural and non-agricultural activities so as to solve the problems of seasonal unemployment and labour shortage. This step again had little effect on the landscape. The next step involved the organization of fixed neighbourhoods, which were characteristically found in China's larger villages, into agricultural producers' co-operatives. Each co-operative may include thirty to forty households. Member households would agree to pool their land and to work according to some central plan that was designed to meet the targets set by the government. One effect of this move on the landscape was the consolidation of the extremely fragmented and uneconomic holdings. By the end of 1955, 63 per cent of peasant households had been grouped into co-operatives. Between 1956 and 1957, co-operatives were consolidated into collective farms which in most cases corresponded to the villages, except where the village

30. *Farms and fragmented farmsteads in South China before consolidation into larger units. Team-work, however, has already been introduced*

size was far below norm. Land became the property of the collective. Rent was no longer paid to the previous owners. The farmer, however, retained private plots as well as barnyard animals and small implements.[1] Since the collective farms correspond to pre-existent villages, collectivization had the effect of accentuating the localism of villagers. By the summer of 1958 there were some 750,000 collective farms in all China.[2]

In traditional China, the socio-economic unit above the village was the area served by the small market town. On the average some eighteen to twenty villages lay within the local marketing area. Its size varied from less than 10 square miles in fertile land close to a city to more than 50 square miles in mountainous or dry regions. During the Great Leap Forward of 1958 the Communist planners took a great leap over the local marketing community and carved an artificial unit nearly three times as large. Rapid merging of the collectives created some 24,000 communes. These ranged enormously in size, from huge communes in the non-agricultural North and Northwest to an average area of c. 77 square miles in agricultural China. In the number of households per commune, the figure varied from less than 1,700 in non-agricultural China to more than 8,000 for the densely settled and productive eastern provinces.[3] Why did the planners aim at a size for the commune so far above that of the local marketing area? One reason may be ideological: the desire to break down the narrow socio-economic outlook of the farmer, the small merchant and the artisan of traditional China. But the rapid conversion of collective farms, based on the traditional socio-economic unit of the village, to huge artificial communes exerted a great strain on the economy; communes could not be maintained in the form in which they were created in 1958 and 1959. By 1961 the subdivision of communes was well under way, and by 1963 the number of communes had been increased to 74,000.[4] The interest of this figure, as Skinner points out, is that it corresponds roughly to the total number of local marketing areas. In Communist China as elsewhere ideology must occasionally yield to the laws of distance and of the market.

Consolidation of holdings began with the formation of agricultural co-operatives, and continued as the higher stages of collectivization were established. Over the flat plains of North China landscapes took on a new geometry. Small fields have gone; the shrub, tree or dyke that marked property boundaries was ploughed out, and so also the numerous trails that led from one tiny plot to another; graveyards which once competed for land with the dire needs of the living on every owner's lot have disappeared, and with them the fine trees that provided shade (Fig. 31). Instead of a patchwork of fields, growing each a different crop and presenting a rich palette of browns, yellows and shades of green, we are likely to encounter a vast unbroken sea of wheat extending to the horizon (Fig. 31). Villages on the North China plain are distributed a mile or so apart; the smaller ones have been combined to form a higher co-operative,

31. Ploughed field east of Chi-nan in Shan-tung province. Disappearance of fragmented plots

though they remain as separate settlements. In South China change in the rural scene is less revolutionary. Grave mounds as well as villages are located on hillsides and dry terraces or on dykes so that they do not encroach on good farmland, and therefore they need not be removed. Land is pooled, but in the more rugged parts of South China the landscape remains fragmented, for the parcellation reflects less the system of land ownership than the adaptation of the water needs of rice culture to the physical environment. The small rice terraces on the hillslopes cannot be mechanized. On the other hand, where the flat plains and deltas of central and South China do permit team work and modest mechanization, the consolidation of fields has taken place – though on a more limited scale than one can see in the North (Fig. 32).

Keith Buchanan visited the Canton delta area in 1964; his description of four communes there gives us some clue as to the character of rural and surburban life in South China at a time when the feverish ideals of 1958 have yielded to the cooler, more practical models born of experience. The Canton communes vary in size from 4,000 acres to 50,000 acres. The largest commune, Fa-tung, lies on the hilly margin of the deltaic plain and has the lowest population density of 1 person per acre. For all four communes the average number of people per

32. Consolidated rice-fields in Hu-pei province, central Yangtze valley

acre of cultivated land is 5. A small portion of the population is engaged in industries or augments its income from remittances from relatives overseas, but 90 per cent of the people depend on farming or fishing for their livelihood. 'It is only by the most meticulous and labour-intensive garden cultivation, involving the use of every scrap of land and, in the case of vegetables, skilful rotations giving six to eight crops a year, that such a high density of population can be sustained.'[5] The most impressive achievement of the communes is the effective control and utilization of the water resources. Here the Chinese have displayed their mastery over nature, their ability to transform the landscape in short order, with a minimum of modern machinery and technical advice. The commune of Xinjiao, for example, was formerly at the mercy of the Pearl River floods but between 1959 and 1960 a major dyke was built which freed 6,000 acres from the flood menace. The construction involved the shifting of 700,000 cubic metres of earth.[6] Another achievement in the years since the establishment of the communes is to push up crop yields through the heavy application of the traditional 'natural' fertilizers, the increasing use of chemical fertilizers (although this is still on a very minor scale), the use of improved seeds and the application of new techniques such as the one that reduces the ditch/ridge ratio. The third achievement is in rural electrification and the consequent spread of rural industries, powered by small generators, through the countryside. The industrial sector is generally under the direct control of the communes. The workshops produce a great variety of goods, from pipes and tiles, rice bowls and tea mugs to simple agricultural machinery and the small parts that are necessary to keep the lorries and tractors in operation.

However, in 1964 private ownership and the family plot have not totally disappeared. Much of the poultry-rearing and part of the pig-rearing is in the care of the individual peasant family. And individual plots, in size about one-twelfth of an acre per family, together amount to some 4–5 per cent of the total cultivated area. These individual plots 'have been carved out along the edges of the fields and the reservoirs, indeed, have been fitted in wherever a scrap of cultivable land could be found'.[7]

Two villages in transition

Two villages, one on the dry loess plateau of northern Shen-hsi and the other on the wet deltaic plain of the Yangtze, may now be described as examples of the kinds of change in local life and scene that took place in the years before and after the Communist take-over. Liu-ling was studied by the Swedish journalist Jan Myrdal who spent a month in close association with the villagers in 1962. His book, *Report from a Chinese Village*, portrays in vivid detail the effect of the Communist revolution on one small community. The detail, however, is not of the kind that enables one to reconstruct the field pattern and the land ownership system of the past and how they have been transformed to fit with the new socio-economic doctrines of China after 1949; it is of the kind that one normally finds in a good novel, personal and tragic, illuminating the unique as well as the cyclic events of time.

Liu-ling in 1962 is a small community of fifty-two households.[8] It is located in a characteristic loess topography of small flat-floored valleys of great fertility, and hills draped in loess which have been deeply gullied here and there to produce dramatic sculptural forms. Cave dwellings appear to be the norm. They are dug into the loess patches on the hillsides and along valley slopes to produce a multi-levelled village. The main crops are millet and winter wheat. The winters are cold, dry and dusty. Frost often damages winter wheat. Drought, frost, and hail are indeed a constant menace, and crop failure is nothing unusual. The extreme hardship of the peasant farmer was compounded of the fickleness of nature and the inadequacy of land to support life much above the subsistence level even in good years. In the past a poor peasant may possess only 10 *mu* (1·65 acres) of land, and that of indifferent quality high up on the hillsides. Some peasants had 100 *mu*, which would have counted as a large property even for landlords in South China. But 100 *mu* would not have sufficed to support a family in northern Shen-hsi if they were in fragments, difficult of access, and did not include good valley soil. (Crop yield on the valley floor is almost ten times that on the hills.) A big landowner, on the other hand, had as much as 600 *mu* of land, and his property included both valley fields and hillside plots.[9]

Following land reform and collectivization the fragmented fields in the valley were combined into larger, more economic units and these were put under the care of labour brigades. The quilted landscape of the valley floor was simplified but it remained a complex mosaic on the hillslopes out of physical necessity, and this held whether the land belonged to the collective or to private families; for in 1962 the peasant farmers could clear hill land in their free time for their own use. Private plots exist even on the valley floor, on good soil, but they appear as bits and pieces in contrast to the common land worked with a tractor. Each person in Liu-ling is entitled to 0·4 *mu* of private land in the valley.[10] On it the peasants grow vegetables, melons, and tobacco. Although the social structure of Liu-ling has been revolutionized, a fact which is clearly reflected in the landscape, the yearly cycle of activities has remained essentially the same. So long as the inhabitants continue to depend on farming for their livelihood and so long as mechanization stays modest, the traditional rhythms of agricultural life – with the traditional festivals – will persist.

K'ai-hsien-kung is a village on the Yangtze delta, south of Lake Tai and about 80 miles west of Shanghai. The social anthropologist Fei Hsiao-tung studied the village in 1936 and reported his findings in a book called *Peasant*

Life in China. Since its publication in 1939 it has become a minor classic in sociological literature. In 1956 the Australian anthropologist W. R. Geddes paid a very brief visit to the same village. For lack of time his record is far from complete, and perhaps not entirely accurate, but it is of great value in that it shows us the sorts of innovation that have occurred in the two crucial decades. It is of interest to note that in 1936 Fei regarded K'ai-hsien-kung as a village community, which like so many others in China, was 'undergoing a tremendous process of change'.[11] It was not a quaint and stagnant community that Fei undertook to study but one that was beginning to respond to the fluctuations of the international market. Yet when Geddes visited it in 1956 he was the first European that the villagers had seen there in living memory. Notwithstanding the village's proximity to Shanghai it remained physically isolated to a remarkable degree. No motor road led to it in 1956; the quickest way to get there was by steamboat from the market town of Chen-tse.

K'ai-hsien-kung is one of the thousands of villages, located 1 or 2 miles apart, that bespatter the delta. For every several tens of villages there is a market town; produce of the countryside goes there and from it come the urban manufactured goods. In 1935 K'ai-hsien-kung's total population of 1,458 was distributed among 360 households.[12] Some 461 acres of land either belonged to the villagers or were rented by them. This meant that there was on the average only 1·2 acres per household, which barely sufficed to support a family of three or four. About 90 per cent of the population had less than 1·5 acres of land that they wholly owned. Many households had surplus labour but not enough land. They rented land and became tenants. The staple crop was rice. Wheat and rapeseed were grown in the drained fields in winter. A typical field was a very flat saucer-shaped piece of mud varying in size from a few acres to tens of acres. The field was subdivided into small plots by dykes and drainage ditches. The minute holding of a farmer consisted of scattered plots in the field and even fractions of a plot. A single fragment of property may measure only a few thousand square feet. As we have noted earlier, whatever the causes of this excessive fragmentation, under the old social order it had the merit of ensuring that a farmer got a variety of soils in different parts of the fields, and that at least some parts of his property received irrigation water early and were among the first to be drained.

In 1956 the population of K'ai-hsien-kung was 1,440. Thus the population of the village had shown no increase in twenty years. The average size of the family also remained the same – four persons – and the excess of males over females among children, characteristic of the village in 1935, became even more pronounced two decades later. In the past, the limitation on the number of children and the imbalance of the sex ratio were maintained by abortion and selective infanticide. Presumably, these practices continued despite thunderous governmental prohibitions. However, food supply had noticeably increased.

Geddes calculates the improvement in food production to be 25 per cent of that in 1935.[13]

K'ai-hsien-kung exemplified the earlier stages of agricultural transformation that we have seen for China as a whole; thus land reform and the experiment in mutual aid teams led to the pooling of holdings to form co-operatives; and by 1956 the village had reached the stage of the higher agricultural producers' co-operative or the collective. K'ai-hsien-kung's land was combined with that of two other smaller villages. In 1936 each household possessed some three to seven pieces of land, and sometimes it took the farmer twenty minutes to go by boat from one piece of property to another.

The draconian measure of public ownership removed at one stroke the wastefulness of time and energy and of land itself; wastefulness that is endemic in a system of private ownership in which excessive parcellation was a necessary evil. Following collectivization farmers found time to reclaim land that was formerly flooded; they were also able to increase the acreage under cultivation somewhat by removing the banks that separated individual properties and the trails that led to them. Contrary perhaps to expectations, land use became even more intensive under public ownership. Again one cause of this was the immediate release of time and energy; paddy land could be ploughed three times and harrowed six times, and the application of river mud as fertilizer was far more widespread than it had been in 1936. Moreover, by 1956 the buffalo-drawn plough could be used in the larger fields; twenty years ago man had to do all the work with the four-toothed iron hoe on his minuscule plot. And instead of the inefficient treadle pumps used of old, in 1956 all paddy land was irrigated by motor-powered air pumps.[14]

Afforestation, erosion control, and water conservancy

Forests occupy only 8·5 per cent of China. Two-thirds of the forested land is in the northeastern provinces and much of the remainder lies in the less accessible parts of the southwest. The total timber resource of the country amounts to no more than 5·4 billion cubic metres, which would last about thirty-five years. To conserve the forests and meet future needs for timber a national programme was announced at the end of 1955. It called for the planting of some 105 million hectares of land in the next twelve years so as to give China a forest cover of 20 per cent of its total surface. Earlier, in 1953, the Ministry of Forestry drew up a document which sought to establish organizations that would exercise fire control in the natural forests and pursue a vigorous programme of afforestation in the hills and wastelands. By the end of the first five-year plan (1957), the Chinese claimed to have planted more than 10 million hectares.[15]

The most ambitious project in this first flush of enthusiasm for tree-planting is the establishment of a 'great green wall' or shelter belt in the semi-arid country of northern and northeastern China. One tree belt is planted roughly parallel with the Great Wall, and extends from Chiu-ch'uan near its western limit for a thousand miles eastward to Yu-lin in Shen-hsi. Its average width is about 1 mile. Another forms a horseshoe around the margins of the central Manchurian plain. Although the shelter belts stretch over country with different soils and climates, yet throughout the chief limiting factor for tree growth is the lack of moisture. For this reason, relatively few species are involved in this gargantuan project. The principal species are the hardy *Populus simonii*, *Ulmus pumila*, *Salix matsudana*, and *Elaeagnus angustifolia*. In Manchuria the tree belts, 100 to 150 feet wide, cross one another to form diamond-shaped enclosures, each of which is about 38·5 square miles in area. Within the major enclosures smaller divisions are made, depending on the need of the crops for further protection against the wind. In parts of northern Shen-hsi and Kan-su, where the shelter belt has the primary function of checking sand movement, a solid barrier about 1 mile wide faces the desert.[16] The success of this venture, especially the firm establishment of trees on the steppes of Inner Mongolia, is uncertain.

If by the end of the first five-year plan some 28 million acres had been planted in trees, it is claimed that in 1958 alone a nationwide drive resulted in the afforestation of 69 million acres. Much of the work done on the North China plain and in South China was piecemeal, in contrast to the massive shelter-belt project of the semi-arid marginal lands. Forest brigades of the individual communes have planted billions of trees around villages, in cities (transforming even raw, newly built towns into oases of green), along roads and river banks, and on the hillsides. By April 1959 a further 39 million acres had been planted. Keith Buchanan reported in 1960 that as seen from the air the new plantings spread 'a mist of green' over the once bare hills of South China, and they emphasized the scale at which the vegetation cover of a country could be transformed within a mere decade.[17] However, this view reflects the extreme optimism of the Great Leap Forward. The excessively dry years between 1959 and 1961 led to severe food shortages and reminded China that nature was not quite so easily subdued. Government attention turned to the deficiencies of the more amateurish efforts in silviculture and to the poor growth of the newly planted trees in some areas. As from 1960, measures were adopted to raise the standard of afforestation practices and to emphasize the need to tend and maintain the existing plantations.

Afforestation, erosion control, and water conservancy are three closely linked efforts to restore, and then increase, the productivity of a land that has supported the Chinese civilization for more than three millennia. Together they have altered the landscape on a scale and at a speed that is unique in history. The most dramatic soil erosion problems in China arise in the semi-arid

forthwest, on the steppes threatened by moving sand dunes and wind de-
ation, and on the loess plateau threatened by proliferating gullies and sheet-
ash. The shelter belt is an attempt to check the movement of sand dunes
nd wind speed in the open Ordos region. Topographic diversity in the loess
lateau requires that different approaches be adopted to tackle erosion prob-
ems. On the gentle flanks of exposed hills, trees, mostly elms and poplars,
re planted in small pits aligned along contours. On slopes in excess of 25°
everal ingenious but labour-intensive measures have been adopted, such as
he making of semicircular pits or fish scales, double furrows, level-grade steps,
nd level ditches. Fruit trees are sometimes planted, including the apple, the
herry, the walnut, and the Chinese date (*Zizyphus jujuba*). And on the loose
oil of the tipped bank from the cut, vegetables may be sown. The lower
lopes of the loess hills are invariably terraced and cultivated and have been so
or several hundred years. On low hills the terraces may extend right to the
ummit, giving them an artificial look, like stepped pyramids. In order to
chieve the maximum use of land, the Chinese have attempted to plant fruit
rees and shrubs even on the earth-retaining walls of the loess terraces and in
he ditches that lie immediately below the walls.[18] In South China similar
methods have been used to check soil erosion, but in the main they are prac-
ised with less care than they are in the North. Simple benches, 4 to 8 feet wide,
nay be cut into the hillsides and the trees sown (broadcast) or in rows along
hem.

In the twelve-year period since 1949, it is claimed that the Chinese people
ave built more than a million small reservoirs and ponds, dug 9 million wells,
nd developed new canals and storage basins which increased the irrigated
rea by 120 million acres.[19] There is little doubt that significant progress has
een made in tackling the age-old problems of water conservancy in China.
One New Zealand geographer describes 'the great proliferation of small-scale
projects', which 'strikes the traveller all over China, and especially in the south;
een from the air the countrysides of Kwangsi and Kwangtung glitter with
countless man-made surfaces'.[20] However, many of the smaller irrigation
acilities have proved to be badly planned. For example, half the 50,000 reservoirs in the hilly regions of Chiang-su ceased to be of any use by August 1959.
And the figure for the acreage of new land put under irrigation is more an expression of potential, based on the ponds and canals in process of construction,
han of achieved fact. Since 1961, although official sources still emphasize the
virtues of local initiative, state control of irrigation projects, irrespective of
size, is tightening.

The larger projects in water conservancy must necessarily be under central
control and directed by highly trained technicians. One of the most ambitious
undertakings in China is the attempt to harness the Huang Ho. The river has
been a challenge to the Chinese since the legendary times of the Great Yu.

Whereas the tributaries can be tamed and put to human use, the Huang H
itself has never been subjugated. Its channel can be temporarily confined k
dykes but such a measure amounts to holding the future in ransom for prese
security. The Huang Ho project is a multipurpose operation which requir
the construction of forty-six dams on the main river, twenty-four large rese
voirs along the major tributaries, and numerous small check dams on the sic
streams to hold back the immense amount of silt in the loess plateau. Afforest
tion in this area is part of the total effort to check the movement of silt into th
Huang Ho. The entire scheme will take decades to complete. A good start h
been made. Thus, of the four big multipurpose dams, three are already con
plete or nearing completion. Two are in the upper Huang Ho Valley, abov
Lan-chou, and one is at the San-men gorge where the river cuts throug
the bedrock before it reaches the North China plain. The San-men dam an
reservoir is perhaps the single most impressive engineering achievement i
China. The dam backs up the waters of the Huang Ho to a distance of 1c
miles, almost to the outskirts of Hsi-an (old Ch'ang-an). The surface area
the artificial lake is some 900 square miles, which makes it one of the large
bodies of inland water in eastern Asia. Water from the reservoir is designed t
irrigate some 6·5 million acres of land.[21] The hope of the nation is that th
Huang (Yellow) Ho will soon be a misnomer, for it is to become a blue ribbo
as blue as the water of the San-men reservoir. The task is immense and achiev
ment is not yet assured.

The development and relocation of industries

Industrial development under the Nationalist government was severe
hampered by the almost continuous civil strife and the very primitive con
munications system inherited from the lethargic Ch'ing dynasty near the en
of its mandate. China had known only a brief decade (1927–37) of relativ
peace under Nationalist rule; nevertheless, important sectors of the moder
economy had shown rapid and constant expansion. For example, railwa
mileage grew at 10 per cent a year from 1894 to 1937. The production c
iron by modern mines increased at nearly 10 per cent a year from 1900 to 193
and that of coal at 8 per cent between 1912 and 1936. The cotton textile in
dustry, the most significant modern industry in pre-1937 China, increased (t
judge by the number of cotton-yarn spindles) at nearly 12 per cent a year fron
1890 to 1936.[22] But the growth rate is impressive because China had so littl
at the beginning of the twentieth century. For example, in 1881 the first per
manent railway was installed; in 1913 the total mileage was already 5,40c
and it rose to 8,950 in 1937. Even in 1926 motor roads hardly extended ver
far beyond the Westernized port cities; but by 1937 the total mileage was sai
to be 50,000. Another point to remember is that prior to 1937 the moder

ectors of the economy were almost entirely coastal. The major textile centres vere the ports; Shanghai was supreme but T'ientsin, Ch'ing-tao, Canton, and Ian-kou also had concentrations of textile mills. As to iron and steel, southern Manchuria was unchallenged. In 1937, two-thirds of the iron and almost nine-enths of the steel produced in China came from Manchuria. Outside of Man-huria the total output of steel was only 50,000 tons. About half of China's oal output came out of the small Manchurian fields while one of the world's great coalfields – that which underlies the loess plateau – remained practically untouched.

After the conquest of China the Communist government saw that the first step towards economic recovery must be the restoration of the communications system that had been widely disrupted during the prolonged wars, and the rehabilitation of the ravaged industrial centres, in particular, those of Man-churia. The first step was successful; by the end of 1952 the total value of the output of industry and agriculture was said to show a 77·5 per cent gain over 1949, which was a particularly bad year. Coal output reached 63 million tons, that is, just above the highest pre-1949 figure. Pig-iron production reached 2 million tons and steel 1·35 million tons. Manchuria remained the supreme centre in 1952; it probably produced half the coal and 90 per cent of the iron and steel of the country.[23]

One of the objectives of the first five-year plan (1953–57) was to break the coastal concentration of industries by locating new centres close to the sources of raw material, thus new textile mills were built in the cotton-growing areas of Ho-pei, Shen-hsi and Ho-nan. The northwest region (Hsin-chiang, Ch'ing-hai, Kan-su, and Shen-hsi) was being developed primarily for its mineral wealth; we see, for example, the great expansion of the Yu-men oilfields in Kan-su and the opening up of new oilfields like those of Karamai and Tushan-ze in Hsin-chiang (Sinkiang or Chinese Turkestan). However, the landscape of the Lop-nor, the place where China loudly announced her entry into the nuclear age, must be left to the imagination.

In Lan-chou, Kan-su province, a new industrial landscape has grown around its oil refineries. In the central Yangtze basin (Hu-pei), the rich iron ore of Ta-yeh was mined as long ago as the tenth century. In the modern period an iron and steel plant was established by Chang Chih-tung at Han-yang in 1891 to manufacture weapons. But despite the proximity of the rich ore, its location on the Yangtze River, and the early start in modern manufacturing, the Han-kou–Han-yang–Wu-ch'ang' area (or Wuhan) never became a big centre, until now. Han-kou is now the site of a large iron and steel complex with a steel capacity of 1·5 million tons. Smaller works were built at Ta-yeh. Near the mouth of the Yangtze River, at Shanghai, steel ingot output increased from 75,000 tons in 1952 to 480,000 tons in 1957, as the result of new facilities and the renovation of existing ones.[24] Some other centres of manufacturing in

South and Southwest China are Ch'eng-tu and Ch'un-ching in the Ssu-ch'uan basin (Fig. 33); Ch'ang-sha and Heng-yang in Hu-nan; Kun-ming, Kuei-yang Liu-chou in the southwestern provinces, and Canton and Fu-chou along the south coast.

In North China, two major iron and steel centres have been established, one at T'ai-yuan in the Fen Ho Valley of Shan-hsi province and the other at Pao-t'ou, near the Huang Ho where it reaches northwards into Inner Mongolia T'ai-yuan is located on the great anthracite and bituminous coalfield of China Iron ore also occurs in small pockets but they are deeply buried. The region is designated a major centre of heavy industry. It has iron and steel works, heavy machine plants and factories for electrical and aeronautical equipment. Pao-t'ou lies in a desolate country some 650 miles by air from the Yellow Sea. Its inland location commends itself for strategic reasons but it has also economic justification in the large and rich iron-ore beds about 100 miles to the north, in Yin Shan. Coking coal has to be imported from northern Shan-hsi. In 1951 there were only two industries at Pao-t'ou, a power plant of 500-kilowatt capacity and a mill that turned out 200 tons of flour a year. In 1962 there were 273 state and municipal enterprises and more than 1,000 small-scale production units. Pao-t'ou was producing railroad equipment, lathes, heavy machinery, all kinds of building materials, processed foods (including packed beef and mutton) and textile machinery.[25] The Pao-kang steel complex, built under Russian supervision and in operation since the early part of 1960, covered 5 square miles with belching smokestacks, pipes, sidings, cranes, and different kinds of plants. It then had a turnout rate of nearly a million tons of steel and 700,000 tons of iron a year. However, despite the successful establishment of new industrial cities inland the pre-eminence of southern Manchuria was unimpaired at the end of the first five-year plan; this situation is the result of the revival of the An-shan complex. In 1960, for example, the An-shan works produced 5 million tons of steel, which was at least five times that of its nearest inland competitor.

The promise of over-fulfilment of the targets set forth in the first five-year plan encouraged the government to launch, in the winter of 1957, a campaign to surpass Britain in major heavy industrial output, as well as a national programme in agricultural development. The mass mobilization of people for this purpose probably made way for the euphoria of the Great Leap Forward. This gargantuan effort to transform the economy of China was not an unqualified success; and it was closely followed by a succession of dry years that disrupted the agricultural programme and threatened the country with starvation. People were told to go to agriculture whereas in the late summer of 1958 they had been told to move to the iron and steel works. However, notwithstanding the strains of the commune movement and despite the havoc that drought caused in food yield, scholars now appear to agree that there was indeed a 'great leap forward' in industrial growth from 1957 to about 1960 when the rate in these three years is compared with that in the preceding five years. The rate of increase fell in 1960, though the absolute magnitudes still showed an increase.[25] When the production figures for 1957 and 1962 are compared, we find that in coal output, for example, the gain was from 130 to 348 million tons; in steel, from 5·35 to 8·63 million tons; in cotton yarn from 4·65 to 8·20 million bales.[26]

The growth of cities

The census of 1953 reports 103 places with a population exceeding 100,000, and nine cities with a population of more than 1 million each. In descending order of size these urban giants are: Shanghai, Peking, T'ientsin, Shen-yang (Mukden), Ch'un-ch'ing, Canton, Wuhan, Harbin, and Nan-ching.[27] The central facts of urban geography in Communist China are the rapid growth of old towns and cities, the establishment of new centres, and the altered character of urban life throughout. The most powerful force in promoting urban growth in the last fifteen years is the pull of rapid industrialization. A less but still powerful force is the push from the countryside that has experienced the strains of collectivization, and that is, moreover, still vulnerable to the natural calamities.

The population of many towns and cities increased dramatically in a mere decade. In the more remote parts of the country the first appearance of a modern highway linking a town with the economic and population heartland of China signalled a period of explosive growth. Thus the city area of Chamdo, gateway into southern Tibet, is said to have expanded by six times since the completion of the Ssu-ch'uan-Tibet highway in 1954.[28] The population of Urumchi, capital of Chinese central Asia, increased from 131,000 in 1949 to 402,000 in 1959. In 1949 Urumchi was a long and narrow triangle stretching from north to south, and composed of three adjoining towns: the main walled Chinese town in the north, followed by the walled Muslim quarter and then a bazaar section at the narrow southern tip of the triangle. The bazaar was congested with shops and with people of different ethnic origins from central Asia. In all, the entire pre-Communist municipality of Urumchi covered an area of about 29 square miles. By 1958 it had been enlarged to 266 square miles to accommodate the influx of people, industrial plants, governmental, educational and other buildings. The old and dilapidated city wall had been demolished. At the site of the old South Gate a park now stands, with a new theatre that can seat 1,200 spectators. Streets have been paved with asphalt and lined by willows. And 'along a six-mile stretch of road running . . . in the western sector of the city there is a succession of newly built office buildings, schools, theatres, movie houses, and hospital buildings'.[29]

By 1962 the railway from Peking had reached as far west as Urumchi. In

1923 it terminated at Pao-t'ou, a bleak frontier town of traders, artisans and immigrant farmers, living in tumbledown adobe houses along a dusty main street. By 1949 its population was still less than 100,000. In a mere decade it had increased thirteen times, so that Pao-t'ou must now be numbered among cities with more than a million people. A new town arose next to the old. The railway station for the new Pao-t'ou is now about 5 miles west of the old town. As Edgar Snow observed in 1960: 'The area in between was rapidly filling up with factories, residences and streets connected with the new steel town by a wide macadamized road which would soon be the main thoroughfare of a single city. Scores of tall chimneys on the horizon told the story of the older town changing at a pace to match the new.'[30]

Lan-chou at the northeastern edge of the Tibetan plateau is a large oasis of the Kan-su corridor. It lies approximately midway between the deserts and steppe of the far west and the great cities of the east coast. Although a railway first reached Lan-chou only in 1952, it is now served by four trunk lines and several major highways. The largest oil refinery in China went into operation there in 1958. It is to become the interior's manufacturing centre. Already rubber, aluminium, and chemical manufacturing plants have been established. A locomotive plant was under construction in 1962, and seven textile mills were to be moved to Lan-chou from Shanghai. The population of the city soared from 190,000 in 1949 to over a million ten years later.[31]

Urumchi, Pao-t'ou and Lan-chou are examples of extremely rapid growth but in this respect they are distinguished from the other urban centres only in degree. A new city may appear, so to speak, overnight in connection with the need to house workers for a vast engineering project such as the San-men dam and reservoir; or an old city – already swelled with people – may yet double or triple its population in a decade. Peking, for example, had 2·36 million people in 1949 and 6·8 million in 1959. It is true that this remarkable growth is partly the result of its new status as the national capital and partly the result of the expansion of the municipal boundaries. The growth, however, was real. In 1949 the population of Peking lay almost entirely within the ancient walls, beyond which spread the small farms of the countryside; in 1959 the built-up area outside the walls was as large as that inside. There was in fact little room for construction within the enclosed compound, and most of the new buildings that had appeared there after 1949 were erected in the less crowded parts of the Southern City. Two things may be said about the built-up areas beyond the walls: one is that they do not yet form a continuous ring but occur as irregular blocks, some contiguous with the ancient city, others appear as isolated units separated by strips of the countryside. The other point to notice is that the growth of Peking is not only the result of its political pre-eminence but also because of its rapid industrialization. Modern industries were established in Peking in fulfilment of the stated aims of the first five-year plan. By the autumn

33. *Iron and steel works in Ch'ung-ching, Ssu-ch'uan province. There is nothing that is specifically Chinese in this scene*

of 1959 there were 97 industrial units that employed more than 1,000 workers each. Most of them are to the east and south of the walled city, and they produce a great variety of machinery, including precision and electrical instruments, cranes, locomotives, automobiles, harvesters, and mining and printing machines.[32]

The new urban landscapes of China have a certain sameness because most of them have come into being in response to industrial development, because they were built in haste, and because they reflect the social and economic doctrines of Chinese Communism. Thus, in nearly all the expanding cities one can expect to find most of the following elements of the urban mosaic: a factory complex of international mien (Fig. 33); huge residential blocks made of red brick, functional but of no aesthetic pretensions, grouped in geometric pattern and relieved somewhat by grassed squares where the children can play; streets that are far broader than they need be for the through traffic, lined with trees which hide some of the architectural rawness behind them (Fig. 16); modern but plain and monolithic buildings housing government offices, educational institutions, recreation facilities for workers, hospital, and department store; an outdoor stadium; and in the bigger cities, where distinguished visitors occasionally call, there may be a large and surprisingl luxurious hotel adjoined, perhaps, by a garden enlivened with fountains an flowerbeds.

By the mid-1950s the rich, seething life that foreigners used to associat with the port cities of pre-Communist China had been transformed, it woul seem, into the orderly pulsations of comrades in their earnest cycles of work study and play. This, at least, is the ideal picture of the new urban style, bu among official circles there remains the persistent fear that the gaudy hues o the past – now painted over with 'democratic' monochrome – may yet re emerge.

References

Introduction

References repeated within a chapter are given with the author's name only, with distinguishing date where necessary, or in some cases (e.g. *Shi Chi*) with short title, without full publication details.

Introduction

1 Kuo Hsi, *An Essay on Landscape Painting*, trans. Shio Sakanishi, 1935, pp. 54, 55.

Chapter 1

1 J. S. Lee, *The Geology of China*, London, 1939, pp. 211–81; see also L. P. Wu, 'Salient latitudinal geotectonic zones in China with notes on the related magneto-gravity anomalies', *Scientia Sinica*, **13**, no. 6 (1964), pp. 979–992.

2 C. C. Wang, 'An outline of the geological structure of Shansi', *Bull. Geol. Soc. China*, **4** (1925), pp. 67–80.

3 C. Y. Hsieh, 'Note on the geomorphology of the North Shensi basin', *Bull. Geol. Soc. China*, **12** (1933), 181–97; T. C. Wang, 'On the Wei Ho graben', *Acta geologica sinica*, **45**, no. 4 (1965), pp. 371–82.

4 De Filippi, *The Italian Expedition to the Himalaya, Karakorum and Eastern Turkestan* (1913–14), London, 1932, p. 507; quoted by H. de Terra in 'Physiographic results of a recent survey in Little Tibet', *Geog. Rev.*, **24** (1934), p. 12.

5 R. D. Oldham, *Records Geological Survey of India*, **21** (1888), p. 157.

6 E. Norin, 'Quaternary climatic changes within the Tarim basin', *Geog. Rev.*, **22** (1932), p. 597.

7 F. Bergman, 'The Lop-Nor region in historical time', *Sino-Swedish Expedition, Publ.* **7**, Stockholm, 1939, pp. 41–50, 147, 156.

8 Sven Hedin, *The Wandering Lake*, London, Routledge, 1940.

9 Sir Aurel Stein, 'Innermost Asia: its geography as a factor in history', *Geog. Journ.*, **65** (1925), p. 391.

10 There exists an extensive literature on loess. See, however, the standard articles by G. B. Barbour, 'The loess of China', *Annual Report, Smithsonian Inst.*, Washington, 1926, pp. 279–96, and 'Recent observations on the

loess of North China', *Geog. Journ.*, **86** (1935), pp. 54–65. More recen
works include that of T. H. Chang, 'New data on the loess rocks of China'
International Geological Review, **3** (1960), pp. 1143–9; and V. V. Popov
editor, *Loess of Northern China*, Jerusalem, 1964.

11 W. H. Wong, 'Sediments of the North China Rivers and their geologica
significance', *Bull. Geol. Soc. China*, **10** (1931), p. 258; J. F. Gellert, 'Tek-
tonisch und klimatisch-morphologische Beobachtungen und Problem
in östlichen China', *Petermanns geographische Mitteilungen*, **107** (1963)
pp. 81–103.

12 W. H. Wong, 'Earthquakes in China', *Bull. Geol. Soc. China*, **1** (1921), p. 39

13 G. B. Barbour, 'Physiographic history of the Yangtze', *Geog. Journ.*, **87**
(1936), p. 26.

14 Sig. Eliassen, 'The topographic map and related river questions of the
North China plain', *Norsk Geografisk Tidsskrift*, **15** (1955), pp. 117–18.

15 Sven Hedin, *Through Asia*, New York and London, Harper, 1899, p. 1028.

16 G. B. Cressey, *Land of the 500 Million*, New York, McGraw-Hill, 1955
p. 329.

17 Owen Lattimore, *Nomads and Commissars*, Oxford Univ. Press, 1962, p. 26.

18 Sven Hedin, *Through Asia*, p. 1232.

19 S. Cammann, *The Land of the Camel*, New York, Ronald Press, 1951, p. 11.

20 Co-ching Chu, 'Southeast monsoon and rainfall in China', *Collecte*
Scientific Papers, Meteorology 1919–1949 [*CSPM*], Academia Sinica,
Peking, 1954, pp. 475–93.

21 H. Y. Hu, 'A geographical sketch of Kiangsu province', *Geog. Rev.*, **37**
(1947), p. 609.

22 P. K. Chang, 'Climatic regions of Szechuan province', *CSPM*, pp. 393–
434.

23 *Ibid.*, p. 412.

24 *Ibid.*, p. 406.

25 Science abstracts of China; *Geomorphological Abs.* (London), **21** (1964),
pp. 279–80.

26 T. K. Chêng, 'Shang fauna and the climatic condition', in *Shang China*,
Univ. of Toronto Press, 1960, pp. 83–7.

27 K. A. Wittfogel, 'Meteorological records from the divination inscriptions
of Shang', *Geog. Rev.*, **30**, 1940, pp. 110–33.

28 Co-ching Chu, 'Climatic changes during historic time in China', *CSPM*,
pp. 265–72.

29 In the following discussion on vegetation, and in chapter 3, I have drawn
liberally on several basic sources, among them being: (1) C. W. Wang,
The Forests of China, with a Survey of Grassland and Desert Vegetation,
Maria Moors Cabot Foundation Publ. no. 5, Harvard Univ. Press, 1961;
(2) S. D. Richardson, *Forestry in Communist China*, Baltimore, Johns

Hopkins Press, 1966; (3) J. Thorp, *Geography of the Soils of China*, Nanking, 1936: henceforth noted as Wang, Richardson, and Thorp (1936), respectively.

30 Richardson, p. 17.
31 Wang, p. 86.
32 Wang, p. 110.
33 Wang, p. 108.
34 Wang, p. 129.
35 Wang, p. 133.
36 Wang, pp. 155–6.

Chapter 2

1 Thorp (1936), p. 456.
2 Thorp (1936), p. 450.
3 Thorp (1936), p. 439.
4 See F. H. King, *Farmers of Forty Centuries*, New York, 1926.
5 G. F. Winfield, *China: The Land and the People*, New York, Sloane, 1948, pp. 45–6.
6 Thorp (1936), p. 431.
7 Richardson, p. 14.
8 Richardson, p. 5.
9 A. de C. Sowerby, *The Naturalist in Manchuria*, 3 vols., T'ientsin, 1922–23; quoted in Wang, p. 35.
10 Wang, p. 41.
11 Richardson, p. 123.
12 *Ennin's Travels in T'ang China*, trans. Edwin O. Reischauer, New York, Ronald Press, 1955, pp. 153–5.
13 Wang, pp. 80–6.
14 *Le Tcheou-li*, trans. E. Biot, Paris, 1851, vol. 1, pp. 371–4.
15 *Mencius*, Bk. I, Part I, Ch. 3:3, trans. Legge, *The Four Books*, New York, Pargon Reprint Co., 1966, p. 438.
16 W. C. Lowdermilk, 'Forestry in denuded China', *Annals of American Academy of Political and Social Science*, **152** (1930), 129.
17 *Ibid.*, p. 137.
18 Richardson, p. 151.
19 A. de C. Sowerby, *Nature in Chinese Art*, New York, John Day Co., 1940, p. 143.
20 Richardson, pp. 152–3.
21 E. H. Wilson, *A Naturalist in Western China*, 2 vols., London, 1913.
22 Thorp (1936), p. 60.
23 Wang, p. 110.
24 Richardson, p. 31.

25 Wang, pp. 135–6, 142.

26 T. K. Chêng, *Prehistoric China*, Cambridge, Heffer, 1959, p. 24.

27 C. O. Sauer, 'Early relation of man to plants', *Land and Life*, Univ. of California Press, 1963, pp. 159–60.

28 *Shi King*, trans. J. Legge, *The Chinese Classics*, Hong Kong, 1871, vol. 4, pt. 1, p. 129.

29 *Shi Chi* (Ssu-ma Ch'ien), chap. 102; trans. Burton Watson, in *Records of the Grand Historian of China*, Columbia Univ. Press, 1961, vol. 2, p. 490.

30 *Mencius*, Bk. III, Part I, ch. 4:7, trans J. Legge, p. 628.

31 Thorp (1936), p. 128.

32 A. N. Steward and Cheo Shu-yuen, 'Geographical and ecological notes on botanical explorations in Kwangsi province, China', *Nanking Journal*, 5 (1935), p. 174.

33 R. Hartwell, 'A revolution in the Chinese iron and coal industries during the Northern Sung, A.D. 960–1126', *Journal of Asian Studies*, 21, no. 2 (1962), p. 159.

34 A. C. Moule, *Quinsai with other notes on Marco Polo*, Cambridge Univ. Press, 1957, p. 50.

35 *Shi King*; J. Legge, *Chinese Classics*, vol. 4, pt. 2, p. 646.

36 In the *Fan chou wen chi*; quoted by L. S. Yang in *Les aspects économiques des travaux publics dans la Chine impériale*, Collège de France, 1964, p. 37.

37 J. Gernet, *Daily Life in China on the Eve of the Mongol Invasion 1250–1276*, London, Allen & Unwin, 1962, p. 114.

38 J. P. Lo, 'The emergence of China as a sea power during the late Sung and early Yuan periods', *Far Eastern Quarterly*, 14 (1955), pp. 489–503.

39 E. H. Schafer, 'The conservation of nature under the T'ang dynasty', *Journ. of the Economic and Social History of the Orient*, 5 (1962), pp. 299–300.

Chapter 3

1 Summaries in English of the recent archaeological work in China appear in T. K. Chêng, *Prehistoric China*, Cambridge, 1959, *New Light on Prehistoric China*, Univ. of Toronto Press, 1966, and K. C. Chang, *The Archaeology of Ancient China*, Yale Univ. Press, 1963. All three works are fully documented.

2 Hsia Nai, 'Archaeology in New China', *Antiquity*, 37 (1963), p. 177.

3 John Maringer, 'Contribution to the prehistory of Mongolia', *Sino-Swedish Expedition, Archaeology 7, Publ. 34*, 1950, pp. 206–7.

4 Chang, pp. 41–2.

5 Chêng, (1959), p. 57.

6 Chang, *op. cit.*, pp. 59–60.

7 J. G. Andersson, *Children of the Yellow Earth*, New York, Macmillan; London, Routledge, 1934.

8 J. G. Andersson, 'Prehistoric sites in Honan', *Bull. Mus. Far Eastern Antiquities*, **19** (1947), pp. 20–2.

9 J. G. Andersson, 'Prehistory of the Chinese', *Bull. Mus. Far Eastern Antiquities* (1934), p. 34.

10 Andersson (1943), pp. 109–10.

11 Chêng (1966), p. 18.

12 Chang, *op. cit.*, pp. 61–2.

13 Chêng (1959), pp. 75–81; (1966), pp. 17–22.

14 Chang, *op. cit.*, p. 64; Andersson, (1943), p. 116.

15 Chêng (1966), p. 28, reports that Lung-shan villages were in general smaller than those of Yang-shao. Chang (p. 94), says they were larger.

16 Chêng (1959), p. 87.

17 Clearest summary and interpretation in Chang, pp. 77–109.

Chapter 4

1 *Shi Chi* (Ssu-ma Ch'ien), chap. 29, trans. Burton Watson, *Records of the Grand Historian of China*, Columbia Univ. Press, 1961, vol. 2, p. 70.

2 K. A. Wittfogel, 'Meteorological records from the divination inscriptions of Shang', *Geog. Rev.*, **30** (1940), p. 130.

3 J. G. Andersson, 'Geographical setting of proto-Chinese', *Bull. Mus. Far Eastern Antiquities* (1943), pp. 39–40.

4 E. H. Schafer, 'Cultural history of the Elaphure', *Sinologica*, **4** (1956), pp. 250–8.

5 K. C. Chang, *The Archaeology of Ancient China*, Yale Univ. Press, 1963, pp. 150–3.

6 T. K. Chêng, *Shang China*, Univ. of Toronto Press, 1960, p. 21.

7 W. Eberhard, *A History of China*, Univ. of California Press, 1960, p. 21.

8 Chêng (1960), p. 198.

9 *Shi King*, trans. J. Legge, *Chinese Classics*, Hong Kong, 1871, vol. 4, pt. 1, p. 129.

10 *Shi Ching, The Book of Songs*, trans. Arthur Waley, Grove Press, 1960, pp. 167–8.

11 Chêng (1960), *op. cit.*, p. 89.

12 *Ibid.*, p. 197.

13 Chang, p. 150.

14 W. Eberhard, *Social Mobility in Traditional China*, Leiden, 1962, p. 269.

15 Y. L. Chang, 'Feudal system during the Chou dynasty', *Tsing Hua Journal*, **10** (1935), pp. 803–30.

16 M. Granet, *Chinese Civilization*, New York, Meridian Books, 1958, pp. 237–46.

17 *Shi Ching*, trans. Waley, p. 248.
18 *Ibid.*, p. 158. Waley's introduction to the agricultural poems.
19 C. S. Hsu, 'The well-field system in Shang and Chou', in *Chinese Social History*, ed. E-Tu Zen Sun and John de Francis, Washington, D.C., American Council of Learned Societies, 1956, pp. 9–11.
20 *Shi Ching*, trans. Waley, p. 162.
21 *Ibid.*, p. 212.
22 C. Y. Hsu, *Ancient China in Transition*, Stanford Univ. Press, 1965, p. 108, 111.
23 *Mencius*, Bk. IV, Part I, ch. 14:3, trans. J. Legge, *The Four Books*, New York, Pargon Reprint Co., 1966, p. 714.
24 *Mencius*, Bk. I, Part I, ch. 3:3, trans. Legge, p. 438.
25 N. Swann, *Food and Money in Ancient China . . . Han Shu 24, with related texts, Han Shu 91 and Shih-chi 129*, Princeton Univ. Press, 1950, p. 138.
26 V. A. Rubin, 'Tzu-ch'an and the city state of ancient China', *T'oung Pao*, **52**, 1965, p. 10.
27 J. Hutson, 'The Shuh Country', *Journ. Royal Asiatic Soc., North China Branch*, **54** (1923), pp. 25–53; T. Torrance, 'The origin and history of the irrigation works of the Chengtu plain', *Journ. Royal Asiatic Soc., NCB*, **55** (1924), pp. 60–5.
28 *Shi Chi*, chap. 29, see D. Bodde, *China's First Unifier*, Leiden, E. J. Brill, 1938, p. 59.
29 *Mencius*, Bk. III, Part I, ch. 3:7, trans. Legge, p. 614; *Chou Li*, 30/11–12; given in Hsu (1965), p. 133.
30 Hsu (1965), p. 133.
31 *Shi King*, J. Legge (1871), vol. 4, 2.5.9.
32 Hsu (1965), p. 118.
33 *Shi Chi*, chap. 29, trans. Watson, p. 71.
34 K. C. Chang, *op. cit.*, p. 181.
35 *Shi Ching*, trans. Waley, p. 281.
36 C. Y. Hsu (1965), p. 111.
37 *Mencius*, Bk. II, Part II, ch. 1:2, trans. Legge, p. 559.
38 C. Y. Hsu (1965) pp. 135–8; 'Reconnaissance and trial diggings on the site of Yen Hsia-tu', *Kao Ku Hsueh Pao*, **1**, Peking (1965), 83–106.
39 *Shi Ching*, trans. Waley, pp. 138, 213, 147.
40 Chang, *op. cit.*, p. 230.
41 H. G. Creel, 'The role of the horse in Chinese history', *American Historical Rev.*, **52** (1965), pp. 647–72.
42 Chang, *op. cit.*, pp. 255–75.
43 Hsu (1965), p. 120.
44 S. S. Ling, 'Dog sacrifice in ancient China and the Pacific area', *Bull. Institute of Ethnology, Academia Sinica*, **3** (Spring, 1957), pp. 37–40.

45 C. W. Bishop, 'Long houses and dragon-boats', *Antiquity*, **12** (1938), pp. 411–24.

Chapter 5

1 *Shi Chi*, trans. Chavannes, *Mémoires historiques de Se-ma Ts'ien*, Paris, 1895–1905, vol. 2, p. 220. A general reference for chapters 6, 8 and 9 is: A. Herrmann, *An Historical Atlas of China*, New edition, edited by N. Ginsburg, Chicago, Aldine, 1966.

2 H. Wiens, *China's March Toward the Tropics*, Connecticut, Shoestring Press, 1954, pp. 132–3.

3 *Shi Chi*, trans. Chavannes, vol. 2, p. 139 and footnote 6.

4 *Ibid.*, p. 178.

5 *Ibid.*, p. 283. D. Bodde, *China's First Unifier*, Leiden, Brill, 1938, pp. 116 17, 163.

6 H. Bielenstein, 'The restoration of the Han dynasty', *Bull. Mus. Far Eastern Antiquities*, **26** (1954), p. 93.

7 *Shi Chi*, trans. Burton Watson, *Records of the Grand Historian of China*, Columbia Univ. Press, 1961, vol. 2, p. 490.

8 H. Bielenstein, 'The census of China during the period A.D. 2–742', *Bull. Mus. Far Eastern Antiquities*, **19** (1947), p. 135.

9 Lao Kan, 'Population and geography in the two Han dynasties', in *Chinese Social History*, ed. E-Tu Zen Sun and John de Francis, Washington, D.C., American Council of Learned Societies, 1956, p. 90.

10 *Shi Chi*, trans. Watson, p. 73.

11 *Ibid.*, pp. 73–4.

12 *The Fan Shen-chih Shu*, trans. with commentary by Shih Shêng-han, Peking, Science Press, 1959, p. 61.

13 *Ibid*, pp. 51–2.

14 *Ibid.*, p. 56.

15 *Ibid.*, pp. 29–39.

16 N. L. Swann, *Food and Money in Ancient China*, Princeton Univ. Press, 1950, pp. 184–5.

17 A. G. Haudricourt and L. Hedin, *L'homme et les plantes cultivées*, Paris, 1943, p. 153.

18 Shih, *Fan Shen-chih Shu*, p. 39.

19 *Ibid.*, p. 19.

20 Y. S. Yu, *Trade and Expansion in Han China*, Univ. of California Press, 1967, pp. 21–2.

21 *Ch'ien Han Shu*, Bk. 24, trans. Swann, in *Food and Money in Ancient China*, p. 163.

22 L. Carrington Goodrich, *A Short History of the Chinese People*, 3rd ed., New York, Harper, p. 39.

23 Lao Kan, pp. 91–2.

24 J. Needham, *Science and Civilization in China*, Cambridge Univ. Press, 1961, p. 183.

25 E. H. Pritchard, 'Thoughts on the historical development of the population of China', *Journ. of Asian Studies*, **23** (1963), p. 16.

26 Bielenstein (1954), p. 148.

27 Bielenstein (1947), pp. 139–41.

28 D. Hawkes, *Ch'u Tz'u, The Songs of the South*, Beacon Paperback, 1962, pp. 119–20.

29 L. S. Yang, 'Great families of Eastern Han', in *Chinese Social History* ed. E-Tu Zen Sun and John de Francis, Washington, D.C., 1956, p. 114.

30 *Ibid.*, p. 113.

31 A. Waley, 'Life under the Han dynasty: Notes on Chinese civilization in the first and second centuries A.D.', *History Today*, **3** (1953), p. 94.

32 L. S. Yang, 'Notes on the economic history of the Chin dynasty', *Harvard Journ. of Asiatic Studies*, **9** (1945), p. 113.

33 Yang (1945), p. 115.

34 Li Chi, *The Formation of the Chinese People*, Harvard Univ. Press, 1928, p. 233.

35 Mabel P. H. Lee, *The Economic History of China, with Special Reference to Agriculture*, New York, 1921, p. 196.

36 Goodrich, p. 95.

37 Amano Motonosuke, 'Dry-farming and the Ch'i-Min Yao-Shu', *Silver Jubilee Volume of Zinbun-Kagaku-Kenkyusyo*, Kyoto Univ., 1954, p. 456. S. H. Shih, *A Preliminary Survey of the Book Ch'i-Min Yao-Shu*, Science Press, Peking, 1962, p. 107; on forestry, p. 61.

38 P. Pelliot, in review of 'A Manual of Chinese metaphors' (by C. A. S. Williams), *T'oung Pao*, **21** (1922), p. 436.

39 Alexander Soper, 'Architecture', in *The Art and Architecture of China*, Baltimore, Penguin Books, 1956, p. 227.

40 K. Ch'en, *Buddhism in China, a Historical Survey*, Princeton Univ. Press, 1964, p. 136.

41 Soper, p. 228.

42 Ch'en, p. 259.

43 Soper, p. 229.

44 W. Willetts, *Chinese Art*, Harmondsworth, Penguin Books, 1958, vol. 2, p. 724.

45 Soper, p. 230.

46 Bielenstein (1947), p. 146.

47 E. Balazs, *Le traité économique du 'Souei-chou'*, Leiden, Brill, 1953, p. 309.

48 W. Bingham, *The Founding of the T'ang Dynasty*, Baltimore, 1941, pp. 14–15.

49 G. W. Roy, 'The importance of Sui and T'ang canal systems with regard to transportation and communication', *Phi Theta Papers*, 8 (1963), p. 38.

50 C. T. Chi, *Key Economic Areas in Chinese History*, New York, Pargon Reprint Co., 1963, pp. 117–18.

51 Pritchard, p. 17.

52 T. T. Li, *Tibet: Today and Yesterday*, New York, Bookman Associates, 1960, p. 9.

53 D. L. Snellgrove, *Buddhist Himalaya*, Oxford, Cassirer, 1957, p. 145.

54 C. Bell, *People of Tibet*, Oxford Univ. Press, 1928, pp. 12–15.

55 E. H. Schafer, *The Golden Peaches of Samarkand*, Univ. of California Press, 1963, p. 58.

56 D. Twitchett, 'Land under state cultivation under the T'ang', *Journ. of the Economic and Social History of the Orient*, 2 (1959), pp. 162–203; quotation from p. 172.

57 Chi, p. 125.

58 *Ibid.*, p. 126.

59 P. T. Ho, *Studies on the Population of China*, Harvard Univ. Press, 1959, p. 177.

60 Schafer (1963), pp. 19–20.

61 Lee, p. 229.

62 K. T. Wang, 'The system of equal land allotments in medieval times', in *Chinese Social History*, Washington, D.C., 1956, p. 172.

63 Twitchett, p. 184.

64 R. Payne, trans., *The White Pony*, New York, Mentor Books, 1960, p. 163.

65 E. H. Schafer, 'The conservation of nature under the T'ang dynasty', *Journ. of the Economic and Social History of the Orient*, 5 (1962), 298–9.

66 Schafer (1962), p. 295.

67 E. O. Reischauer, *Ennin's Travels in T'ang China*, New York, Ronald Press, 1955, p. 154.

68 Reischauer, p. 155.

69 Waley, p. 90.

70 Ichisada Miyazaki, 'Les villes en Chine à l'époque des Hans', *T'oung Pao*, 48 (1960), pp. 378–81.

71 *Ibid.*

72 W. Eberhard, *A History of China*, Univ. of California Press, 1960, pp. 32–3; *Conquerors and Rulers*, Leiden, 1965, pp. 34–7.

73 Miyazaki, pp. 383–9.

74 Schafer (1963), p. 15.

75 *Ibid.*, p. 18.

76 *Ibid.*, p. 15.

77 *Chou li* 43. Biot trans. *Le Tcheou-li*, Paris, 1851, vol. 2, pp. 555–7; A. F. Wright, 'Symbolism and function: reflections on Ch'ang-an and other

great cities', *Journal of Asian Studies*, **24** (1965), pp. 670–1; T. C. Peng, *Chinesischer Stadtebau*, Hamburg, 1961, pp. 6–20.

78 A. Waley, *Chinese Poems*, London, Unwin Books, 1911, p. 161.
79 E. H. Schafer, 'The last years of Ch'ang-an', *Oriens Extremus*, **10**, 1963, pp. 133–79.
80 *Ibid.*, p. 138.
81 *Ibid.*, p. 154.

Chapter 6

1 A. C. Moule, *Quinsai, with other notes on Marco Polo*, Cambridge Univ. Press, 1957, p. 23.
2 H. Fugl-Meyer, *Chinese Bridges*, Shanghai, 1937, p. 33. This section on Chinese bridges leans heavily on Fugl-Meyer's book.
3 Chen Tzu-teh, 'The Chauchow stone bridge', *People's China*, **15** (August, 1955), 30–2; Andrew Boyd, *Chinese Architecture and Town Planning, 1500 B.C.–A.D. 1911*, Univ. of Chicago Press, 1962, p. 155.
4 J. Needham, *Science and Civilization in China*, Cambridge Univ. Press, 1961, vol. 1, p. 231.
5 Fugl-Meyer, pp. 17–19.
6 Fugl-Meyer, p. 57.
7 J. E. Spencer, 'The houses of the Chinese', *Geog. Rev.*, **37** (1947), pp. 268–272; G. D. Su, *Chinese Architecture: Past and Present*, Hong Kong, 1964, pp. 227–37.
8 See Chapter 5: Landscape and life in Chinese antiquity.
9 K. C. Chang, *The Archaeology of Ancient China*, Yale Univ. Press, 1963, p. 193.
10 W. Willetts, *Chinese Art*, Harmondsworth, Penguin Books, 1958, vol. 2, p. 716.
11 Boyd, p. 45.
12 H. G. Creel, *The Birth of China*, Ungar, 1937, p. 68.
13 Boyd, diagram on p. 80.
14 Boyd, p. 93.
15 Alexander Soper, 'Architecture', in *The Art and Architecture of China*, Baltimore, Penguin Books, 1956, p. 221.
16 Boyd, pp. 87–92.
17 Moule, p. 26.
18 J. Gernet, *Daily Life in China on the Eve of the Mongol Invasion 1250–1276*, London, Allen & Unwin, 1962, p. 114.
19 Boyd, pp. 103–8.
20 N. I. Wu, *Chinese and Indian Architecture*, New York, George Brazilier, 1963, p. 48.

21 M. Sullivan, *The Birth of Landscape Painting in China*, Univ. of California Press, 1962, pp. 29–30.

22 O. Siren, *Gardens of China*, New York, Ronald Press, 1949, p. 117.

23 Robert Payne, trans., in *The White Pony*, New York, Mentor Books, 1960, p. 144.

24 Sullivan, p. 84.

25 Siren, p. 6.

26 S. Y. Ch'en, 'Chinese houses and gardens in retrospect', in *Chinese Houses and Gardens* by Henry Inn, ed. S. C. Lee, New York, Hastings House, 2nd edn., 1950, pp. 8–9.

27 E. H. Schafer, 'The conservation of nature under the T'ang dynasty', *Journ. of the Economic and Social History of the Orient*, **5** (1962), pp. 280–1.

28 Gernet, pp. 51–2.

Chapter 7

1 W. Eberhard, *Conquerors and Rulers: Social Forces in Medieval China*, 2nd edn., Leiden, 1965, p. 20.

2 E. A. Kracke, *Civil Service in Early Sung China 960–1067*, Harvard Univ. Press, 1953, p. 12.

3 E. H. Pritchard, 'Thoughts on the historical development of the population of China', *Journal of Asian Studies*, **23**, no. 1 (1963), p. 18.

4 D. C. Twitchett, *Land Tenure and the Social Order in T'ang and Sung China* (inaugural lecture), Oxford Univ. Press, 1962, p. 31.

5 C. T. Chi, *Key Economic Areas in Chinese History*, New York, Pargon Reprint Co., 1963, p. 136.

6 H. S. Ch'üan, 'Production and distribution of rice in Southern Sung', in *Chinese Social History*, Washington, D.C., 1956, p. 223.

7 Chi, p. 137.

8 W. Eberhard, *Social Mobility in Traditional China*, Leiden, 1962, p. 269.

9 Ch'üan, p. 223.

10 P. T. Ho, *Studies on the Population of China, 1368–1953*, Harvard Univ. Press, 1959, p. 178.

11 Twitchett, p. 31.

12 Ho, p. 321.

13 Ch'üan, p. 231.

14 R. Hartwell, 'A revolution in the Chinese iron and coal industries during the Northern Sung, A.D. 960–1126', *Journ. of Asian Studies*, **21**, no. 2 (1962), pp. 153–62.

15 E. A. Kracke, 'Sung society: change within tradition', *Far Eastern Quarterly*, **14** (1955), pp. 481–2.

16 Kracke (1953), p. 13.

17 Kracke (1955), p. 481.

18 A. C. Moule, *Quinsai . . .*, Cambridge Univ. Press, 1957, p. 12.

19 J. Gernet, *Daily Life in China . . .* London, Allen & Unwin, 1962, p. 32.

20 *Ibid.*, p. 47.

21 For the geomantic properties of Peking, see T. C. Peng, *Chinesischer Stadtebau, unter besonderer Berücksichtigung der Stadt Peking*, Hamburg, 1961, pp. 42–61.

22 *The Travels of Marco Polo*, trans. R. Latham, Harmondsworth, Penguin Books, 1958, pp. 98–100.

23 C. O. Hucker, *The Traditional Chinese State in Ming Times (1368–1644)*, Univ. of Arizona Press, 1961, p. 23.

24 S. D. Chang, 'Historical trend of Chinese urbanization', *Annals Assoc. American Geographers*, **53** (1963), p. 137.

25 Pritchard, p. 18.

26 H. F. Schurmann, *Economic Structure of Yuan Dynasty*, Harvard Univ. Press, 1956, p. 29.

27 Chi, pp. 143–6.

28 Ho, p. 139.

29 *Ibid.*, p. 264.

30 *Ibid.*, pp. 191–2.

31 *Ibid.*, p. 203.

32 *Ibid.*, pp. 184–8.

33 W. C. Lowdermilk and D. R. Wickes, *History of Soil Use in the Wu T'ai Shan Area*, Monograph, Royal Asiatic Society, North China Branch, 1938, pp. 4–5.

34 Chi, p. 22.

35 Lowdermilk and Wickes, p. 5.

36 *Ibid.*, p. 23.

37 W. W. Rockhill, 'Explorations in Mongolia and Tibet', *Smithsonian Inst. Annual Report*, Washington, D.C., 1892, p. 663.

38 Ho, p. 142.

39 Ho, pp. 145–8, 'The development of the Yangtze highlands'.

Chapter 8

1 A. G. H. Keyserling, *Travel Diary of a Philosopher*, London, 1925, p. 71.

2 F. H. King, *Farmers of Forty Centuries*, Penn., Organic Gardening Press, p. 16.

3 The most serious rebellion was the holocaust set in motion by Chang Hsien-chung in the middle of the seventeenth century which nearly destroyed the richly humanized landscape of Ch'eng-tu.

4 G. B. Cressey, *Land of the 500 Million: A Geography of China*, New York, McGraw-Hill, 1955, p. 248.

5 J. G. Andersson, *Children of the Yellow Earth*, New York, Macmillan, 1934, p. 128.
6 M. L. Fuller and F. G. Clapp, 'Loess and rock dwellings of Shensi', *Geog. Rev.*, **14** (1924), pp. 215–26.
7 S. D. Gamble, *Ting Hsien: A North China Rural Community*, New York, Inst. of Pacific Relations, 1954, p. 210.
8 S. D. Gamble, *North China Villages*, Univ. of California Press, 1963, p. 29.
9 M. C. Yang, *A Chinese Village*, Columbia Univ. Press, paperback edn. 1965, pp. 4–6.
10 Gamble (1963), p. 16.
11 Yang, p. 7.
12 H. C. Sha, 'The cultural landscape of the Szechwan basin', *Geographical Studies* (Taiwan), **1** (1966), pp. 3–15.
13 Cressey, pp. 190–2.
14 H. T. Fei, *Peasant Life in China*, London, Routledge, 1939, pp. 155–65.
15 *Ibid.*, p. 12.
16 G. B. Cressey, 'The Fenghsien landscape: a fragment of the Yangtze delta', *Geog. Rev.*, **26** (1936), pp. 402–3.
17 Fei, pp. 120–1.
18 C. P. Fitzgerald, *Tower of Five Glories*, London, Cresset Press, 1941.
19 T. R. Tregear, *A Geography of China*, Chicago, Aldine Publishing Co., 1965, p. 258.
20 Gamble (1954), p. 460.
21 G. William Skinner, 'Marketing and social structure in rural China, Part II', *Journal of Asian Studies*, **24**, no. 2 (1965), pp. 195–6.
22 Skinner, pp. 196–206.
23 G. William Skinner, 'Marketing and social structure in rural China, Part I', *Journal of Asian Studies*, **24**, no. 1 (1964), pp. 32–43.
24 S. Y. Yao, 'The geographical distribution of floods and droughts in Chinese history 206 B.C.–1911 A.D.', *Far Eastern Quarterly*, **2** (1943), pp. 357–378.
25 P. T. Ho, *Studies on the Population of China . . .*, Harvard Univ. Press, 1959, pp. 232–3.
26 W. H. Mallory, *China: Land of Famine*, New York, American Geographical Society, Special Publ. no. 6, 1926, p. 2.
27 C. T. Hu, 'The Yellow River administration in the Ch'ing dynasty', *Far Eastern Quarterly*, **14** (1955), pp. 505–13.
28 O. J. Todd, 'The Yellow River re-harnessed', *Geog. Rev.*, **39** (1949), pp. 38 56.
29 W. H. Wong, 'Earthquakes in China', *Bull. Geol. Soc. of China*, **3** (1921), p. 39.

30 W. H. Wong, 'Sediments of North China Rivers and their geological significance', *Bull. Soc. of China*, **10** (1931), p. 258.

31 Baron von Richthofen, *Letter on the Provinces of Chekiang and Nanghwei*, Shanghai, 1871, pp. 12–14, quoted in Ho, p. 243.

32 Ho, p. 157.

33 P. H. Stevenson, 'Notes on the human geography of the Chinese Tibetan borderland', *Geog. Rev.*, **22** (1932), pp. 599–616.

34 Y. H. Lin, *The Lolo of Liang Shan*, New Haven, HRAP Press, 1961, p. 11.

35 R. B. Ekvall, *Cultural Relations on the Kansu-Tibetan Border*, Univ. of Chicago Publ. *Anthropology*, Occasional Papers, no. 1, 1939.

36 O. Lattimore, *The Desert Road to Turkestan*, London, Methuen, 1928, p. 35.

37 *Ibid.*

38 S. Cammann, *The Land of the Camel: Tents and Temples of Inner Mongolia*, New York, Ronald Press, 1951.

39 Cammann, p. 28.

40 Cammann, pp. 50–1, pp. 114–15.

41 O. Lattimore, *Inner Asian Frontiers of China*, Boston, Beacon Press, paperback edn., 1962, p. 108.

42 O. Lattimore, 'Chinese colonization in Manchuria', *Geog. Rev.*, **22** (1932), pp. 177–95.

43 Lattimore (1962), p. 13.

44 Cressey (1955), p. 289.

45 Lattimore (1932), p. 188.

46 I. Bowman, *The Pioneer Fringe*, New York, American Geographical Society, Special Publ. no. 13, 1931, p. 290.

47 A. Feuerwerker, *China's Early Industrialization*, Harvard Univ. Press, 1958, p. 2.

48 Cressey (1955), p. 302.

49 A. Rogers, 'The Manchurian iron and steel industry and its resource base', *Geog. Rev.*, **38** (1948), pp. 41–54.

50 J. E. Orchard, 'Shanghai', *Geog. Rev.*, **26** (1936), p. 25.

51 E. M. Hinder, *Life and Labour in Shanghai*, New York, Inst. of Pacific Relations, 1944, p. 30.

52 P. Bure, 'Tientsin', *Société royale Belge de géographie, Bull.*, **23** (1899), p. 244.

53 Quoted in R. Murphey, *Shanghai: Key to Modern China*, Harvard Univ. Press, 1953, p. 6.

54 Hinder, p. 81.

55 Murphey, p. 12.

56 Based on statistics of 1923 for China, 1914 for India and U.S.A. J. E.

Barker, 'Transportation in China', *Annals, American Journal of Political and Social Sciences*, **152** (1930), p. 166.
57 Skinner (1965), pp. 211–28.
58 *Ibid.*, pp. 213–20.

Chapter 9

1 K. R. Walker, *Planning in Chinese Agriculture*, London, Cass, 1965, pp. 3–13.
2 G. William Skinner, 'Marketing and social structure in rural China: Part III', *Journal of Asian Studies*, **24**, no. 3 (1965), p. 382.
3 *Ibid.*, pp. 386–9.
4 *Ibid.*, p. 397.
5 K. Buchanan, 'The people's communes after six years', *Pacific Viewpoint*, **6** (1965), p. 56.
6 Buchanan, p. 59.
7 *Ibid.*, p. 62.
8 J. Myrdal, *Report from a Chinese Village*, New York, Random House, 1965, p. 38.
9 Myrdal, p. 126.
10 Myrdal, p. 7.
11 H. T. Fei, *Peasant Life in China*, London, Routledge, 1962, p. 1.
12 Fei, pp. 22, 29.
13 W. Geddes, *Peasant Life in Communist China*, The Society for Applied Anthropology, Cornell University, Monograph no. 6, 1963, p. 19.
14 *Ibid.*, p. 37.
15 *Peking Review*, 22 April, 1958, p. 15.
16 S. D. Richardson, *Forestry in Communist China*, Baltimore, Johns Hopkins Press, 1966, p. 123.
17 K. Buchanan, 'The changing face of rural China,' *Pacific Viewpoint*, **1**, no. 1 (1960), p. 26.
18 Richardson, p. 116.
19 E. Snow, *The Other Side of the River*, New York, Random House, 1962, p. 502.
20 Buchanan (1960), p. 19. See, however, a less enthusiastic evaluation in Wen-shun Shi, 'Water conservancy in Communist China', *The China Quarterly* **23** (July–Sept., 1965).
21 Snow, p. 508.
22 C. M. Hou, 'Some reflections on the economic history of modern China (1840–1949)', *Journal of Economic History*, **23** (1963), p. 597.
23 T. J. Hughes and D. E. T. Luard, *The Economic Development of Communist China: 1949–1958*, Oxford Univ. Press, 1959, p. 97.
24 R. Hsia, 'Changes in the location of China's steel industry', in *Industrial*

Development in Communist China, ed. C. M. Li, New York, Praeger, 1964, p. 128.
25 Snow, p. 52.
26 C. M. Li, 'China's industrial development 1958–1963', in *Industrial Development in Communist China*, p. 14.
27 T. Shabad, 'The population of China's cities', *Geog. Rev.*, 49 (1959), 32–42.
28 J. S. Prybyla, 'Transportation in Communist China', *Land Economics*, 42, no. 3 (1966), p. 274.
29 H. J. Wiens, 'The historical and geographical role of Urumchi, capital of Chinese Central Asia', *Annals Assoc. American Geographers*, 53 (1963), p. 456.
30 Snow, p. 51.
31 K. S. Chang, 'Geographical basis for industrial development in north-western China', *Economic Geography*, 39 (1961), pp. 341–50.
32 S. D. Chang, 'Peking: The growing metropolis of Communist China', *Geog. Rev.*, 55 (1965), p. 324.

Index

afforestation, 34–5; roadside trees in Chou period, 65; *Cunninghamias* in deforested South China, 144; Communist China, 195–6

agriculture: beginnings of, 47; Neolithic, 47–8, 52; Shang, 58–9; Western Chou, 60–2; Eastern Chou, 62–4; Former Han empire, 81–3; Later Han empire, 86–8; Period of Disunion, 89–91; military-agricultural colonies, 97–8; T'ang dynasty, 99–100; Sung dynasty, 128–30; Yuan dynasty, 138; Ming dynasty, 138–140; Ssu-ch'uan basin, 154–5; Yangtze plains, 155–7; southwest China, 159–60; South China, 160–2; Tibet, 170; Mongolia, 172; Manchuria, 175–6; influence of modern cities on, 183–5; Communist land reform, 189–92; changes in agricultural practice, 193–5

Andersson, J. G., 48

Arabs, 95, 97, 104, 105, 119

architecture, 109–25; bridge, 109–13; house, 113–15; courtyard, 115–19; Hakka, 119; gardens and parks, 121–5; Buddhist temples in Mongolia, 173; urban architecture under Communism, 203–4. *See also* cities, walls, pagoda

Boyd, A., 117

Bridges, 109–13, 159

Buchanan, K., 191, 196, 197

Buck, J. L., 139

Buddhism: Tarim basin, 95; protected trees, 35, 101; contributions to landscape, 10, 92–4, 177; gardens, 123–4, 125

Cammann, S., 173

canals: Han-kou canal (Eastern Chou), 65; Ch'eng-kuo canal, 62–3, 75; Yangtze-Hsi river canal, 77; Han (Wei Valley) canal, 80–1; Sui dynasty, 95; T'ang

dynasty, 98; Grand Canal, 138; Yangtze plains, 155, 157

Canton, 99, 104, 105, 201

Chang Ch'ien, 84

Chang, K. C., 50

Ch'ang-an, Han dynasty 103–4; T'ang dynasty, 99, 105, 106–8, 134

Chao Kuo, 82, 83, 87

Chia I, 75

Chin (Jurchen) dynasty (A.D. 1115–1234), 135, 137, 138

Ch'in empire (221–207 B.C.): irrigation, 75; wall, 76; colonization of South China, 77; canal, 77; Hsien-yang (capital), 77–8

China, 1850–1950: stability and innovation, 147; types of landscape, 148–62; types of population and landscape change, 162–4; natural and manmade disasters, 164–8; expansion and adaptation at the frontiers, 168–76; impact of the West, 177–85; early industrialization, 177–8; south Manchurian 'industrial landscape', 178–9; urban manufacturing, 179; treaty ports, 179–82; impact of modernized cities on countryside, 182–5

Ch'ing (Manchu) dynasty (A.D. 1644–1911), 136, 137, 138, 140, 142, 143, 144, 163, 165–6, 167

Chou, Eastern (722–222 B.C.): irrigation works and agricultural techniques, 62–64; commerce and transportation, 64–5; cities, 65–8

Chou, Western (1127–723 B.C.): landscape and life, 59–62

Ch'u, state of, 69, 70, 71, 79

cities: Shang, 55–7; Western Chou, 60; Eastern Chou, 65–8; Ch'in (Hsien-yang), 77–8; Han metropolises, 80; Sui capitals, 94–5; Ch'ang-an, 99, 106–8; Hang-chou, 109–10, 132–5; K'ai-feng,

cities—*cont.*
132; Peking, 135, 136, 202–3; Nanching, 135–6; Ming and Ch'ing urbanization, 135–7; treaty ports, 179–84; urban manufacturing, 179; under Communism, 201–4
climate: western and northwestern China, 19–21; humid and subhumid China, 21–23; climatic fluctuations, 23–4, 45–6
coastline, advance of, 18
colonization: Eastern Chou, 68; Ch'in dynasty, 77; Former Han dynasty, 84; T'ang dynasty, 97–8; Ming dynasty, 112, 139; Ch'ing dynasty, 136, 140; Mongolia, 172–3; Manchuria, 173–6
Communist ideology and landscape, 186–204; stages in agrarian reform, 186–92; two villages in transition, 192–5; afforestation, erosion control and water conservancy, 195–8; development and relocation of industries, 198–201; growth of cities, 201–4
conservation: Mencius on conservation, 62; nature and conservation, 100–1; Manchuria, 176; erosion control, 196–7; water conservancy, 197–8. *See also* forestry
courtyards, 115–19
Cressey, G. B., 149, 158

deforestation, 31–7; causes of, 37–41; neolithic, 49; Ch'in dynasty, 78; Northern Sung dynasty, 131; Ming dynasty, 141–2; Ch'ing dynasty, 144
disasters, natural and manmade, 164–8
drought, 24, 165, 196

earthquakes, 16–17; 166–7
Ennin, 101, 141
erosion, 29–31; loess, 15–16, 17; neolithic, 49; North China plateau, 140–2; southern highlands, 144, 196–7
European impact, *see* West, impact of

Fan Shêng-chih, 81, 82, 83, 87
Fei, Hsiao-tung, 193
flood, 24; Huang Ho, 19, 53; Later Han empire, 85; effect on population and land use, 165–6; Canton delta, 192

forestry: ancient practice, 34; Communist China, 35; in *Ch'i Min Yao Shu*, 90; tree belts, 195–6
frontier: Han dynasty territorial expansion, 84–5; T'ang dynasty frontier, 95–8; expansion and adaptation, 168–76
Fugl-Meyer, H., 110, 113

Gardens, nature preserves, parks, 121–5; Chu-chiang park in Ch'ang-an, 108; Hang-chou, 134
Geddes, W. R., 194–5
Grand Canal, 105, 138, 166
graves, disposal of the dead: Shang culture, 56–7; cremation, 39–40; North China plain, 153; Yangtze delta, 158–9; Tibet, 170–1; removal of, 189
Great Leap Forward, 187, 189, 196
Great Wall, *see* walls
Great Yu (Ta Yu), 53, 54

Hakka architecture, 119
Han empire, Former (202 B.C.–A.D. 9): population, 79; cities, 80, 102–4; canal, 80–1; agricultural techniques and landscapes, 81–3; territorial expansion, 84–85
Han empire, Later (A.D. 25–220): population changes and migration, 85–6; land-use, 86–8; cities, 102–4
Hang-chou (Quinsai), 109–10, 119, 132–5
Harbin, 175, 177
Hartwell, Robert, 39
Hedin, Sven, 20
Ho, Ping-ti, 139, 167
house types, 113–15; neolithic, 50, 114; Shang, 56, 114–15; long-house, 71; Later Han empire, 87; courtyard, 115–119; Hang-chou, 134; cave-dwellings, 151, 193; North China plain, 153; Yangtze delta, 158; Tibet, 170, 171; Mongolia, 172–3
Hsien-yang, 77, 78, 102
Huang Ho (Yellow River): deposition, 17–18; course changes, 18–19; silt and flood (early historic), 53; course changes, effect on land use and population, 165–166; harnessing of, 197–8

Ice-age, 9, 13, 23
industries: Shang bronze, 56; Chan-kuo (462–222 B.C.) iron foundries, 68; in Ch'u state, 69; T'ang dynasty, 105; Northern Sung industrial revolution, 130–1; in K'ai-feng, 132; shipbuilding, 41; early modern industrialization, 177–178; south Manchuria's industrial landscape, 178–9; urban manufacturing, 179; development under Nationalist government, 198–9; under Communism, 199–201
irrigation: Eastern Chou, 63–4; Ch'eng-tu plain, 63; Han dynasty, 80–1; wet rice (terraces?), 82–3; South China, 89; Sung dynasty, 129, 130; Ssu-ch'uan basin, 154; Yangtze plains, 155, 157; Inner Mongolia, 172; under Communism, 197

K'ai-feng, capital of Northern Sung, 132
K'ai-hsien-kung village, 193–5
K'ang-hsi, emperor, 122, 142
King, F. H., 147
Kracke, E. A., 127
Kublai Khan, 135, 138
Kuo Hsi, 4, 5

Lamaseries: Tibet, 171; Mongolia, 172
Lan-chou, 202
land tenure: organization of labour in Shang period, 59; feudal Chou, 60; great estates of Han dynasty, 86–7; t'un-t'ien (military agricultural colonies), 97–98; Period of Disunion 'equal-land allotments', 99; large estates of T'ang dynasty, 99–100; great estates of Sung dynasty, 127–8; North China plain, 152–3; Yangtze plains, 157; pre-Communist China, 187; land reform, 187–192; communes, 189–92
landforms, 9–19; chequerboard pattern, 9–13; hydrologic changes, 13–14; loess, 14–17; deposition and subsidence, 17–18; Huang Ho, 18–19
Lattimore, O., 171
Lee, J. S. (Li, S. K.), 9
Li K'uei, 62, 63
Li Ping, 63, 75
Li Po, 100

Liu-ling village, 192–3
Lo-yang, 67, 89, 92, 95, 103, 105
loess, 15–17; cave-dwellings, 151, 193
loessic uplands, see North China plateau
Lowdermilk, W. C., 34
Lung-shan, neolithic, 51–2

Manchuria, 173–6; landforms, 11–12, 16; vegetation, 26–7, 32; immigration into, 173–5; Russian and Japanese influence, 175; population increase, 175; agriculture, 175–6; industrial landscape, 178–179
Marco Polo, 109, 110, 119, 135, 180
Ming dynasty (A.D. 1368–1644): country houses, 119; urbanization, 135–6; population, 137, 139; agricultural expansion, 138–40; North China, 140–2; Ssu-ch'uan basin, 142–3
Miyazaki, I., 103, 104
Mongolia, 171–3; climate, 20–1; prehistoric landscape, 46; Eastern Chou, 68; desiccation, 69; agriculture, 172; house types, 172–3
Moule, A. C., 110
Murphey, R., 182
Muslim, 96, 135, 167
Myrdal, Jan, 192

Nan-ching (Nanking), 98, 135–6
Needham, J., 112
neolithic landscapes: Yang-shao, 48–51; Lung-shan, 51–2
North China plain: appearance, 11; rivers, 19; climate, 21–2; vegetation, 27, 33; Lung-shan culture, 51–2; wet environment, 53–4; Shang countryside, 57; population in Former Han dynasty, 79; under Mongols, 137–8; in the 1930s, 151–3; villages (Ting county), 163
North China plateau: structure, 12; loess, 15–17; natural vegetation, 27; agriculture during Han dynasty, 81; deforestation in Ming dynasty, 140–2; loessic uplands in the 1930s, 150–1

Pagoda, 92–4
Pan Ku, 121
Pao-t'ou, 172, 202

pasturelands: T'ang dynasty, 97; Jurchen and Mongol, 138; Min-chia of Yun-nan, 160; Tibet, 170; Mongolia, 171, 173
Peking, Cambaluc or Ta-tu, 135; Ming dynasty, 136; under Communism, 202–203
Peking Man (*Sinanthropus pekinensis; H. erectus pekinensis*), 13, 16, 23, 38
Period of Disunion (*c*. A.D. 220–589): population changes and migration, 88–89; agriculture, 89–91
Po, Chü-I, 108, 124
population: neolithic village, 49; Shang China, 57; Chan-kuo, 79; Former Han empire, 79; Later Han empire, 85; Period of disunion, 88–9; Sui dynasty, 94; T'ang dynasty, 95; Sung dynasty, 127; Ming dynasty, 137, 139; Ch'ing dynasty, 144; North China plain, 151; Ssu-ch'uan basin, 154; Yangtze plains, 155; Tali plain, southwest China, 159; South China, 162; natural population increase and landscape change, 163–4; marketing areas, 164; disasters, 165–8; Manchuria, 175

rebellions: Red Eyebrow, 85; Huang Ch'ao, 137; T'ai-ping, Nien, and Muslim, 167–8
Richardson, S. D., 31
roads, *see* transportation and commerce
Rockhill, W. W., 142

Sauer, C. O., 37–8
Schafer, E. H., 41, 99
Shang culture: cities, 55–7; countryside, 57–9
Shanghai, 177, 179–84, 199
Shih-huang-ti ('First Emperor'), 76, 77, 84, 87, 96
Sinkiang, *see* Tarim basin, Urumchi
Skinner, William G., 163, 185
Soil processes, 29–31. *See also* erosion
South China: landforms, 12–13; climate, 21–3; vegetation, 27–8; soil processes, 30; Eastern Chou, 71–2; population increase during T'ang dynasty, 96–7; population dominance during Southern Sung dynasty, 127; southern highlands

during Ch'ing dynasty, 143–4; in the 1930s, 160–2
Southwest China, 112, 139, 159–60
Snow, E., 202
Sren-tsen-gampo, 96
Ssu-ch'uan (red) basin: landforms, 12; climate, 21, 22; vegetation, 27; soil processes, 30; irrigation, 63; Ch'eng-tu population centre, 80; early intensive agriculture, 130; population in Chan-kuo period, 142; population changes in Ming and Ch'ing dynasties, 143; altitudinal crop pattern, 143; stability of landscape, 147; in the 1930s, 154–5
Ssu-ma Ch'ien, 38, 53
Su, Tung-p'o, 125
Sui dynasty (A.D. 589–618): population changes, 94; Great Wall, canal, capitals, 94–5
Sung dynasty (A.D. 960–1279): agricultural economy and landscape, 127–30; population, 127; industrial revolution, 130–1; commerce and Sung cities, 132–5
Swann, N. L., 82

Tai-tsu, emperor, 99
T'ang dynasty (A.D. 618–907): population, 95, 99; changing frontier scenes, 95–8; relations with Tibet, 96; military agricultural colonies, 97–8; economy and landscape of prosperity, 98–100; nature and conservation, 100–1; forested landscapes, 101–2; cities, 104–8
T'ao, Yuan-ming, 123
Taoism: landscape sentiment, 88, 122
Tarim basin, 13, 14, 20, 23, 95, 96, 149
Tea, 90–1; in Tibet, 96
Terraces, 83, 149, 150, 154, 160, 162
Tibet, 168–71; Tibetan plateau, 13–14; climate, 20; vegetation, 26; relations with T'ang China, 96
T'ientsin, 180
Transportation and commerce: Eastern Chou, 64–5, 72; Ch'in dynasty, 76, 77; Former Han dynasty, 84; Sui dynasty, 95; T'ang dynasty, 98–9; Yuan dynasty, 138; Ming dynasty, 112; Yangtze plains, 155, 157; trade with Tibet, 168; Manchuria, 175; Shanghai, 183; Yangtze river, 184; road and railroad mileage in